KARL A. PLANK

MOTHER OF THE WIRE FENCE
Inside and Outside the Holocaust

Book design by Drew Stevens
Cover design by Kevin Darst, KDEE Design Inc.

First edition

Published by Westminster John Knox Press
Louisville, Kentucky

This book is printed on acid-free paper that meets the American National Standards Institute Z39.48 standard. ∞

PRINTED IN THE UNITED STATES OF AMERICA
94 95 96 97 98 99 00 01 02 03 — 10 9 8 7 6 5 4 3 2 1

Library of Congress Cataloging-in-Publication Data

Plank, Karl A. (Karl Andrews)
    Mother of the wire fence : inside and outside the Holocaust / Karl
A. Plank. — 1st ed.
        p.   cm.
    Includes bibliographical references and index.
    ISBN 0-664-25219-2
    1. Holocaust, Jewish (1939-1945), in literature.   2. Jews—
Poland—Łódź—Persecutions—Photographs.   3. Holocaust, Jewish
(1939-1945)—Poland—Łódź—Photographs.   4. Holocaust
(Christian theology)   5. Holocaust survivors.   I. Title.
PN56.H55P53   1994
808.81'9358—dc20   94-15667

*This book is dedicated
to three teachers*

*John B. Mathews
Lou H. Silberman
Paul W. Meyer*

CONTENTS

ACKNOWLEDGMENTS

I acknowledge with appreciation the permission to reprint, quote, or reproduce images from the following sources:

Photograph on title page and facing page 1 is from *With a Camera in the Ghetto* by Mendel Grossman. Copyright © Michael Grossman. Reprinted by permission of Schocken Books, published by Pantheon Books, a division of Random House, Inc.

"Ash Wednesday" by Karl A. Plank (vol. 74 [1992]: 68–69); and "Empty Tomb" by Karl A. Plank (vol. 75 [1993]: 116–17) are reprinted by permission of *Anglican Theological Review*.

Photograph on page 142 courtesy of The Art Institute of Chicago: Marc Chagall, French, born in Russia, 1887–1985, *White Crucifixion*, oil on canvas, 1938, 154.3 x 139.7 cm, gift of Alfred S. Alschuler, 1946.925.

Reprinted by permission of Bloodaxe Books Ltd. from: *An Empty Room* by Leopold Staff, translated by Adam Czerniawski (Bloodaxe Books, 1983).

"Broken Continuities: *Night* and 'White Crucifixion,'" by Karl A. Plank. Copyright 1987 Christian Century Foundation. Reprinted by permission from the November 4, 1987 issue of *The Christian Century*. Published here as Chapter 6, "Procession of the Crucified: A Lenten Devotion."

"A Poor Christian Looks at the Ghetto" © 1988 Czeslaw Milosz Royalties, Inc. From "The Collected Poems 1931–1987" by Czeslaw Milosz. Published by The Ecco Press. Reprinted by permission.

Reprinted by permission of Farrar, Straus & Giroux, Inc.: excerpt from "Chorus of the Rescued" translated by Michael Roloff from *O The Chimneys* by Nelly Sachs. Translation copyright © 1967 by Farrar, Straus & Giroux, Inc.; excerpt from "A dead child speaks" translated by Ruth and Matthew Mead from *O The Chimneys* by Nelly Sachs. Translation copyright © 1967 by Farrar, Straus & Giroux, Inc.; and excerpt from untitled poem translated by Michael Hamburger from *The Seeker* by Nelly Sachs. Translation copyright © 1970 by Farrar, Straus & Giroux, Inc.

Excerpt from "Work Song" in *Clearing*, copyright © 1977 by Wendell Berry, reprinted by permission of Harcourt Brace & Company.

Reprinted by permission of the publishers from *Against the Apocalpyse: Responses to Catastrophe in Modern Jewish Culture* by David G. Roskies, Cambridge, Mass.: Harvard University Press. Copyright © 1984 by David G. Roskies.

Reprinted by permission of *Hobart Park*: "Michaelmas" by Karl A. Plank (vol. 12 [1991]: 14).

Reprinted from *Iron Mountain Review* 4/1 (Fall 1987), with permission of the editor: excerpts from the poetry of Michael Martin.

Reprinted by permission of The Jewish Publication Society: excerpts from "*Lekh-Lekho*" by Simkhe Bunem Shayevitsh and "A Night" by Moyshe-Leyb Halpern, in *The Literature of Destruction*, ed. David G. Roskies, copyright © The Jewish Publication Society, 1989; and "Written in Pencil in the Sealed Railway-Car" by Dan Pagis, trans. Stephen Mitchell, in *Points of Departure*, copyright © The Jewish Publication Society, 1981.

Reprinted with permission of JUDAISM: "The Survivor's Return: Reflections on Memory and Place" by Karl A. Plank (vol. 38/3 [1989]: 263–77). Published here as chapter 5.

Reprinted and revised by permission of *Journal of Literature and Theology*: "Scripture in a Sealed Railway-Car: A Poem of Dan Pagis" by Karl A. Plank (vol. 7, no. 4 [1993]: 354–64). Published here as chapter 2, "Eve of the Boxcar."

Reprinted by permission of *The Lyricist*: "Birkenau Nativity" by Karl A. Plank (vol. 25 [1991]: 14).

Excerpt from "I did not manage to save . . . " by Jerzy Ficowski in *A Reading of Ashes*, The Menard Press, © 1981. Reprinted by permission of The Menard Press.

Excerpts from the unpublished manuscript of "Approaching History," by J. M. Martin. Reprinted by permission of the author.

Excerpts from *Poems of Paul Celan*, translated by Michael Hamburger. Copyright © 1972, 1980, 1988, by Michael Hamburger. Reprinted by permission of Persea Books.

Reprinted from *Shenandoah: The Washington and Lee University Review*, with the permission of the editor: excerpts from "Return Letter," by Michael Martin (vol. 43, no.2 [1993]); and "Unbroken Trains: Reflections on Michael Martin's *Approaching History*," by Karl A. Plank (vol. 43, no.2 [1993]). Published here as chapter 4, "Unbroken Trains."

Excerpts from *Lodz Ghetto* by Alan Adelson and Robert Lapides. Copyright © 1989 by The Jewish Heritage Writing Project. Used by permission of Viking Penguin, a division of Penguin Books USA, Inc.

PREFACE

If writing requires solitude, it also seeks company and draws upon the nearness of other voices to challenge and sustain. I am immensely aware that I have written this book in the presence of family, friends, and colleagues whose words have helped call forth my own. The debt I owe them I cannot simply pay with expressions of appreciation. Instead, this book itself must bear my gratitude as a response to our common life. I cannot guarantee a good book, but should the words of this volume be deemed honest or to have registered a worthy concern, let that give tribute to those who have summoned such in these pages.

I have been helped by many. Gail Gibson, David Kaylor, Sandy McKelway, Bill Mahony, Lynn Poland, and Max Polley have been the best sort of colleagues at Davidson. They have read this material at various stages of its writing, have been generous with criticism and, more important, have maintained the kind, good humor that has made our corner of the college habitable. To work in the midst of friends is a boon.

In Holocaust seminars and courses in Jewish studies that I have taught at Davidson, I have received the kind of challenge and support that the best of students offer. In particular, the insights and questions of the following persons have helped to shape this book in important ways: Amy Cohan, Suneya Gupta, Meredith Hammons, Cyndi Hess, Kyle Kinner, Chris Pace, Sarah Sadowski, Wallace Sanders, and Anne Zirkle.

At Westminster John Knox Press I have been well served by the patience and editorial insight of Jeff Hamilton. In addition, the longtime support of Davis Perkins has spurred me to bring this manuscript to final form and buoyed the process with friendship.

Two persons warrant special mention: Mike Martin and Trent Foley. Each in his own way has offered me a most extraordinary company. They are the readers I first imagine myself writing for and whose responses ever matter. As chapter 4 indicates, the poetry of Mike Martin converges powerfully with the interest of this book. This connection has enriched me in immeasurable ways. Trent Foley has been my near companion for virtually every intellectual effort I have attempted and for undertakings that have ventured much more. His disdain for pretense, passion for honesty, and unfettered humor have made it possible to survive the dog days and to think the occasionally unsettling thought.

I am deeply indebted to Bill Warren, Mark Plank, Steven Plank, Charles Plank, Joyce Plank, and most of all to Kathleen Blackwell-Plank for their distinct gifts of care that have steadied, encouraged, and strengthened in this season of writing, as in so many other seasons.

To all of you mentioned above, I offer my thanks. While supporting the writing of this book, it was ultimately me you kept from falling.

A final acknowledgment. I dedicate this volume to three teachers who planted the seed from which these words have grown. At Hanover College, John B. Mathews opened my eyes to the dismay of the Holocaust and to the importance of storytelling in its aftermath. At Vanderbilt, Lou H. Silberman brought me near the structure and sensibility of Jewish life, its lasting mystery and power. Paul W. Meyer, then also at Vanderbilt, revealed to me the durability of biblical texts that invite and require wrestling until the break of day. For the story, the tradition, and for the Book, I am most grateful. I have written in the echo of your words.

KAP
Erev Chanukah 5754
Feast of the Blessed Mother 1993

MOTHER OF THE WIRE FENCE

Leave-taking before deportation. Photographed by Mendel Grossman in the Lodz Ghetto.

INTRODUCTION

A face is a message.
Abraham Joshua Heschel[1]

When I built upon sand
The house fell down.
When I built upon a rock
The house fell down.
This time I shall start
With chimney smoke.
Leopold Staff[2]

This book begins with an image, a photograph of a Jewish mother speaking to her youngest child through a wire fence. Mendel Grossman took this photograph in the Lodz Ghetto during the fall of 1942. Watched by the Gestapo and himself wary of intruding in scenes of privacy, the photographer must have felt compelled by what he was witnessing that September day. With hands in his pockets, he aimed his coat-hidden lens toward the mother's face and released the shutter on the poignant image.[3]

The mother leans toward her son who, under the age of ten, has been claimed for deportation. Separated from mother and siblings, the boy soon will be herded onto a wagon or truck that will take him to the trains; and the trains, to the death-*Lager*, Chelmno. Grossman's photograph captures the moment of leave-taking and preserves the mother's gesture. She grasps the wire on bent knee, as if to draw the fence toward her and, with it, the child who sits beyond. Hand curled, she reaches to embrace the other side.

The intent of these pages is both simple and complex. At its simplest, the book meditates on Grossman's photograph and other textual images kin to it. Each chapter responds to questions raised by viewing the photograph: What is the meaning of the mother's gesture? What is the significance of the intruding fence? The simple questions, however, involve other complex issues.

First, the fence creates a boundary that divides the world of the photograph into an inside and an outside. This division marks more than spatial separation. It reflects a deep chasm between what the boy will experience and what his mother and siblings, at this point, know on their own side of the

1

fence—the outside. Inside the fence, reality manifests a quality of difference that distinguishes it from life on the outside. The boy's ordeal defies comparison. He faces a crisis unlike that of his brothers and sisters who huddle with their mother, although their situation, too, will change. No stories or scenes from his people's past accurately describe his predicament or prepare him for what lies ahead at the end of track and ramp.

Such difference burdens our use of analogy and metaphor to understand the inside. It resists the language with which we have spoken of other afflictions and enormities. Any comparisons depend too much on categories that belong peculiarly to the outside. As such, they are remote from the ordeal inside the fence. In fact, interpreters of the Holocaust have understood the Jewish experience of the inside to be so dramatically particular that they speak axiomatically of its unprecedentedness and singularity.[4] But if the inside is unprecedented, can those on the outside ever forge a meaningful connection to it? If the affliction of ghetto and *Lager* is unique, can those who approach it in the aftermath ever know it in a way that does not trivialize and reduce its scandal? And if they cannot, does this condemn the survivor to a silent isolation that hauntingly maintains the fence at Lodz?

Second, while the photograph depicts separation and difference, it also conveys connection. It reveals most visibly the mother's gesture that links her to her child. Further, the photograph's construction—the way it shapes the scene—implies a more subtle linkage. The photograph creates its image typologically by expressing a recognizable pattern. As it groups mother and children, the photograph takes on a strangely familiar quality that may lead viewers to conclude that they have witnessed this scene before. When a photograph or literary text uses a type, it draws on a people's stock of images that have organized its experience into meaningful patterns. If effective, the type stimulates a viewer or reader to recall the fund of comparable instances and relate them to the present expression.

The child in the photograph is a Jewish boy. He bears the six-pointed star. The grouping of his family in this scene may call to mind broad associations of family, but, as type, it evokes a particular stream of Jewish tradition. Viewed within this tradition, the photograph opens itself to connection with images of mothers and children in crisis that have been inscribed in Jewish literature. From the Hebrew Bible to writings of the Lodz Ghetto, the literary tradition has preserved a rich store of maternal types. But if framed by this tradition, does the scene at Lodz forfeit its difference? Or does that difference reassert itself, breaking apart the continuities of the frame that, in turn, must be viewed in light of the difference? Can both continuity and difference coexist in a single image?

The tension of difference and connection complicates the simple questions of the photograph. These questions also may become complex when we consider the situations from which we view the scene. We approach the photograph only from its aftermath. For the Jewish survivor of ghettos and camps, memory may grant privileged access to the photograph's inside and enable him or her to identify with the young boy about to be deported. For Jews of the second generation, who did not experience directly the ordeal but intimately know its toll, the photograph provides an ambiguous point of entry. Like the mother, these Jews witness the suffering of one whose need and kinship are paramount, but whose place they cannot now share. At the same time, however, they can identify with the vulnerability of the boy and realize that, in 1942, their place may well have been his.

Christian viewers necessarily approach the photograph from a more distant outside. They are neither the Jewish mother nor the child. If the fence keeps the mother outside her son's plight, the photograph's compound image of mother and son draws the edge of another inside. Within the world of the photograph, mother and son share an estrangement wrought by the fence that admits no non-Jew to the company of their anguish: The Christian stands outside the photograph. In another way, however, the non-Jew enters the photograph as the unseen outsider who may have maintained the fence or looked upon its scene with apathy. That the photograph depicts no Christians tearing down the fence emerges as the starkest portrayal of their distance from the inside. Still, even when seen from afar, the face of a young boy implicates and summons.

Standing before the photograph, the Christian viewer may share the vantage and quandary voiced by Czeslaw Milosz as he observed the Warsaw ghetto in 1943. Considering the fate of the Warsaw Jew, Milosz asks:

> What will I tell him, I, a Jew of the New Testament,
> Waiting two thousand years for the second coming of Jesus?
> My broken body will deliver me to his sight
> And he will count me among the helpers of death:
> The uncircumcised.[5]

The photograph counts the Christian or the non-Jew "among the helpers of death." Its particular image does not dismiss the heroism of righteous Gentiles in other times and places, but shows that no rescue comes forth here to aid *this* Jewish family. That is enough. Whether from timidity, indifference, or collaboration, the Christian stands outside this wire fence among "the uncircumcised" and faces in the photograph an ongoing demand to be no longer a helper of death.

Although it depicts a scene of a moment now past, the photograph itself hosts still another moment, the present of its viewing. As viewer meets image, the photograph returns outsiders to a trace of the wire fence. There, although they cannot alter its outcome, they face the challenge to turn away from the fear, indifference, or will to harm that would again make them "helpers of death." The photograph brings the onlooker to a point where humility, compassion, and vigilance might begin and thereby mark the outsider with the scar of the inside. Transformed, the non-Jewish outsider may find the photograph to evoke confession and vow, such as the words of Jerzy Ficowski:

> I did not manage to save
> a single life . . .
> I run to help where no one called
> to rescue after the event
> I want to be on time
> even if I am too late.[6]

Inevitably, we contend with this photograph from within our own situations. I write this book from the outside, because I can do no other—I am an outsider. Yet, by turning, the outsider can listen to voices that have spoken from inside the wire fence and speak to others of their call or of the silencing gap itself. If bold, such speaking comes from no prerogative, but only from an awareness that the aftermath claims all for the mending repair, that it is important to be on time, even if now too late. I wager that difference can yet host connection, that their relation in Holocaust image and testimony is also the condition for my writing about them. But outsiders must everywhere follow the lead of the particular. They must listen for the voice that speaks with difference and yet with address. Responding, they must proceed with care, for in every attempt to speak a sufficient word, something of the wire fence falls or stands.

My guiding convictions are twofold. On the one hand, the fence must be overcome, for its perpetuity grants "posthumous victory" to Hitler and continually segregates the surviving Jew.[7] No less does it maintain the non-Jewish outsider as a "helper of death" whose own humanity lies in jeopardy. If the fence is to be overcome, connection must be forged between the inside and the outside; not only between mother and son but between this family and those who, as latecomers and onlookers, view the photograph already outside its frame. On the other hand, the fence must not be overcome in such a way that robs the Holocaust's victims and survivors of their particular identity, for to do so would only replicate, in another way, the Holocaust's basic condition. Sequestered by their difference, Jews were made to die divested of the markers of human identity that difference warrants and expresses. If our connection is to be genuine, we must honor and not obliterate the difference of the inside.

On its own, the photograph cannot answer the questions it poses. We must gather many images to understand this single one. Jewish literature contemporary with and after the Holocaust has wrestled with the same issues that are at stake in the photograph. Poets such as Simkhe Bunem Shayevitsh, who wrote in the Lodz Ghetto, and Dan Pagis, a survivor who wrote later in Israel, have provided poems that focus these issues. In particular, Pagis's "Written in Pencil in the Sealed Railway-Car" and Shayevitsh's "*Lekh-Lekho*" recast features of the photograph's image and echo its underlying tone. Forsaking abstractions, the poets depend upon concrete images, structure of language, and narrative scenes to respond to the quandary of continuity and difference. Their poems, set in contexts of boxcars and deportations, exemplify the dynamics of tradition and subversion. Both texts re-create the effect of these dynamics by requiring the reader to experience the works' inside and outside, their manifestations of continuity and discontinuity.

Both poets tie their perception of Holocaust scenes to biblical types and allusions. For Pagis, the occupants of the boxcar are Eve and her younger son, Abel; for Shayevitsh, the pending deportation of the girl Blimele and her parents echoes the saga of Abraham who himself heard unyielding commands to "go!" (Gen. 12:1; 22:2). Thus, in their poems, the tradition that bears continuity and faces the assault of difference is no vague past, but a biblical legacy of image, pattern, narrative, and liturgy. The poems both claim and put at stake the scripture common to Judaism and Christianity, leaving neither free to detach its canon from the Holocaust's challenge (or conversely, to separate the Holocaust from a theological frame).

The poetry engages the tradition in its complexity. No mere correlation of biblical affirmation and Holocaust dissent, the hermeneutic of both poets takes seriously the Bible's own entanglement of confidence and utter dismay. As biblical tradition attests its own moments of fracture, it furnishes an ironic precedent for Holocaust testimony and its reckoning of difference. If, for its part, the Bible emerges as a precursor for the Holocaust writings, they create, in turn, what Primo Levi named "stories of a new Bible."[8] They are the leaves of a newer testament and the echoes of the photograph's other side.

Part 1 follows the path from photograph to poem, from the problem of the wire fence to the dynamics of new scripture. The first chapter interprets Grossman's photograph, its history, typology, and vectors of meaning. Beginning with the fence's rupture in the world of mother and son, the chapter proceeds to discern the mother's resistance in acts of word and gesture. Chapters 2 and 3 also focus upon scenes of parents and children as they continue to probe the interrelation of continuity and discontinuity. Chapter 2 provides a reading of Pagis's "Written in Pencil in the Sealed Railway-Car"; chapter 3 contains an interpretation of Shayevitsh's "*Lekh-Lekho.*" As indicated, both poems manifest a biblical hermeneutic and reflect the pattern of a rewritten scripture.

The book's second part, "Connection," considers various modes of responding to discontinuity and, in the aftermath of the Holocaust, bridging the gap of inside and outside. These chapters examine the power of artifacts, writing, memory, place, and religious symbol to contend with the persistent crisis of discontinuity. Chapter 4 explores Michael Martin's "Mountain-City," a poem cycle that offers a vision of the poet's vocation to channel the connections of disparate experience. In its Blue Ridge setting, the work yokes the sounds of passing trains with the legacy of other boxcars, tracks, and ramps. Chapter 5 reflects upon the significance of memory and the particularity of place as it discusses the return of Jewish survivors to the landscape of the Holocaust. Whereas the fifth chapter describes the survivor's return to the outsider's world, the sixth addresses the Christian outsider's need to turn to the inside. This final chapter takes up the symbol of the crucified as a tangent point between outside and inside. When placed in the setting of the Holocaust, as seen in Elie Wiesel's *Night* and Marc Chagall's *White Crucifixion*, the symbol connects crosses and hanging deaths with the plight of the Jewish victim. As such, it calls Christian readers back to the photograph to face the Jewish child at the wire fence and, in doing so, to receive the challenge of their own identity. A poetic epilogue concludes the volume.

A final word of prologue. Speaking to a group of Quaker leaders in Frankfurt on the Main, Abraham Joshua Heschel quoted the midrash that "When Israel approached Sinai, God lifted up the mountain and held it over their heads, saying: 'Either you accept the Torah or be crushed beneath the mountain.'" Heschel continued, in conclusion: "The mountain of history is over our heads again. Shall we renew the covenant with God?"[9]

The year was 1938, a time that was soon to erupt with fire and broken glass; the word, a Jewish word seeking to meet the other with challenge and overture. Now, more than fifty years have passed since Heschel's address. We need again to hear its voice. The mountain of history remains overhead and has added to its shadow the scenes of mothers kneeling at wire fences and leaving messages to sons on boxcar walls. It grows weighty with the burden of a father preparing his daughter for deportation. If we are not to be crushed, we must attend to this memory and renew a certain covenant: to sustain the life of that child who sits before us, precious in kinship and difference. Like the mother of the wire fence, we must reach for the other side.

NOTES

1. Abraham Joshua Heschel, *Who Is Man?* (Stanford, Calif.: Stanford University Press, 1965), 38.

2. Leopold Staff, "Foundations," in *An Empty Room*, trans. Adam Czerniawski (Newcastle upon Tyne: Bloodaxe Books, 1983); also published in *The Poetry of Survival: Post-War Poets of Central and Eastern Europe*, ed. Daniel Weissbort (New York: Penguin Books, 1993), 62 (hereafter referred to as *The Poetry of Survival*).

3. On Grossman and his means of photographing in the ghetto, see Arieh Ben-Menahem, "Mendel Grossman—The Photographer of the Lodz Ghetto," in Mendel Grossman, *With a Camera in the Ghetto*, eds. Zvi Szner and Alexander Sened (New York: Schocken Books, 1977), 97–107.

4. See, for example, Emil Fackenheim's "The Uniqueness of the Holocaust," in *The Jewish Thought of Emil Fackenheim: A Reader*, ed. Michael L. Morgan (Detroit: Wayne State University Press, 1987), 135–39; "Concerning Authentic and Unauthentic Responses to the Holocaust," in *Holocaust and Genocide Studies* 1 (1986): 101–20; and, earlier, *God's Presence in History* (New York: New York University Press, 1970), 70–71 and 100 n. 10. For perceptive discussion, note Michael Berenbaum's reflections on the uniqueness and universality of the Holocaust. See *After Tragedy and Triumph* (New York: Cambridge University Press, 1990), 17–32.

5. Czeslaw Milosz, "A Poor Christian Looks at the Ghetto," in Czeslaw Milosz, *The Collected Poems 1931–1987* (New York: Ecco Press, 1988); also in *The Poetry of Survival*, 52–53.

6. Jerzy Ficowski, "I did not manage to save . . . ," in *A Reading of Ashes*, trans. K. Bosley and K. Wandycz (London: The Menard Press, 1981); also in *The Poetry of Survival*, 132–33.

7. On such "posthumous victory," see Emil Fackenheim's formulation of a "614th Commandment": "The authentic Jew of today is forbidden to hand Hitler yet another, posthumous victory" (*The Jewish Thought of Emil Fackenheim: A Reader*, 159).

8. Primo Levi, *Survival in Auschwitz*, trans. S. Woolf (New York: Collier Books, 1961), 59.

9. Abraham Joshua Heschel, "The Meaning of This Hour," in *Between God and Man*, ed. Fritz A. Rothschild (New York: Free Press, 1959), 258.

PART 1. MOTHERS AND FATHERS

1 THE MOTHER OF THE WIRE FENCE

My mother held me by the hand.
Then someone raised the knife of parting:
So that it should not strike me,
My mother loosed her hand from mine.
But she lightly touched my thighs once more
And her hand was bleeding.

Nelly Sachs[1]

Mothers run through the streets, only one shoe on, hair
barely combed, shawls dragging on the ground. They still
keep their children at their sides. They can clasp them even
more tightly to their emaciated breasts. They can still pour
kisses onto the bright little faces, the dear eyes.

But what will happen tomorrow?

Jozef Zelkowicz[2]
September 1, 1942

FAMILY PORTRAIT IN NIGHTMARISH DAYS

The photographer is a "poet of memory, an elegist of ruined
hopes."[3] In the making of certain pictures, moments become artifacts and
instants endure. What the eye may miss, the camera lens brings to intense
focus, exposing patterns and a sense of image to vision otherwise obscure.
The focused image summons memory. In the viewer's mind, it draws to itself
clusters of associations evoked by its own imagery and tone. It forges connection between captured scenes, moments now passed from view, and the present of the viewer who must re-member the lost and broken history. Still, no
past returns to memory with innocence. The photograph shapes the memory
it calls forth, giving recollection a pattern and a frame. The photograph
creates a visual poem that gives presence to the past and meaning to its
recollection.

In its ability to preserve a vestige of the precious, photography gives
remembrance a sense of poignance. Once lost to sight, a human scene may
take on added significance, bearing the freight of the unrecoverable. Photographs render the faces, the gestures, and the landscapes to which one no

longer has living access and thereby may move those who have eyes to mourn and to value. Where loss is final or immense, photographs may express an "[elegy] of ruined hopes," a witness to the passing of human lives and to the scars of their struggle.

Photographs from a time of great devastation may horrify in their revelations of violent wreckage. In their exposure of the obscene ruin of the precious, such images may scandalize. More subtly, however, other photographs may bear witness to catastrophe by portraying the scenes and settings that violence has interrupted. There in the portrayal of life suspended, one confronts the particular image of what has been lost—not the aftermath of destruction, but the scenes to which destruction allows no return. It is one such photograph that concerns us here.

An artifact from a time of ruin, this photograph preserves an image of lives caught in the process of profound interruption. No scene of savagery, this sight does not rattle with the storm of nightmare, but haunts with human gesture. The photograph depicts an aproned mother kneeling on the ground with her children. The camera captures her leaning forward, mouth open in a moment of speech. Now she bends toward the smallest of the children, the boy sitting opposite her, as if to touch him with the breath of her words. What she says, we cannot know. We know only that these words are private, spoken in the huddle of a family drawn together.

At first glance, the scene suggests a domestic quality. The composition of the photograph as a family circle, here a mother and children seated or kneeling on the ground, invites associations of household and home. On another day, this mother and children might have gathered in the same manner around a picnic basket, the mother kneeling on a spread blanket to offer her son an item freshly baked for the occasion; or, in just this way, they might have walked through a grassy field and sat down to look closely at a wildflower, an animal track, or a weather-worn stone; or in a warm room of their house, they might have circled similarly on the floor to play a board game and pass the wintry night.[4] The composition of the figures in the photograph looks much the same as it would in these other settings and generates an expectation of tranquility. Yet any such expectation crumbles in the clutch of complicating features. The photograph does indeed picture a family circle, intimate and close. And the scene would be serene were it not for the wire fence that separates the mother and her smallest child, the one who sits cross-legged in the scrabble, the one whose jacket bears on its right shoulder the sewn fabric of a six-pointed star.

If the photograph's composition conceals distress, its details yet disturb. The photograph, in and of itself, is neither obscene nor graphically horrible. On the contrary, the poignant interaction of these figures displays unusual depth and beauty. Still, an underlying evil has brought mother and children together in this way and remains unavoidable in the photograph's vertical grid, the criss-crossing of the wire fence that isolates the young boy from his family and separates the kneeling mother from her most vulnerable son. We see the scene's horror mirrored in the eyes of an older son, whose gaze into the vague distance appears frozen and desperately frightened.

The photograph was taken by Mendel Grossman in the ghetto of Lodz. It survives as part of the archives through which the Lodz Jews documented the detail of their life within the sealed boundaries of the ghetto.[5] In a 1942 entry of the daily *Chronicle*, one of the writers notes that "during the first twenty days of September the weather was lovely and sunny, with only a few brief showers."[6] Fine weather notwithstanding, the beginning of September was "nightmarish," according to Jozef Zelkowicz, another chronicler whose diary intones the solemn chord, beginning with these words: "Son of man, go out into the streets. Soak in the unconscious terror of the newborn babies about to be slaughtered. Be strong. Keep your heart from breaking, so you'll be able to describe, carefully and clearly, what happened in the ghetto during the first days of September in the year one thousand, nine hundred and forty-two."[7]

The terror Zelkowicz sees in the streets of Lodz originated in the so-called "*Gehsperre*," a general curfew enforced by the Nazis from September 5–12 for the purposes of rounding up nearly twenty thousand Jews for deportation to Chelmno, and there, extermination. Earlier in the year, between January 16 and May 15, other deportations to Chelmno had occurred, sending as many as fifty-five thousand Jews to their death along the river Ner.[8] The heinousness of these earlier deportations, however, was masked by the participation of Mordecai Chaim Rumkowski and the community's Council of Elders who were forced to create the roster of deportees and secure their assembly. Moreover, at this point in time, the sealed isolation of the ghetto made it impossible for any to foresee the fate of those "resettled" beyond the ghetto walls.[9]

The September *Gehsperre* introduced starkening elements to the scene of deportation. Earlier in the year, the community's *Aeltestenrat*, or Council of Elders, presided locally over the deportations, providing a sense of rationale and security, albeit groundless. Now, however, the increased presence of German force compelled resettlement with open brutality and the ghetto's own police could only echo the harsh cries of "*Alle Juden raus!*" ("All Jews, out!").[10] Moreover, the *Aeltestenrat* itself played a more ambiguous role in the September 1942 events. If previously the Council of Elders filled the deportation lists with "undesirables," prisoners and persons on welfare, the September action saw Rumkowski negotiating a roster that jeopardized the community's children and elderly. On September 4, Rumkowski delivered a speech to some

1500 people in the square. Confessing his anguish, he expressed his concern that it would be better for the community to provide its own selection than to suffer such unmediatedly at the hands of the Germans; and that some must be sacrificed in order to save a larger portion of the community—"I must cut off limbs in order to save the body itself!" The limbs, in this case, were to be children under the age of ten and persons over the age of sixty-five.[11]

Rumkowski's role, like that of the Council generally, is controversial.[12] For some, his actions scarcely fell short of collaboration and treachery; for others, his decision to provide the deportation lists and internal selection was more heroic, an attempt to rescue what Jewish lives might be saved and, where possible, to ease what he perceived to be the ordeal of resettlement. The plain summary of one chronicler, Oskar Rosenfeld, following Rumkowski's September 4 speech, exposes the difficulty: "The Eldest gave numbers: 13,000 elderly, 8,000 children, a total of 21,000. That's 20% of the ghetto in order to save 80%."[13] Rumkowski envisioned the September deportations as nothing short of an *Akedah*, an unavoidable sacrifice of the children and the elderly—in his words, "the best we possess."[14] He was wrong, of course, in his perception that no more deportations would follow: eventually, the ghetto would be liquidated. And he was wrong in thinking that his compliance and administration would buffer the deportation process: Nazi forces conducted the violent September round-up for themselves. But even had he been right, Rumkowski would still be condemned by the dis-ease surfacing in Rosenfeld's comment: "*That's 20% of the ghetto. . . .*" At what cost would sacrifice redeem? And at what point would such cost make of redemption itself a questionable end? The criteria are more than mathematical. In this case, the scandal of sacrifice derives from the identity of the chosen group: the aged parents whom one was to sustain and honor (Deut. 5:16); and the children, whose presence was a sign of promise and a sacred obligation to protect. This sacrifice profanes in the destruction of the deepest of created bonds.[15]

One of the "limbs" to be cut off sits opposite his mother in the Grossman photograph.[16] Theirs is a bond not yet broken, although breaking in the autumn ravage. The photograph captures an apparent moment of leave-taking between the young boy, his mother, and his siblings. Sometime in the hours or days immediately before, revolver shots would have rung out in their courtyard and loud German voices would have barked at them to rush outside with all their neighbors—an "insane, wild rush of frozen corpses hurrying to carry out the command."[17] Placed in two rows, the assembly of families and generations would have faced the inspection of Gestapo authorities. Any word of plea or protest would have met only their violent rebuke: The mother who refuses to surrender the hand of her four-year-old is shot to death with her child; and the "child who wants to call out *Mama!* He will get out *Ma* and never finish."[18] Selection made, the child in Grossman's photograph and thousands of others would have been placed in horse-drawn wagons and brought over cobblestones to an assembly point, either the hospital on Drewnowska Street or the hospital on Lagiewnicka Street.[19] There, on the other side of a fence, families perhaps might have found them for a moment before more wagons or five-ton trucks with high, plank siding would have arrived to take them to the trains, to Chelmno, and to death.[20]

THE FENCE: EDGE OF DEATH, BORDER OF CONNECTION

The photograph displays both the fundamental threat of deportation and a moving attempt to respond to it. Although neither mother nor child yet reflect torment, they now face each other through the openings of a wire fence that mediates their connection and holds them apart. The fence is a barrier; it divides. Where previously mother and child shared a common world, they now meet on uncommon ground. The boy has been cast out from the world that mother and son had formerly known as their own. Separated, they no longer have a place that is "theirs," a loss that uproots their bond, making it homeless and increasingly vulnerable.

The fence imposes a stubborn difference upon the worlds of mother and son and thus, also, creates an unnatural estrangement in the condition of their meeting. Caught on separate sides of the fence, they face situations that cannot readily be assimilated to each other. Sitting alone, the son confronts the ordeal of deportation, the journey away from home and, ultimately, toward death. The mother, at least in this moment, faces the challenge of survival on her own side of the fence, of living in the diminished, familiar place with others, all the while knowing that she can no longer reach her youngest child in the moment of his greatest need. Thus this most obvious fact of the photograph—the intrusion of the fence—reflects not only a spatial separation, but the imposition of an existential difference. Cast in estranged circumstances, mother and son find their roles set over against each other, all will of their own to the contrary. On the one hand, the departing son is made to increase his mother's anguish, to make her survival a matter of loss as well as of life; on the other hand, the mother's survival is forced to bring to his deportation a dimension of forsakenness. She remains behind. In this way, the fence has done more than separate mother and child; it has made of their very connection a source of fracture.[21]

Awaiting deportation, the displaced child sits on unfamiliar earth. There, in the dusty scruff of grass, forces of exile have already begun their work. The imposition of the fence initiates a process that will radicalize conditions al-

ready present in the world of the photograph. Unimpeded, the tracks that
lead to Chelmno start here:

> in separation
> of mother and son
> becoming absence
> becoming final
> in death
>
> in the severance
> of a mother's touch
> becoming loss of
> human connection
> becoming complete
> in death
>
> in the uprooting
> of children from homes
> becoming exile
> from the world itself
>
> as death gives flesh and bone to smoke
> as smoke vanishes in the sky.

No smokestack appears in the photograph; no striped cloth nor shaven head.
Still, the death camp's shadow looms large, for the photograph depicts realities that are but the germ growing to monstrosity as ghetto yields to *Lager* and
Lodz to Chelmno. Separation and isolation, uprootedness—in their limited
forms these describe existential conditions of life in its finitude. Made absolute, however, they are the conditions of death itself and signature markings
of the "Final Solution" that ran rampant on narrow-gauge rails to Auschwitz
and Treblinka. The Grossman photograph reflects a murder in progress. Here
any reassertion of a human bond is not only vulnerable; it is miraculous.

Something in the bond between mother and son does persist, however,
even in the midst of its breaking. Those who sit on either side of the lattice
share a common boundary that links them even as it holds them apart: They
meet on two sides of some *one* thing. Thus, although the fence slices the bond
between mother and son, it also ties them together in the mirrored loss of
each other, jointly defined by the single intruding reality. A similar reciprocity
implicates a group that only seems absent from the photograph. The fence
delineates not only those it has separated, but those who have constructed it,
maintained it, and used it to territorialize the living and the dead. The same

fence that divides son and mother identifies this other group as captors and tormentors, yoked to its victims by the agency of its own deeds. As it segregates some for death, the fence marks others as murderers and situates them in the photograph along with the impending shadow of Chelmno.

The moment of the photograph, however, reveals a greater constancy in the bond of mother and son than the common mesh explains. The enduring quality emerges in the mother's gesture, an act willed and irreducible. Here, we see the mother approaching the boundary to defy separation in the only means available to her: a word, a look, a motion. The unseen guardians of the fence do not turn toward the boundary except to enforce its barrier, to push the other away at farther and farther distance. In utter contrast, the mother neither turns away from nor polices the critical edge. She draws near, extending herself toward her son. Grasping the wire, she joins herself to the very boundary that would separate them. As a spoken word might penetrate the barrier, so does her gesture reach out for the other side.

MOTHERS AND CHILDREN:
THE MATERNAL GESTURE

The photograph constructs the mother as no isolated entity, but as part of a triangle of figures that emerges from the family circle. She and the son who is two figures to her right are the only persons whose faces have been revealed to the camera. Along with the central figure who sits on the near side of the fence, these figures constitute a triad within the larger group and attract the greatest attention: the mother and youngest son through their interaction; the older son through his facial expression that threatens to interrupt the line established between the other two figures. These lines of relation shape the mother's situation decisively. To understand her gesture, we must see her first as mother and, in particular, as the mother of *these* two sons.[22]

We do not approach this woman innocently. Recognizing her as mother, we bring to the photograph the grid of other stories, images, and experiences to assist us in speaking of her situation. The photograph's composition evokes certain images or types of maternal response to crisis, each offering a pattern in which to place the mother at the wire fence. As mother, her situation resonates with other mothers who have sought to protect their sons and daughters from harm or who have found it necessary to contend with separation and the loss of precious children. With a sense of common predicament, the types may suggest a language to name this mother from Lodz. At the same time, however, that which is rare in her gesture may simply require a language of its own. The types, like the bond of this mother and child, may be on the verge of fracture, their wholeness broken by the severing fence.

The mother's resemblance to certain types is strong and suggests her undeniable kinship. With respect to other types, her difference suggests the incomparability of circumstance or, where that is shared, a contrast in intent or reaction. Whether with kinship or difference, however, she occupies a place on the line of antecedent types and can be identified in its terms. Those types, themselves reflections of experience, reveal themselves in the scripture, the art, and the chronicle of a given culture's tradition; they reify the fleeting impressions of experience and give form to the imagination. Grossman's photograph, as it prominently displays the child's Star of David, leaves no doubt about the Jewish identity of the mother. It invites us to name her within that tradition. Yet, Jewish tradition is itself no one thing, and the heritage of its mothers in crisis creates a wide spectrum ranging from the weeping of Rachel to the martyrdom of the Maccabean mother, from the mothers of mercy at Mainz to the comforting mother of Blimele in Shayevitsh's "Lekh-Lekho." Where is the mother of the fence among these women of tears and defiance, comfort and tragedy?

Rachel, the Weeping Mother

Before the mother of the fence faced her child in September 1942, the Lodz Ghetto had already witnessed the resumption of mass deportations earlier in the year. As many as fifty-five thousand Jews had been sent from Lodz to Chelmno between January 16 and May 15.[23] Simkhe Bunem Shayevitsh, a mitten maker in Lodz and a self-educated writer, responded to the anguish of these deportations in two lengthy poems: "Lekh-Lekho," a father's final words to his daughter on the eve of their deportation; and "Spring 5702 [1942]," a rendering of the deportation and murder of the Lodz Jews against the ironic backdrop of the resurging vitality of spring.[24] Although we will return to "Lekh-Lekho," the later poem concerns us here in its evocation of the matriarch Rachel as a maternal type.

In the ninth canto of "Spring 5702 [1942]," Shayevitsh summons the spirit of the poet, Chaim Nachman Bialik, whose poem "City of Slaughter" (1904) had challenged Jewish passivity and piety in the face of the Kishinev pogrom. Shayevitsh bids the "poet of wrath and vengeance" to walk with him through this ghetto and to observe the desperate features of its situation that have surpassed the crisis of "the other 'City'" and humbled the rhetoric of revenge. Only one thing Shayevitsh asks of the "great poet":

What I require of you?
I ask that you wake from their sleep
Our mother Rachel,

And the saint of Berdichev
And that the three of you go together before God.
You will thunder and demand.
Rachel will weep and plead,
And Levi Yitzhak will argue his lawsuit, proclaiming:
—If, Lord of the Universe, You will not be the Savior
Of Living Jews,
You will, God forbid, be the Savior of Corpses.[25]

In his call for Bialik to waken "our mother Rachel," Shayevitsh alludes to and imitates the prophet Jeremiah's appropriation of the figure Rachel: "A voice is heard in Ramah, / lamentation and bitter weeping. / Rachel is weeping for her children; / she refuses to be comforted for her children, / because they are no more" (Jer. 31:15). As Jeremiah personifies his land as the inconsolable mother, weeping for her lost children, he allows the image of Rachel to function as a type or metaphor. The Assyrian deportation of the northern tribe of Ephraim (722–21)—Rachel's children—poses an unmitigable grief for the nation like that which Jeremiah must face in the context of the Babylonian captivity. Yet, as Yahweh consoles this inconsolable mother with the hope of her children's return (31:16–17), so the prophet can offer comfort in his time.[26]

Like Jeremiah, Shayevitsh appeals to the image of the weeping mother. As type, Rachel is not confined to her epoch (nor to Jeremiah's), but emerges in the poem as "our mother," even as a ghetto mother whose child has been torn from her arms in rage.[27] Where Jeremiah, however, had used the image of Rachel's inconsolable weeping to prepare the prospect of a radical comfort, Shayevitsh leaves the tears unrelieved. For it is in her weeping, the poem suggests, that she adds her voice to the thundering protest of the poet and the contending of the Berdichever rebbe. In weeping, her voice becomes a powerful plea.

The weeping Rachel protests and intercedes. This emphasis of Shayevitsh's "Spring 5702 [1942]" echoes other texts that had themselves built upon Jeremiah's trope. Writing between the world wars, the Yiddish-American poet Moyshe-Leyb Halpern offered a nightmarish, apocalyptic response to the pogroms in his native Galicia. In "A Night," he creates a harrowing lullabye that juxtaposes soothing sounds with harsh images of violence and inversions of religious symbols. Like Shayevitsh, he draws upon Jeremiah's weeping Rachel and understands her weeping to be no less than a plea that "will put an end / To the Messiah's patience." But the tone and the meaning of "A Night" differs considerably from Shayevitsh's poem. Halpern writes,

If you slouch down on some rock,
Blaming yourself, flailing away,

Ay lyu-lyu, lyu-lyu,
Mother Rachel will take stock
And weep for your black fate.
So make with the shut-eye, you.
Ay lyu-lyu, lyu-lyu.

Her wailing will put an end
To the Messiah's patience.
Ay lyu-lyu, lyu-lyu.
He will shatter his chains,
Then hit his head on a stone.
So make with the shut-eye, you.
Ay lyu-lyu, lyu-lyu.[28]

The human lament may move Rachel to weep and, in turn, her wail may stir the Messiah. But, in Halpern's vision, even that provocation is futile. Messianism crashes, as does any other ideology, on the hard rock of catastrophe. The tears of this mother are ultimately as absurd as the lyu-ing round tones of lullabye in the midst of civilization's nightmare.

Shayevitsh and Halpern, in their renderings of the weeping Rachel as one who intercedes, both follow a rabbinic precedent and, in their own way, provide commentary to it. The homily of Rabbi Samuel ben Nahman, preserved in the Midrash on Lamentations, marshals a series of intercessors who, after the destruction of the Temple, go before the Holy One to lament, challenge, and testify—in short, to plead Israel's case and move the Holy One toward mercy.[29] Abraham and the letters of Torah themselves give their witness, as does Moses. But it is the matriarch Rachel who singularly stirs the Holy One with her lament and brings about the divine turning that restores Israel. The midrash, in narrative, develops the prooftext to which it finally appeals: "A voice is heard in Ramah, lamentation and bitter weeping. Rachel is weeping for her children. . . . Thus says the Lord: Keep your voice from weeping, and your eyes from tears; for there is a reward for your work . . . and your children shall come back to their own country" (Jer. 31:15–17, NRSV).

The modern poets and the ancient rabbi differ significantly in their appraisal of the Rachel type. For Shayevitsh, the weeping Rachel protests the condition that has caused her lament and, in so doing, retains a certain human quality. Whether God responds as "Savior of Living Jews" or as "Savior of Corpses," the meaning of the Rachel type lies in the wailing itself that refuses to accept the great loss imposed in the spring of 1942. For Halpern, "our mother Rachel" takes note of the current misery and her tears vent the

plea that ends "the Messiah's patience." Where Shayevitsh, however, left open
the consequence of Rachel's wailing, Halpern notes its ultimate absurdity. The
Messiah, stirred by her cry, has no power to end the nightmare, but only
"hit[s] his head on a stone." The midrash of Samuel ben Nahman, like Halpern's poem, renders Rachel's weeping in terms of its consequence, only in
this homily an unqualified confidence emerges in the power of the mother's
testimony to provoke a divine turning and restoration of the lost children.
Differences notwithstanding, each text conserves Jeremiah's Rachel-type and
expresses two constant features: Rachel is a mother who meets loss with tears
and lament; her weeping pleads and intercedes. It protests.

Mother as Martyr

On March 7, 1944, Nazis began the murder of some 3800 Czech Jews in
the gas chambers of Birkenau. What distinguished this group from others that
had preceded them to Auschwitz crematoria was that the Czech Jews went to
their death as families. Deported from Theresienstadt with families relatively
intact, the Czech Jews were maintained for six months in Camp B2b as a
Family Camp, unique in its privilege of food and clothing, as well as family
structure. No result of kindness, this pretense of civility was created as a Nazi
ruse. When, in the first week of March, a Red Cross delegation visited the site,
they were shown only this Family Camp and no more. The appearance of
families together, working in their own clothes with children nearby, masked
for outsiders the atrocity of the Birkenau death factory. Having served their
purpose, the Czech Jews were sent to the gas chambers before a week had
come and gone.[30]

One of the witnesses to their death, Zalmen Gradowski, a member of the
Sonderkommando, chronicled their murder.[31] Gradowski portrays the procession of mothers with children in arms, and notes the defiance of their mien:
"All glanced scornfully at the line of officers, not wishing to grace them with
direct gazes. No one pleaded, no one sought mercy. . . . They didn't want to
give them the pleasure of watching them beg for their lives in despair."[32] The
scornful glance erupts into an angry oracle. One mother, standing with her
daughter of nine (Gradowski describes the girl poignantly as having long,
intricately plaited braids), denounces the German officers:

> "Murderers, thieves, shameless criminals! Yes, now you kill innocent
> women and children. You blame us, helpless as we are, for the war. As if
> my child and I could have brought this war upon you.
>
> "You think, murderers, that with our blood you can hide your
> losses on the front. But the war is already lost. . . . You will be carved
> up alive. Our brothers all over the world will not rest until they have

avenged our innocent blood. . . . Remember, murderers! You will pay
for everything—the whole world will take revenge on you."

Then she spat in their faces and ran into the bunker with her
child.[33]

This scene, from the mother's refusal to beg for mercy, to her open defiance,
to her entry into the chamber of death with her daughter, depicts the mother
as a martyr. Hers is the "innocent blood"—hers and her daughter's—that
indicts the persecutor and leaves behind a testament to summons justice.

This particular story resonates within the tradition of martyrdom. In its
maternal witness, it most closely echoes the narrative of the nameless Maccabean mother who dies defiantly with her seven sons (2 Maccabees 7).[34] Set in
the context of the persecutions by Antiochus IV, the narrative of the nameless
mother and her sons defines the martyr-type, especially in its familial form.
The Maccabean mother, declared to be "admirable and worthy of honorable
memory" (2 Macc. 7:20), becomes, in remembrance, a paradigm for the maternal martyr. Her actions furnish a pattern that, in certain respects, the
Czech mother reenacts as she defies her persecutor unto death.

The scenario for the Maccabean narrative centers on the arrest and torture of the mother and her seven sons. Compelled to eat prohibited food, an
act tantamount to the renunciation of their faith, the family declares a readi-
ness to die before submitting to any violation of the Torah. The story then
narrates the deaths of the seven sons, one by one, as the surviving siblings
and mother witness the executions until all have died. The mother must view
the death of each of her sons. Her death is the final one.

In its simplest pattern, the story depicts the mother's role as witnessing
her children's death and, finally, sharing their fate. Yet, a third action accompanies these and sets the decisive tone for the martyrdom. The mother transmits to each son a message, encouraging his faithfulness even and especially
at the moment of death (7:21, 27–29). In turn, each son delivers a final word,
prolonging the message of his mother as a testament.[35] Their witness, repeated in various ways, affirms God's power over life and death and boldly
curses Antiochus (who rightly perceives it as contempt [7:24]). Voiced
through her sons, the testament of the Maccabean mother blesses God but
utterly defies the murdering Antiochus.

Understood in another way, however, the mother's message is not just
spoken through the sons, but to them. Her words, filled with intimations of
resurrection and the power of God to create from nothing (7:22–23, 28), seek
to preserve a connection between them: "Accept death," she tells the seventh
son, "so that in God's mercy I may get you back again along with your
brothers" (7:29). The martyr's words here prepare for and encourage a restoration of life in the future.

As maternal martyrs, the nameless Maccabean mother and her Czech counterpart share, in their respective stories, at least three features: Each knows of and must observe the death of a child; each must die with sons or a daughter; and each dies with a testament of defiance. The defiant death finds the Czech mother indicting her murderers and announcing revenge upon them as she spits in their faces. For the Maccabean mother, the words of defiance—comparable words of curse and revenge—are uttered by her sons, but at her inspiration. For both, defiance robs the murderer of a certain power to control the terms of death. Having made her testament, the martyr wills or accepts death on her terms (2 Macc. 7:29) rather than receives it as simple victimization. The Czech mother does not give her killers the satisfaction of struggle: She runs with her child into the bunker. So, too, the Maccabean mother, we can assume, dies not by being robbed of life as much as by "[giving up] body and life for the laws of [her] ancestors" (7:37).

The similarities between the two mothers, however, should not obscure a persistent difference that qualifies the Birkenau death as a martyrdom. Where we overhear the Maccabean mother address her children with a faithful confidence of reunion, we do not know what the Czech mother says to her child, or even what she could say.[36] Her oracle of the future, while it includes the just downfall of her killers, is understandably silent on the prospect of any restoration.[37] The context of the two martyrdoms differs significantly. The Maccabean mother participates in her death with a degree of choice that the *Lager* context does not afford. By recanting her faith, the Maccabean mother could choose not to die and could act to save her sons from death. The Czech mother knows no such choice. Whether faithful or not, whether compliant or defiant, her death and that of her child is certain. Only the terms of her death are open and that in the most limited manner. To choose whether to run into the gas chamber or to be herded into it like an animal may express a final vestige of freedom, but unlike the Maccabean sacrifice, this choice does not ennoble or sanctify the scandal of such a death. Indeed, it scarcely deserves to be called a choice at all.[38] The martyrdom of the Czech mother contends not only with evil, but with profound absurdity; and that absurdity breaks the category of faith or any other frame of reference through which she might console her daughter, claim the future, or understand her death as meaningful.[39]

Mother as Comforter

During the resumption of the deportations from Lodz between January and May of 1942, Simkhe Bunem Shayevitsh wrote two poems that responded to the crisis enveloping him and his community. Both involve maternal imagery. In "Spring 5702 [1942]," Shayevitsh appealed to the image of a Rachel who weeps for her children. In "*Lekh-Lekho*," his maternal image springs from a more immediate setting, yet also retrieves a biblical type.

"*Lekh-Lekho*," the earlier of the two poems, portrays a father speaking to his daughter Blimele on the night before their deportation is to occur. As they pack their necessities, the father reminds Blimele to bring her nit-comb and adds to this a rush of increasingly powerful associations, all of them involving the figure of Blimele's mother.

> And don't forget to bring
> The white nit-comb, that we talked about before;
> Every night mother will use it
> To straighten out your hair
>
> And take good care of you
> Lest, God forbid, you get lousy,
> And sing to you "Bibl, bibl
> Little louse"—and hold you on her lap
>
> And tell you stories
> Of the past that is like today
> And she herself will be Jeremiah
> Who comforts all, though the heart fears and weeps.[40]

The father envisions the mother maintaining familiar roles with the daughter: The mother will comb Blimele's hair and take good care of her; she will hold Blimele on her lap and tell her stories. Yet each customary act takes on additional freight in the new setting that he imagines. No simple nod to appearance, combing the hair here battles lice and wagers the prospect of cleanliness and thereby dignity. Storytelling, no idle diversion, forges a connection between the past and the ominous present that addresses the heart's fears and cry. In these acts of caretaking, the mother becomes prophet. Indeed, she stands in place of Jeremiah as comforter of all.

The mother's comfort looms large in this setting, for Shayevitsh has charged it with the guardianship of dignity and continuity—features without which human identity erodes and withers. Such comfort, however, rests upon a prior act that the prophetic allusion illumines. Earlier in the poem, the father likens their deportation to the Exile, but notes: ". . . there is no Jeremiah / To lament the Destruction. / He does not go with them into Exile / To comfort them by Babylon's streams."[41] Only the one who accompanies can comfort; only the one who shares the exile can prophesy. Blimele's mother will journey with father and daughter to the "strange, strange land." There, by the streams of the new Babylon, the mother will comfort. The father can imagine it in no other way.

Later in 1942, during the September *Gehsperre*, Zytnia Street in Lodz would provide stark backdrop for such an act of accompaniment. No imagined scene, this moment occurs during the same week as that of the Grossman photograph. Jozef Zelkowicz describes the scene in his diary.[42] During one of the selections aimed to separate and deport the ghetto's children, the widow of a Doctor Tzamber walks out into the courtyard, holding the hand of her four-year-old daughter. Zelkowicz notes, "They smiled to one another." The mother continues to smile and hold her daughter's hand, even when the German officer calls for the child. Perceiving her resistance—"No, she won't give away the child. As long as she lives, she won't let the child be torn away from her"—he gives her a three-minute stay. Three minutes to decide whether to give up her daughter, or what? As Zelkowicz notes, "She had nothing to decide. . . . She would not relinquish the child's hand as long as she lived."

This resolve—"SHE WILL NOT GIVE UP HER CHILD"—Zelkowicz repeats four times in less than a page's writing, once in capital letters. In the repetition, the reader confronts the building suspense of the scene and the strength of the mother's will to accompany. But Zelkowicz pauses and allows for something else to be noticed as well. During the three minutes,

> their neighbors were seized with convulsions. Neighbors who stood in the central row and stole glances with their weeping eyes at the two, set off by themselves, who stood and smiled at each other. The child from the satisfaction of still being with her mother, and that her mother was still holding her hand. And the mother from satisfaction that she still had her child with her and in her.[43]

During the three minutes, the presence of one to another, hand in hand, comforts. It satisfies. And it strengthens the resisting resolve of the mother: "She would not relinquish her child's hand as long as she lived. Nothing had changed for her during those three minutes—not even the smile."

At the end of the stay, the smile and the handclasp speak all that is to be spoken. Only one more sentence will be uttered, and this from the officer who shrieks for them to "*Turn to the wall!*" If now the mother holds the child's hand "more convulsively," if now the child "lift[s] up her head to her mother" in query, no one will find any other than the intensification of their bond to one another, the mother's devoted accompaniment and desire to comfort. No one will deny that their murder was of "a young, vivacious mother with her four-year-old child, hand in hand."

Mothers of Mercy

The images of maternal martyrs and of comforting mothers share an awareness of death's imminence. If the Maccabean mother chooses death for herself and for her sons, she does so because the alternative of profaning God's Torah is simply unthinkable. For her to choose life while sacrificing its source of meaningfulness would only create another form of death and, at that, a less noble one. Her Czech counterpart and the Lodz widow, however, do not even have that choice to make. Regardless of any decision on their part, death will claim their children. Given their context, they cannot rescue their children from death, leaving open only acts that would respond to the death that draws near: in the martyr's case, a spitting indictment of the murderers; in the comforter's, an act of accompaniment, a holding of the child's hand.

When facing the inevitability of a child's death and its certain cruelty, a mother's mercy may compel her to consider actions unimaginable in any other context. To save the child from the Nazi murderer, she may use her own gentler hands to place the child at death's safe remove from further harm. Her mercy may take the form of euthanasia, an act that does not rescue the child's life, but saves his or her death from basic violations.[44]

An anonymous, medieval *selicha* or penitential verse describes the Crusaders' murder of the Jews of Mainz in 1096. The poem narrates the death of more than one thousand Jews who had retreated to the protection of the bishop's courtyard only there to meet massacre as they refused conversion. The poet justly understands the murder as a martyrdom and uses imagery of slaughter and sacrifice to underscore its connotation. Invoking the *Akedah*, the poet shows a "mother binding her son, lest he profane the sacrifice by shuddering." Another nuance emerges, however, in a subsequent line: "Compassionate women strangle their own children."[45] The mother may kill the child, not to keep the sacrifice holy, but to express what compassion requires. Where a child's death is certain, mercy may dictate the extraordinary measure to rescue that death from the stranger's brutality. If the child must die, then let death come from the more familiar hand—so wills the mother of mercy—that her child's final moments may know a certain kindness and humanity, that they may not be savaged.

Within a Holocaust context, Judith Sternberg Newman, a nurse interned at Auschwitz, recalls witnessing there the drowning of a Jewish infant:

> Two days after Christmas, a Jewish child was born on our block. How happy I was when I saw this tiny baby. . . . Three hours later, I saw a small package wrapped in cheese cloth lying on a wooden bench. Suddenly it moved. A Jewish girl employed as a clerk came over, carrying a pan of cold water. . . . She picked up the little package—it was the baby, of course—and it started to cry with a thin little voice. She took the infant and submerged its little body in the cold water. . . . After about eight minutes the breathing stopped.[46]

Olga Lengyel, a Jewish physician imprisoned at Auschwitz, herself assisted in infanticide. Attending women prisoners at the moment of childbirth, she would kill the newborns, pretending that they had been stillborn.[47]

We should not misunderstand the instances recalled by Newman and Lengyel. In neither case does death occur at the hands of the mother herself, though in each the act takes place through the agency of a maternal surrogate, a woman expected, if not entrusted, to act in the mother's behalf. Emphasis belongs, however, not on the women's capacity for killing, but on the conditions of a system that seemingly required such of its prisoners. As Lengyel notes, "The Germans succeeded in making murderers of even us."[48]

As epitomized in these instances, one of the most scandalous features of *Lager* existence, and perhaps its grossest symptom, was the inevitability of a prisoner becoming this murderer in some form or another. Within the *Lager*, any move to sustain or rescue life could endanger one's fellow prisoners and undermine in oneself or others the humanity one would salvage. To this point, Lawrence Langer recalls the testimony of a survivor who remembers her mother's revealing insight: "'This is no life; it's a chess game, in which you play the white pieces and the black pieces at the same time!'" Langer goes on to comment, "each move one made in the 'game' of survival *included* a gesture that insured, for another if not for oneself, a form of human defeat."[49] Accordingly, the context of *Lager* existence freights action with dilemma and paradox, and makes choices absurd, although perhaps necessary.

The infanticides witnessed by Newman and participated in by Lengyel capture the dilemma. The Jewish clerk declares to Newman, "'We had to save the mother; otherwise she would have gone to the gas chamber.'"[50] Similarly, Lengyel reflects, "The only meager consolation is that by these murders we saved the mothers. Without our intervention they would have endured worse sufferings, for they would have been thrown into the crematory ovens while still alive."[51] To condemn a mother to such a death, or to kill her child? Langer rightly questions: "Is this choice between two horrors any choice at all?"[52]

Still, the women act not only with respect to the mothers, but to their children and, here, function as the compassionate surrogate. Like the mothers of Mainz, they minimize the brutality of a child's certain death, although they themselves must become death-agents in order to do so. Stanislawa Leszczynska, a midwife at Auschwitz, testifies to the fate of infants who survived their birth. Even if hidden from Nazi view, the newborns were vulnerable to the attack of rats and to the plague of inescapable filth. Even where protected from Nazi hands, starvation would ensure their death. Babies received no food rations, and the starved mothers were themselves unable to provide for them. Accordingly, Leszczynska notes, "[The infants] died a slow hunger death. Their skin turned thin, like parchment, transparent, so that one could see the tendons, veins and bones."[53] Where seized by guards, babies could be burned alive, tossed in the air "like a length of wood, to land in the blazing pit, while the murderers watched the results of their bravery with great pleasure." [54] At Sobibor, the SS

> stomped on little children and smashed in their skulls. . . . The Jewish workers found a child among the clothing rags. A guard rushed over, took a shovel, and "split open the baby in pieces." Babies born were thrown directly into garbage pits or "were torn apart down the middle by their legs, or just flung up and shot in the air."[55]

To kill a child oneself, or to surrender it to death by crueler hands? To echo Langer, this is a choiceless choice, yet one made necessary within the context of *Lager* existence. If becoming the agent of death is murderous, it yet expresses in the hands of these Jewish women an undeniable will for compassion, a will that children might not die as if there were within them no human breath becoming faint and extinguished.

The Surrendering Mother

Each of the maternal types so far discussed has acknowledged a basic separation between mother and child: The tears of the weeping mother reflect already the child's absence; the presence of the comforting mother consoles, but not apart from her anticipation of the time when her touch may no longer reach the child to accompany and confirm. Where the mother in the Lodz courtyard resists unto death the surrender of her child's hand, that death will yet part them, even as it will separate the maternal martyr and women of mercy from their children. In these instances, the reality of separation is imposed upon the world of mother and child, a given in the condition in which others have forced them to live and die. The mothers do not choose separation, except perhaps in the most limited sense of the "choiceless choice" exercised by the women of mercy.

Another dimension of separation, however, involves a greater degree of intention on the part of a mother as she yields her child to the care of another or simply to the reality of his or her own fate. Such an act still occurs in an imposed context that radically limits alternatives or renders them absurd. However, within this context, a sense of purposefulness seems to shape, in some cases, a mother's willful separation from her child, her release of its hand and refusal any longer to accompany. Like Moses' mother, as she places her baby's basket among the river reeds (Ex. 2:2–3), other mothers may choose to surrender a child into a keeping not their own.

In July of 1942 mass arrests of Jews began in Paris. French police rounded up nearly thirteen thousand foreign Jews (including four thousand children) and interned them within the *Velodrome d'Hiver*. From there they were moved to the assembly camp at Drancy and then deported to the east, to Auschwitz. These developments dramatized the growing vulnerability of Jews in France and created an immediate crisis for those foreign Jews not yet seized. Among them were the parents of Saul Friedlaender, who was then a young boy of ten years. Aware that her son's greatest chance for survival lay in his being apart from her, Elli Friedlaender writes a letter to a non-Jewish woman, imploring her help:

> I beg you, dear madame, to agree to look after our child and assure him your protection until the end of this terrible war. I don't know how he could best be safeguarded, but I have complete confidence in your goodness and your understanding. . . . If we must disappear, we will at least have the happiness of knowing that our beloved child has been saved. . . . We can no longer exist legally. . . . I beg you to excuse the appearance of this letter. My hands no longer obey me.[56]

In this case, protection was secured, eventually taking the form of refuge in a Catholic seminary. The trembling hands that could no longer write legibly or "obey" had yet found a way to let go of the son, to wager the prospect of his survival.

A later episode in the Friedlaender story accents the difficulty of this task. Running away from Saint-Beranger, the son finds his parents, a situation that only required a second act of separation. Friedlaender recalls,

> Nothing was definite yet; others had risked taking their children with them. My parents had put me in a safe place, but here I was, a runaway who had gone straight back to them, unable to bear being separated. Could I be dragged away from them a second time? I clung to the bars of the bed. How did my parents ever find the courage to make me loosen my hold, without bursting into sobs in front of me?[57]

Surrender, the loosening of a hold, had prepared the path for the son's rescue. Such turning away, a courageous act, especially in the face of the child's own resistance, had turned the child toward life. The parents did not survive the war; their son yet lives.[58]

In Friedlaender's case, the surrender recognizes that the parents' presence jeopardizes the son. In other situations, however, it is the presence of children that endangers, most especially during the initial *Selektion* that accompanied a transport's arrival into the *Lager*. Here, a mother's separation may take the form of more overt abandonment, an act that, although cruel, testifies more to

the desperateness of the situation than to the hardness of the mother. A story
by Tadeusz Borowski depicts precisely this scene:

> Here is a woman—she walks quickly, but tries to appear calm. A small
> child with a pink cherub's face runs after her and, unable to keep up,
> stretches out his little arms and cries: "Mama! Mama!"
> "Pick up your child, woman!"
> "It's not mine, sir, not mine!" she shouts hysterically and runs on,
> covering her face with her hands. She wants to hide, she wants to reach
> those who will not ride the trucks, those who will go on foot, those who
> will stay alive. She is young, healthy, good-looking, she wants to live.
> But the child runs after her, wailing loudly: "Mama, mama, don't
> leave me!"
> "It's not mine, not mine, no!"[59]

The testimony of a survivor confirms Borowski's scene. In Langer's words,
Anna G.

> tells of a ten-year-old girl who refused to go to the "left" (toward death)
> after the selection. . . . Kicking and scratching, the young girl was
> seized by three SS men who held her down while she screamed to her
> nearby mother that she shouldn't let them kill her. According to Anna
> G., one of the SS men approached the mother, who was only in her late
> twenties, and asked her if she wanted to go with her daughter. "No," the
> mother replied. . . .[60]

Langer refers to such scenes and the complexity of their recollection as instances of "maternity infected by atrocity."[61] Such acts violate our expectations
of motherhood, but leave us no ground from which to understand, let alone
judge. The other side of abandonment is the mother's own youthful will to
live, now *Lager*-twisted in absurd combination with her child's pending murder. Abandonment surrenders the child not to the safe keeping of another,
but simply to his or her own fate. The opposite of the caring separation or the
comforting presence, such abandonment reminds that under conditions of
the *Lager* and the wire fence, the strongest maternal gifts are yet placed in
jeopardy.

THE MOTHER OF THE WIRE FENCE

As portrayed in the Lodz photograph, the mother of the wire fence shares
features of certain of the maternal types. A family resemblance links her to the
Jewish mothers who have contended with basic threats to their children's lives
and well-being. The conditions of inhuman separation and loss present themselves no less in the Lodz photograph than they have in the scenes of histori-

cal and literary tradition. So, too, the responses of defiance, message-bearing, and accompaniment find their place in the gesture of the mother of the wire fence. Still, we must see this mother in her own regard, lest family resemblance obscure the identity she here struggles to bear.

The Non-weeping Mother

The mother of the wire fence displays, at first notice, an unusual calmness. Although the context of the scene invites one to expect signs of overt emotion, this particular moment has not given way to fury or wail. On the contrary, the photograph's composition expresses a settled quality through its placement of figures seated on the ground; the mother shares in this repose. Her face, unlike Rachel's, is not tearstained from weeping and lament, although, as the fence reminds, she anticipates a loss comparable to the matriarch's.

Conditioned by the Rachel type, viewers of the Lodz photograph would not be surprised by tears. Nor would a Rachel-like weeping disappoint, for lament satisfies a need to value what has been lost and protest its absence. The photograph, however, asks the viewers to imagine this scene differently and to consider the mother's non-weeping. Admittedly, one cannot always choose to weep or to refrain from weeping. Still, the act of weeping involves a certain assent that opens oneself to the rush of tears and surrenders to their force. Accordingly, that the mother of the wire fence does *not* weep may signify an intention on her part, a non-surrender. No sign of indifference, her dry eyes may mirror another kind of struggle wherein she willingly masks, or in some way suspends, anguish to meet other needs.

The survey of maternal types has shown other mothers who have met anguishing circumstance without tears, a feature noted by their chroniclers. Two in particular, the widow of Doctor Tzamber and the defiant Czech mother, suggest purposes that may summon a resistance to tears. Mrs. Tzamber, a Lodz contemporary, faces a joint execution with her young daughter, stubbornly retaining her smile and holding the hand of her four-year-old.[62] The Czech mother from the Auschwitz Family Camp moves in line with other mothers who neither plead nor seek mercy as they process to their death with children in arms.[63] In Zelkowicz's account, Mrs. Tzamber's composure reflects an intent to comfort her daughter; in Gradowski's, the Czech mother's refusal to plead or beg shows her concern to give her oppressors no satisfaction. Such intentions to comfort and to defy may explain, as well, the non-weeping of the mother of the wire fence.

Neither Mrs. Tzamber nor the mother of the wire fence can yield to weeping because of the continued need of the children in their presence. The eruption of crisis endangers the lives of these children. Before death, however, the children confront a fundamental chaos. From behind the wire fence or in the Lodz courtyard, the world spins in flux, no longer appearing in its familiar order. The hostile climate of change robs the children's setting of reliability, thereby denying them any prospect of trust. Familiar activities that nurtured on a former day, now tangle themselves in unusual jeopardies. The family circle has become a stage on the way to deportation; the walk, hand in hand with the mother, now traces steps toward death. Waking to a scene of chaotic inversion, these children face not only the threat of death but of a world-collapse.[64]

The constancy of the mother's recognizable face—the face unsurrendered to the scarring of hostile change—affords a point of relative stability within the chaos. The maternal constancy furnishes, at least in its moment, an anchorage that defies the pending world-collapse of deportation and execution. All is not change. Here, the child's gaze meets the face that does not show the disfigurement of profound grief and therein finds a recognition that yet may comfort. If only for a moment, a world endures in this human face. In the maternal countenance the child may find the presence of the past's care still visible, still abiding, within the frame of the wire fence.[65]

The face comforts first by no particular look but through its essential recognizability. Amid the spin of radical change, the face asserts itself with defiant constancy, a constancy that assures a familiar point of reference. As such, the mother's face provides a link to a past context of meaning as yet undestroyed in the child's sight. If the fence separates the family, it does not yet obliterate the child's vision of the mother or all that her face may bring into view. The face appears as a living symbol, making visible a sign of the familiar context. Where the mother's face symbolizes the goodness of home, countenance makes present a context wherein life has been sustained and nurtured. The point, however, depends on no sentimentalized ideal. Whatever the domestic quality of the symbol, whatever the connotations of home, the simple familiarity of the mother's face contrasts with the unrecognizability of the wire fence and the S.S. revolver. Whatever the face may portray, it does not convey these realities. In its difference, it resists.

The retrieval of a rival context may comfort in its resistance to the totality of threatening change; but, even more, as the face establishes a context within chaos, it enables an orientation within which signs of comfort (or of warning) might be given and received. It makes possible a grammar of word and gesture that otherwise would have no avail. Where all is hostile, no message can be trusted. Where all is unfamiliar, no message can be understood. The face, familiar in its regard, creates a condition for communication and thus, also, connection—a channel for comfort.

In giving herself to the child's need, the mother of the wire fence supplants her own grief that a constancy of face may comfort. Such a move to comfort, however, also defies the one who would cause grief. Like the Czech mother of the family camp, when the mother of the wire fence resists weeping, she challenges the domination imposed upon her. By refusing to surrender to the pressure of grief, she refuses, as well, to yield her face to the tormentor's control. Not weeping, the mother of the wire fence claims a freedom to *appear* in the world in a particular way. The fence imposes a condition whose limits she cannot finally overcome, but whose tyranny she fights with a will for constancy. The fence stands, but within the wire frame of its mesh a human face appears, maintained and defiant.

The Maternal Dilemma and Presence

The photograph captures on film a single moment. If its image hints at meaningful comfort or resistance, any affirmation that one might derive must yet respect the moment's fragility. The scene cannot maintain the stability it suggests through its seated figures and maternal composure. If the mother's constancy comforts, it is only for the time being; her resistance is limited. Destabilizing features emerge within the photograph to render precarious the balance of the seated group. The stability suggested by the mother's constancy appears less durable, but also more significant, as a counterweight to the situation's inherent instability. The photograph unsettles any static order through several of its details: the complex vectors of vision; the terrified countenance of the only child whose face is visible; and the dynamics of negative space that attach themselves to the child seated opposite the mother.

The photograph calls attention to a triangle of three figures who are prominent within the larger family group: the mother and the youngest son, whose interaction provides the central focus of the photograph; and the older brother, seated at one remove from his mother's right hand, whose face expresses horror. The triangle disrupts the photograph's static order by leading the reader to confront competing angles of vision. If, in their vis-à-vis, the mother and the youngest child share a common line of sight, the older brother follows a different angle that finds him staring off into the distance of another horizon. No viewer can simply concentrate on the mother-child interaction, because of a need to follow as well the older brother's vector. Something has terrified him and seems to wait beyond the photograph's lower right edge. At the least, his line of vision distracts the viewer from the photograph's maternal center; more pointedly, however, it may compel attention in such a way as to become an alternate center, more ominous and riveting than the initial focus on mother and child.[66]

Only two faces appear in the photograph: the mother's, which we have interpreted in terms of a constancy, and the older son's, which shows a fear that must anticipate radical change. More exposed than even the mother's face, the expression of the older son virtually defines the children's reality: No other expression of a child appears in the photograph to distract from this son's horror or to suggest any other way that a child might appear. The photograph's depiction of the youngest son prolongs the fearful uncertainty and reinforces its effect. From the viewer's vantage, the image of the youngest son is filled with negative space. Visible only from the back, his body and face, like the star on his shoulder, appear as a gap or as a hole in the photograph's texture. The photograph constructs his image obliquely. Rather than seeing positive assertion of features such as face and hands, the viewer has access only to the space he occupies. The basic emptiness of that space in the photograph takes away any prospect of seeing comfort received or secured. The essentially negative space leaves the viewer uncertain and suspicious that the face of this child may mirror that of his older brother, the only child's face shown to the camera.

The destabilizing features of the photograph not only unsettle the viewer but, within the scene, complicate the image of the mother. If the need of the youngest son compels her present attention, the horror of the older son seems no less ready to make its claim. As the viewer's eye is drawn in worry to the expression of the older son, so does that stare of terror seem on the verge of pulling the mother's gaze away from its present focus. The stare, intent and powerful in its vector, cuts across the visual line of the mother's vis-à-vis and, like a magnet, seems capable of tugging her vision to the urgency on her own side of the fence.

The two sons sit opposite each other and look askew in different directions. Situated on one side of the fence, the mother cannot meet the gaze of either son without, at the same time, hiding her face from the other. The sons' vectors of vision, each competing for the mother's sight, dramatize again the force of the fence as a dividing barrier. From the mother's vantage no unified perspective can include both sons, a visual feature of the photograph that reminds the viewer that the fence severs the world into two sides and ever acts to exclude. At the wire fence, the mother thus shares features of the same dilemma that freighted the mothers of mercy in their acts of compassion: She cannot comfort the one son without, at least for the time being, denying attention to the other, whose need may grow urgent as the moment lengthens.

A sense of the dilemma sharpens when the viewer interprets the mother's image in terms of the comforter type and its emphasis on accompaniment. Both Blimele's mother in "Lekh-Lekho" and Mrs. Tzamber in Zelkowicz's diary can comfort because of their accompanying presence. They share the journey of their children: In deportation, Blimele still sits on her mother's lap; in the Lodz courtyard, the Tzamber daughter yet knows the grip of her mother's hand. The fence denies the mother in the photograph the possibility of accompanying her youngest child and, moreover, renders the thought futile. Even should she be able to break through the barrier to join her youngest son, she could do so only at the expense of the other children gathered on her side of the fence. To accompany the youngest son would no less forsake the older in his terror. By its authority to place mother and children on separate sides of an unyielding divide, the fence has given the mother no choice. It further torments with the taunt that, whatever she might imagine doing, she will be an outsider to at least one of her children—a "choiceless choice," even if possible.

The mother of the wire fence yet defies the boundary that would make her an outsider to the youngest son. If separated, she will not here betray or simply surrender her child. The very fact of the fence's two sides has, in one sense, already effected her release of the child and set her at distance. It does not seem, however, to have overcome a manifest will to accompany. Although the mother cannot finally surpass the barrier, she acts to establish a presence that joins to the forbidden edge. As noted in other instances, it is possible for her to despair or to turn away. She does not. She speaks; she gestures. In these acts she freights the moment with a tangence that touches the other side.

The mothers of comfort, in their effort to accompany, all seek to overcome the isolation of their children. In the moment of crisis, their children must not suffer alone. Various expressions of touch, from holding the child's hand to rocking the child upon a lap, tangibly assert the accompanying presence. Silence, however, can also isolate; the absence of a word can estrange. Like the Maccabean mother whose message accompanies her sons to their execution, and like the mother of Blimele whose stories accompany her in exile, the mother of the wire fence brings to her child the sound of a human voice. She broaches the silence of wire and post with the thrust of her own word. In the case of the Maccabean mother and the mother of Blimele, speech responds to pending danger with words of continuity. At the wire fence, the viewer does not know what words the mother speaks, only that she is speaking. That must suffice. Where the fence is silent, the voice penetrates the web of wire and offers a human presence. Where a child is alone, the mother's word—heard and remembered—accompanies.

The final expression is not spoken, but given to gesture. With body and hands, the mother of the wire fence offers a visual sign that communicates motion toward the son. Posture, the bearing of the body, discloses intention. She kneels, but leans forward, extending her face and the momentum of her body toward the opposite side of the fence. In unforgettable gesture, her hand curls to clasp the run of wire as if to draw it toward her, and with it, the child who sits beyond; as if, for the moment, to make herself a part of that fence whose line must now channel their connection. Singularly, the mother comes near to embrace, as she can, the realm beyond the wire fence. This, a fleeting gesture, yet fills the moment with a presence that endures in the artifact and in the viewer's mind. Present to her child, the mother's final name is Comforter; her legacy, the dilemma of compassion and the struggle to touch the other side.

NOTES

1. Nelly Sachs, "A dead child speaks," in *O The Chimneys*, trans. Ruth and Matthew Mead (New York: Farrar, Straus & Giroux, 1967), 13.

2. Jozef Zelkowicz, *In These Nightmarish Days*, in *Lodz Ghetto: Inside a Community Under Siege*, eds. Alan Adelson and Robert Lapides (New York: Viking, 1989), 320 (hereafter referred to as *Lodz Ghetto*). *In These Nightmarish Days*, the diary of Jozef Zelkowicz, is a 345-page Yiddish manuscript, the longest sustained writing to survive from the Lodz Ghetto. Zelkowicz was an ethnographer and historian who was involved in the ghetto archive and *Chronicle*, contemporary efforts to document the perilous life of the Jewish community in Lodz from 1941–44. Zelkowicz died at Auschwitz in 1944.

3. Elie Wiesel, in describing the photographer Roman Vishniac. See Wiesel's foreword to the important collection of Vishniac's work, *A Vanished World* (New York: Farrar, Straus & Giroux, 1983).

4. The last scene is not remote from the world of the photograph. On display in the art museum at Yad Vashem, The Holocaust Martyrs' and Heroes' Remembrance Authority (Jerusalem), one finds a Monopoly game made by a child in one of the ghettos. The game board, however, instead of being defined by its usual markings and labels, is shown to bear images and names from the ghetto itself. The child's immediate world is transferred onto the game board, creating at least a temporary sense for the child of being able to negotiate that constricting world.

5. The photograph is reproduced in Mendel Grossman, *With a Camera in the Ghetto*, ed. Z. Szner and A. Sened (New York: Schocken Books, 1977), 46–47; and in *Lodz Ghetto*, 356–57. Grossman's photographs belong within the materials of the Lodz archives, an effort institutionalized by the community's leader (the "eldest of the Jews"), Mordecai Chaim Rumkowski. The work of the Archives, a section of the ghetto's Department of Population Records, included the daily *Chronicle* as well as monographic and encyclopedic documentation of the Lodz Ghetto. Diaries and journals kept by persons such as Jozef Zelkowicz (see n. 2) complement this work and are part of the same collective activity to write and record. On the archives, see *The Chronicle of the Lodz Ghetto, 1941–44*, ed. Lucjan Dobroszycki (New Haven, Conn.: Yale University Press, 1984), ix–xvi (hereafter referred to as *Chronicle*). Upon the ghetto's liquidation, Grossman was taken to the Koenigs-Wusterhausen labor camp where he continued to photograph clandestinely. A few days before the Nazi surrender in 1945, Grossman died in a forced march from the German camp, his camera still

with him. On Grossman, see Arieh Ben-Menahem, "Mendel Grossman—The Photographer of the Lodz Ghetto," in *With a Camera in the Ghetto*, 97–107. On the problematics of Holocaust photography, see Yitzchak Mais in *19.9.41, A Day in the Warsaw Ghetto* (Jerusalem: Yad Vashem, 1988).

6. *Chronicle*, 255.

7. In *Lodz Ghetto*, 320.

8. On the deportations from Lodz, see *Chronicle*, 123–74 and 250–58, and also xx–xxi; *Lodz Ghetto*, 197–265 and 319–59; and Shmuel Krakowski, s.v. "Lodz," in *Encyclopedia of the Holocaust*, ed. Israel Gutman (New York: Macmillan Publishing Co., 1990), 3:905–7.

9. As Dobroszycki notes, it is not until the summer of 1942 that the community seems to gain knowledge of the nearby death camp. On April 12 members of the Gestapo bring to Lodz a falsely consoling description of resettlement life (see *Chronicle*, 145). Later in the summer, however, a letter from the Rabbi of Grabow quoting the eyewitness of one who had managed to escape the camp arrives in Lodz, although we cannot be certain either of the extent of its circulation or of its influence. For the text and discussion see Dobroszycki's introduction to *Chronicle*, xx–xxi. If not through this letter, then clearly, by the open barbarism of the *Gehsperre* the implications of deportation would be spelled out in a way unforeseeable earlier in the year.

10. See the testimony of Irena Liebman, *Lodz Ghetto*, 350.

11. For the text of Rumkowski's speech, see *Lodz Ghetto*, 328–31. The *Chronicle* summarizes the speech bluntly: "In his speech of September 4, 1942 (at 4:00 P.M.), the Chairman announced that, by order of the authorities, about 25,000 Jews under the age of 10 and over 65 must be resettled out of the ghetto" (250). That during this week the actual number of deportees was closer to 15,000 (which the *Chronicle* notes) should not ease the picture of what is here envisioned or is ultimately to occur. On Rumkowski's speech and the situation of Jewish children in the ghettos, see Deborah Dwork, *Children with a Star: Jewish Youth in Nazi Europe* (New Haven, Conn.: Yale University Press, 1991), 155–205, and especially 176–79.

12. Although his authority was virtually unassailable within the ghetto, Rumkowski's contemporaries responded to him on a wide spectrum from hatred to adulation. Harsh criticism can be heard in the lampooning lyrics of Yankev Herszkowicz, one verse of which runs: "Rumkowski Chaim gives us bran-a, / He gives us barley, he gives us life. / Once upon a time, Jews too ate manna. / Now each man is eaten by his wife! / . . . May the devil take him away!" For the full text see the anthology of David Roskies, *The Literature of Destruction* (Philadelphia: Jewish Publication Society, 1989), 471–72. Mendel Grossman also photographed Herszkowicz, a popular street singer. See *With a Camera in the Ghetto*, 38. Controversy over Rumkowski continues in the critical and historical literature. See Isaiah Trunk, *Judenrat: The Jewish Councils in Eastern Europe Under Nazi Occupation* (New York: Macmillan Publishing Co., 1972).

13. From the notebooks of Oskar Rosenfeld, *Lodz Ghetto*, 352.

14. Rumkowski's speech begins in this way: "A grievous blow has struck the ghetto. They are asking us to give up the best we possess—the children and the elderly. . . . I never imagined I would be forced to deliver this sacrifice to the altar with my own hands" (*Lodz Ghetto*, 328). That, in his thinking, the sacrifice would be redemptive of Jewish lives is clear in the speech: "I must tell you a secret: they requested 24,000 victims, 3000 a day for eight days. I succeeded in reducing the

number to 20,000, but only on the condition that these would be children below the age of ten" (330).

15. Rumkowski's role is, I think, ambiguous. Such ambiguity, however, should not obscure either the paucity of his alternatives or the fact that the damnable situation in which he finds himself is not of his own making. To place blame on Rumkowski for the sacrifice evades the Nazi victimization at all levels and its characteristic strategy of compelling choiceless choices, of placing Jews in urgent dilemmas wherein they cannot but be destructive of themselves or someone else. In this regard, see Lawrence L. Langer, *Versions of Survival: The Holocaust and the Human Spirit* (Albany, N.Y.: SUNY, 1982), 67–129 (hereafter referred to as *Versions of Survival*).

16. Here I follow the suggestion of the editors of *Lodz Ghetto*, who include this photograph within their discussion of the September 1942 events. *With a Camera in the Ghetto* identifies the photograph as a leave-taking prior to a deportation, but dates the photograph from 1943. The later date is not likely. There were no deportations from Lodz between September 13, 1942, and May 1944 and, in that relatively stable period, there were very few children or elderly still present in the ghetto (see Krakowski, 905). Moreover, the scene itself, with the isolation of the younger child, presupposes precisely such a situation as reflected in the *Gehsperre* and in the aftermath of Rumkowski's September 4 speech.

17. From the diary of Jozef Zelkowicz, in *Lodz Ghetto*, 341. For this, and the general portrait of the round-up process that follows, I depend on Zelkowicz's account (*Lodz Ghetto*, 336–48) and on the *Chronicle's* description of the action (251). I have extrapolated the process to the particular case of the photograph, but in no instance have I manufactured a feature or detail that is beyond the contemporary accounts.

18. Zelkowicz, especially sensitive to the plight of mothers and children, gives a detailed account of the murder of a Mrs. Tzamber and her four-year-old child who still held her hand. The second image is again from Zelkowicz's diary, this time rendering his sense of the increased violence in the Nazi-executed round-up. See *Lodz Ghetto*, 346–47 and 342. Note, too, the parallel between the second image and lines from Bialik's 1904 Kishinev oracle, "In the City of Slaughter" "Of how a dagger halved an infant's word, / Its *ma* was heard, its *mama* never heard," in *The Literature of Destruction*, 161.

19. Thus the description of the *Chronicle*, 251–52. The wagons in many cases were driven by members of the "White Guard," teamsters of the ghetto who come in for harsh censure by Zelkowicz (*Lodz Ghetto*, 340). Photographs of one children-laden wagon and also the deportation trucks are printed in *Lodz Ghetto*, 358.

20. Thus the *Chronicle*, 252. Dobroszycki's note details the route: "The 5-ton trucks took deportees to a railroad station outside of Lodz, where the victims were loaded onto railroad cars and sent via Kutno to Kolo, and from there taken directly by vehicle to the death camp in Chelmno, a distance of 14 kilometers" (252, n. 80).

21. The only resolution would be for both mother and son to share the same side of the fence, a restoration of a common world—and it is precisely this that neither of them can do. *There are no choices to be made.* The son is powerless to escape his captivity, and the mother to join his exile (which, even should she be able to do, would be futile on the one hand, and abandoning of different children, on the other).

22. The approach followed here takes seriously the challenge and caution advanced by Joan Ringelheim in "Women and the Holocaust: A Reconsideration of the Research," in *Signs: Journal of Women in Culture and Society* 10 (1985): 741–61. In the

same way that one should resist abstracting Holocaust victims and survivors from their Jewishness, so must one ask questions of gender and social role. In the case of the Lodz photograph, we do not elevate gender per se to a primary determinant of the woman's situation, but we do look to her role as mother as providing the fundamental key to understanding the photograph. We do not contrast her suffering as a woman with that of a man, for example, but we do situate her as a mother in relation to her children, and we look to that relation as the single most pertinent feature of the scene. The mother of the wire fence may not suffer because she is a mother, but only as a mother can she respond to the suffering imposed upon her as a Jew.

23. See note 8.

24. "*Lekh-Lekho*," completed February 23, 1942, and "Spring 5702 [1942]," completed on Passover Eve, 1942, were the only two of Shayevitsh's poems to be recovered after the war. In 1946 these two poems were published in Yiddish by the Central Jewish Historical Commission in Lodz. Elinor Robinson's translation of "*Lekh-Lekho*" is included in Roskies, *Literature of Destruction*, 520–30; another translation is given in *Lodz Ghetto*, 216–30. A translation of "Spring 5702 [1942]" is printed in *Lodz Ghetto*, 250–62. Shayevitsh himself was deported to Auschwitz in 1944 and died in the Kaufering camp shortly before the liberation. For biographical sketches, see *Literature of Destruction*, 630, and *Lodz Ghetto*, 504.

25. "Spring 5702 [1942]," in *Lodz Ghetto*, 260–61.

26. Jeremiah's typology is complex. The prophet transforms the figure of Rachel not once, but twice. The metaphor depends upon a double analogy. First, the prophet appeals to the figure of Rachel to provide a metaphor for the eighth-century Assyrian deportation of the tribe of Ephraim, her "child." As the mother Rachel would have mourned for the loss of her children (in this case Ephraim, the son of her son Joseph), so would the land or nation—the personified Rachel—weep for the loss of the tribe of Ephraim. Second, the prophet then allows this figure of the weeping Rachel to provide analogy to the ordeal of the sixth-century Babylonian Exile with which he himself must contend.

27. "Spring 5702 [1942]," in *Lodz Ghetto*, 260.

28. From the translation of "A Night" by Hillel Schwartz and David Roskies; included in *Literature of Destruction*, 237.

29. From *Midrash Rabbah Lamentations*, trans. A. Cohen (London: Soncino Press, 1939), 40–49; Roskies includes this text in *Literature of Destruction*, 52–56.

30. On the Czech Family Camp, see the following witnesses: Filip Mueller, *Eyewitness Auschwitz: Three Years in the Gas Chambers*, ed. and trans. S. Flatauer (New York: Stein and Day, 1979), 90–119; Ota Kraus and Erich Kulka, *The Death Factory: Document on Auschwitz*, trans. Stephen Jolly (New York: Oxford University Press, 1966), 172–74. Note also Martin Gilbert, *The Holocaust* (New York: Holt, Rinehart & Winston, 1985), 657–59.

31. The *Sonderkommando* was that group of Jewish prisoners compelled to work in the crematoria, performing the menial labor of the death factory. It fell to this group, for instance, to cremate the corpses, to maintain the furnaces, and to clean the crematoria between killings. Gradowski, an observant Polish Jew from Suwalki, carefully recorded the narrative of portions of his experience at Auschwitz. He buried his writings in the ash-pits of the crematoria. Four of these chronicles have survived, including his account of the murder of the Czech Family Camp. Gradowski himself died in the revolt of the *Sonderkommando* on October 7, 1944. Excerpts of Gradowski's

chronicle of the family camp, translated by Robert Wolf, are provided in *Literature of Destruction*, 548–64; on Gradowski, see 517–19.

32. Gradowski, in *Literature of Destruction*, 558.

33. Ibid.

34. Thus Roskies, Ibid. 518–19.

35. I infer that the sons' words, at least in part, prolong their mother's message from the instance of the seventh son (7:26–38). In this case, we overhear the message in detail and find him making his public declaration without pause—indeed, when his mother had barely finished speaking (7:30). Note, too, the general correspondence between the summary of the mother's message (7:22–23) and each son's assertion of confidence in God's power.

36. From Holocaust contexts outside the death camps, parallels do exist for the Maccabean mother's act of giving a message and wagering a future connection. For example, note the testimony of Menachem S., whose mother, before entrusting him to a Polish Christian family, transmits a message and a token, her high school identification card. At the moment of their parting, she says, "You keep my picture, so when we meet again . . ." The testimony, excerpted from the Fortunoff Video Archive for Holocaust Testimonies at Yale University, is quoted by Lawrence Langer in *Holocaust Testimonies: The Ruins of Memory* (New Haven, Conn.: Yale University Press, 1991), 110 (hereafter referred to as *Holocaust Testimonies*). This same testimony is discussed in Shoshana Felman and Dori Laub's *Testimony: Crises of Witnessing in Literature, Psychoanalysis, and History* (New York: Routledge, 1992), 86–92.

37. On the problematic character of restoration see the poem of Dan Pagis, "Draft for a Reparations Agreement," in *Variable Directions*, trans. Stephen Mitchell (San Francisco: North Point Press, 1989), 35.

38. On the phenomenon of "choiceless choices" and its relation to categories of moral heroism and martyrdom, see *Versions of Survival*, 67–129. Note also the reflections of Emil Fackenheim, *God's Presence in History* (New York: New York University Press, 1970), 73–76.

39. Note that the structures of faith provide a frame of reference that renders the Maccabean choice nonabsurd: difficult certainly, but meaningful. In the Gradowski text, however, no such structure of faith can be inferred and, moreover, even were it to be manifest it would be powerless to mitigate the fundamental absurdity. The Czech mother's death bears no real relation to her faith, her maternity, or her defiance.

40. Shayevitsh, "*Lekh-Lekho*," lines 170–80; in *Literature of Destruction*, 524.

41. "*Lekh-Lekho*," ll. 121–24; Ibid., 523.

42. On Zelkowicz and his diary, see n. 2. On this particular scene, see *Lodz Ghetto*, 346–47.

43. *Lodz Ghetto*, 347.

44. One might explore the notion of mothers of mercy in other contexts as well, as, for example, in Toni Morrison's novel, *Beloved* (New York: Knopf, 1987), esp. 148–53. Morrison dramatizes the comparable plight and protective instinct of an African-American mother in the time of slavery and its immediate aftermath. I am indebted to Anne Blue Wills for this reference.

45. See "Martyrs of Mainz," in *The Penguin Book of Hebrew Verse*, ed. and trans. T. Carmi (New York: Penguin Books, 1981), 372–73.

46. *In the Hell of Auschwitz: The Wartime Memoirs of J.S. Newman* (New York: Exposition Press, 1963), 42–43 (hereafter referred to as *In the Hell of Auschwitz*).

47. Thus *Versions of Survival*, 42.

48. Ibid.

49. Ibid., ix. This quotation functions as an apt motto for Langer's work that argues at length the problematics of *Lager* existence over-against theories of survival grounded in the prospect of moral heroism (as, for example, in the writings of Viktor Frankl and Bruno Bettelheim).

50. *In the Hell of Auschwitz*, 43. Newman comments, echoing Lengyel's self-appraisal: "This girl had learned well from the SS and had become a murderess herself."

51. Cited in *Versions of Survival*, 42. Note also the comments of Joan Ringelheim on the vulnerability of women with children. See "Women and the Holocaust," 746.

52. *Versions of Survival*, 42.

53. Quoted in Konnilyn G. Feig, *Hitler's Death Camps: The Sanity of Madness* (London: Holmes and Meier, 1979), 184 (hereafter referred to as *Hitler's Death Camps*).

54. *In the Hell of Auschwitz*, 52.

55. *Hitler's Death Camps*, 288; Feig quotes from Isaiah Trunk, *Jewish Responses to Nazi Persecution* (New York: Stein & Day, 1980).

56. Quoted in Saul Friedlaender, *When Memory Comes*, trans. Helen Lane (New York: Noonday Books, 1979), 78; see also, 90.

57. Ibid., 87–88.

58. For parallels to Elli Friedlaender's act, see the testimonies recounted in *Holocaust Testimonies*, 9 and 110.

59. *This Way for the Gas, Ladies and Gentlemen*, trans. Barbara Vedder (New York: Viking Press, 1967), 23.

60. *Holocaust Testimonies*, 12.

61. Ibid., 13.

62. See Zelkowicz's account in *Lodz Ghetto*, 346–47. That Zelkowicz notes that at the end the mother holds the daughter's hand "more convulsively" only accents the fact that throughout this scene the mother had remained calm.

63. See Gradowski, in *Literature of Destruction*, 558.

64. In this regard, see Elaine Scarry's insightful discussion of torture as an assault on a victim's person by first unmaking or dissolving her or his world. See *The Body in Pain: The Making and Unmaking of the World* (New York: Oxford University Press, 1985), 27–59.

65. On the phenomenological significance of "face," see Emmanuel Levinas, *Totality and Infinity*, trans. A. Lingis (Pittsburgh: Duquesne University Press, 1969), 187–247; and, with a theological perspective, the writings of Abraham Joshua Heschel. For depiction of a similar masking of anguish, note Kierkegaard's exordium to *Fear and Trembling*, trans. H. Hong and E. Hong (Princeton, N.J.: Princeton University Press, 1983), 9–14.

66. Note, too, that beyond the triangle of figures, other children look in still a different direction. The girls at either end look toward the photograph's upper right corner. Their perspective is ambiguous: Do they look away with a relaxed indifference to the conversation, or do they function as watch-guards on the lookout for the approach of further threat? Whatever the motive, their vector of vision adds to the instability of the photograph through the distraction of another line of sight.

2 EVE OF THE BOXCAR

> To understand the last collective response of a people in all
> its contradictions, one must look to the writers, who, be-
> cause they shared the same fate and were intimately involved
> in all facets of the people's Armageddon, were able to trans-
> mute the screams into a new and terrible scripture.
>
> —David G. Roskies[1]

> It was The Book for me in the sense Bruno had yearned for
> "that great tome, sighing, a stormy Bible, its pages fluttering in
> the wind like an overblown rose"—and I believe I read it as
> such a letter deserves to be read: knowing that what is writ-
> ten on the page is less significant than the pages torn out and
> lost. . . ."
>
> —David Grossman[2]

THE LAND OF *THERE*

The struggle to touch the other side never ends. Where the
mother of the wire fence and her son, in 1942, faced an unyielding barrier,
survivors were to confront in the aftermath a continuing isolation of those
once severed from human kinship. If he had survived, the young boy would
yet, in certain respects, remain behind the fence, trapped in the loneliness of
an inexpressible experience. Silent where words would betray, he would find
no ready bridge to connect him to those who had not shared his ordeal. He
could not speak and, from the other side, even the willing could not understand. If death was his fate, as surely it was, his dying would be unreachable,
as remote as his living face from the lens of the camera or from his mother's
touch.

The durability of the fence does not grow either from the reluctance of
survivors to testify or, in the main, from outsiders to listen. Rather, the fence
stands as a symptom of the past's lingering estrangement; it is the Holocaust
rendered into perfect tense. Its continuing force feeds on the singular dimensions of what Jews suffered behind the wire fences of ghetto and *Lager*. Where
the Nazi fence separated Jews from the human context of life, that barrier
reasserts itself in the burden of remembrance and testimony. For the survivor,
memory is a form of the wound itself; testimony, a repetition.[3] Where Jews

testify to an incomprehensible or radically distinct experience, their words may reenact a deep sense of isolation, a further moment of being cut off from the community whose ordeal has not been as theirs. And if the Jew's testimony cannot be given and received within that community, then the fence simply remains unbroken; all remain apart.

As a continuing crisis, the fence threatens more than the mother and son of the Lodz Ghetto. Not only does it slice their world into two sides, but it separates the viewer of the photograph from that estranged world. Unless the viewer has sat on either side of that fence, he or she will come to the photograph too late to know its immediate anguish and from too far away to share its dilemma. As the fence makes the mother an outsider to her son's inside of the wire, so it makes of the viewer a stranger to the fragile moment of the photograph. The photograph testifies in its own language. How can we who come late and from afar receive its image, its word? How can we, like the mother of the wire fence, touch the other side?

The other side is a place called "THERE." So infers Momik, the nine-year-old child protagonist of David Grossman's *See Under: Love*.[4] Haunted by the murmurings of his parents and the deranged allusions of a grandfatherly uncle, Momik senses an ominous undertone to the family history. In the days sometime before the year 1959 in this Jerusalem suburb, a time before Momik's birth, something occurred in a land spoken of in whispered tones as "Over There." About that place named THERE, Momik can know only fragments, cryptic echoes that are themselves broken like the old man's immigrant Hebrew. Its danger and awesomeness he knows from the hush and the indirection: "Whatever it was that happened Over There must have really been something for everyone to try so hard not to talk about it."[5]

As Momik's story indicates, however, those around him are, in fact, "talk[ing] about it." The whispers, the vague echoes, the gaps, all testify as part of the language of THERE, a language whose meaning, on the one hand, he can scarcely comprehend, but on the other, hardly escape. If he assumes THERE to be the name of a land whose foreign language is impenetrable, he has not misunderstood. No dictionary exists to secure his knowledge. If he supposes the numbers on Anshel Wasserman's arm to have been written from somewhere within the old man, etched from the inside out, he mistakes only the implementation of the scar. He has not misunderstood the numbers' permanence (scrubbing on the outside provides no remedy) or their link to inner torment. If he reckons the "Nazi Beast" to be a mysterious animal that roamed THERE and now lives in their basement to menace and harm, he has not misunderstood the threat, only the creature's imagined form. Seeking to stalk this beast that makes his father scream in the night, Momik begins to catalog the history, the language, and the topography of THERE. His effort is heroic, but tragic. He collapses under the burden of what he has understood, albeit in his own way, and from proximity to that which he cannot understand in any way: the irreducible there-ness of Over There. Later, as a writer, Momik will return to the raving words of the old man and thereby resume the struggle to touch the other side. He can only succeed by again seeking the elusive language of THERE and the gate through which it passes to become HERE. He must find the opening in that unbroken fence.

STORIES OF A NEW BIBLE

Primo Levi, one of the few Italian Jews to survive Auschwitz, began to write of his ordeal as early as 1947.[6] Written within months of his return home, his memoir compresses the lapse that commonly distinguishes the survivor's recollection from the inmate's contemporary witness. He writes his memoir, however, keenly aware of the death camps' burden on language that would span even this short distance to speak of the past atrocities. The aftermath of Auschwitz, for Levi, threatened to sever the connective tissues of language that would bridge HERE and THERE. He writes:

> Just as our hunger is not that feeling of missing a meal, so our way of being cold has need of a new word. We say "hunger," we say "tiredness," "fear," "pain," we say "winter" and they are different things. They are free words, created and used by free men who lived in comfort and suffering in their homes. If the Lagers had lasted longer a new, harsh language would have been born; and only this language could express what it means to toil the whole day in the wind, with the temperature below freezing, wearing only a shirt, underpants, cloth jacket and trousers, and in one's body nothing but weakness, hunger and knowledge of the end drawing nearer.[7]

In Levi's reckoning, only a different language born of the *Lager* itself, could express the wind-whipping absurdity of his experience; but if it did so, who could understand it? In this case, difference shatters the continuity of language. THERE remains, in Kafkan terms, that realm always "away from here."[8]

Levi offers another nuance, however, when he writes of the inmates' own storytelling. Of one prisoner he notes:

> He told me his story, and today I have forgotten it, but it was certainly a sorrowful, cruel and moving story; because so are all our stories, hundreds of thousands of stories, all different and all full of a tragic, disturbing necessity. We tell them to each other in the evening, and they take place in Norway, Italy, Algeria, the Ukraine and are simple and

incomprehensible like the stories in the Bible. *But are they not themselves stories of a new Bible?*"⁹

With this figure Levi affirms both discontinuity and continuity: these are "stories of a new Bible." On the one hand, the tales prisoners tell differ not only from each other, but from the biblical legacy of the interpreter's world. Their chronicle unscrolls a scripture that is new. On the other hand, even in their difference, these stories constitute a testament—"simple and incomprehensible"—that Levi understands as a Bible, a *megillah* of mysteries. Thus, a thread of likeness integrates that which is THERE into a pattern already HERE.

Levi's trope—"stories of a new Bible"—provokes questions necessary to a discussion of holocaust literature and the language of testimony.¹⁰ First, according to Levi, holocaust testimony requires a *Lager* language all its own and asserts a quality that is "simple and incomprehensible." Thus, he gives testimony connotations of difference and irreducibility that cut the cords of analogy and metaphor.¹¹ In its simple difference, what happened THERE is unlike what has happened HERE and cannot be reduced to or explained by its categories. Accordingly, the patterns of experience fashioned HERE may be unable to furnish viable analogy or metaphor, a language, through which to speak of THERE. If such connotations resist efforts to integrate the Holocaust into antecedent perspectives, what then is the nature of the continuity suggested by Levi's trope? Does it honor the difference of THERE or seek to suppress it? Does it accept the existence of a *caesura*, or does it deny such a gap and its implication of silence?¹²

Second, Levi's trope, in its hint of continuity, encourages thinking of the Holocaust through literary types, a mode of language that involves a network of intertextual relations. The trope concedes that while the Holocaust may defy analogy, any language used to write of it will be tangled in a web of tradition and textual equivalences. The stories told by inmates, although filled with difference, are yet "like the stories in the Bible." As Levi construes biblical narrative as a prototype for the "simple and incomprehensible" testimony, the question of continuity and difference again asserts itself: Can intertextuality, the network of relations between one discourse and another, avoid the compromising of difference? For example, can one name the Holocaust intertextually in terms of the Bible's HERE and yet keep the "simple and incomprehensible" character of THERE? Does intertextuality inevitably subordinate THERE to the qualifying relation of HERE?

Third, the particular trope raises a narrower issue. If intertextuality is possible within *Lager* language, can the Hebrew Bible provide the Holocaust a source for continuity and trope? As "stories of a new Bible," how are the tales that inmates tell related to the tropes and types of the precursor Bible?

THE MESSAGE FROM EVE

The issues of Levi's text find concrete expression in the poetry of Dan Pagis. A Romanian-born Jew, Pagis survived Hitler's camps and in 1946 emigrated to what was then Palestine. With Yehuda Amichai, Nathan Zach, and Abba Kovner, he became one of the leading poets writing in modern Hebrew during the first generation of the state of Israel.[13] His poems embody what Sidra Ezrahi has termed "a poetics of displacement," a use of language that unmoors words from any determinate situation or fixed time and place.[14] In their displacement, Pagis's poems emphasize discontinuity. Suspended in their own coordinates, his poems seldom refer beyond themselves. Thus, it surprises when Pagis employs biblical typology, evoking continuity amid unrelenting dislocation. Where Levi wrote of "stories of a new Bible," Pagis speaks through the persona of an Abel and about a Cain, his fratricide. He reads words scrawled by an Eve, their mother, in a sealed railway-car.[15] Accordingly, the poetry requires a probing of the same issues that emerge from Levi's figure and returns us, as well, to the question of the Lodz photograph: What is the relation between discontinuity and continuity? How are THERE (the experience of the boxcar) and HERE (the language of biblical narrative) connected? Pagis best illumines these questions in the haunting lines of "Written in Pencil in the Sealed Railway-Car." It is the message of another mother with one son beside her and his brother utterly separate from them both.

This is a dark poem, full of white space, an empty page that takes away the wend of our word. It reads in full:

> here in this carload
> i am eve
> with abel my son
> if you see my other son
> cain son of man
> tell him that i

The spare economy of these lines exposes jolting movements. Stark and simple, the poem moves the reader to confront the Holocaust's difference. The scene pushes the reader from a perception of the confinement of the railway-car to the devastating open-endedness of Eve's message. Yet the poem shows a counter direction as well. It moves the reader from a position outside the boxcar to a space within it, a movement that insists that the reader forge a connection with the encountered difference and touch the other side. If Eve's ellipsis breaks every continuity, her mandate to "tell" allows no discontinuity to remain unclaimed.[16]

The Preservation of Difference

Pagis's title expresses the only clear historical allusion in the poem. The "sealed railway-car" evokes images of that time when narrow-gauge tracks led to ramps of death; when the walls of freight trains entombed Jews in passage to other chambers, fast and secure.[17] Further, the title points to a trace of that season by hinting at the survival of an artifact, a text inscribed within the boxcar walls. Through his allusion and the hint of artifactuality, Pagis loads his title with connotations of fixity and closure. The symmetry of the Hebrew title—language enwalled within its own structure—re-creates the train's confinement and serves those connotations.[18] Like the sealed space of the boxcar, the poem appears at first to have definite coordinates and, thus, a capacity to be known and described. The drastic enclosure portends a closure of fact.

Any closure, however, starts to fall apart with the opening lines. The poem begins with a simple deictic marker, "here" (kaan). The deictic grids the poem yet provides no external reference. "Here" simply describes the place of the poem's speaker, the point from which she pencils her fragment. Of "here" we know only two things: It marks the place of the boxcar's human cargo; and it is never "there" where the poem's readers find themselves. Although elusive, the "here" maps a structure within the poem itself. As the poem designates "here" as someplace within the boxcar, it implies an opposing "there" that is outside the car walls, a somewhere else. The mother's message, an address to a reader absent from "here," presupposes a distance between writer and reader, who always comes to these words after and from afar. "Here" is where the reader cannot be; where the reader is cannot be "here."[19]

The sealed chamber further loses determinacy when Pagis names its occupants as Eve and her son Abel. With Eve's words, Pagis introduces a mythic presence or transcendence into the poem, setting it at significant remove from the geography of history and the rhetoric of realism and fact. The boxcar's "here" corresponds to no "where"—at least to no "where" that a reader can control for the purposes of his or her knowledge. Eve's "here," though not apart from the history of sealed railway cars, loads that history with a surplus of difference, elusive and irreducible.

Pagis's invocation of an Eve of the boxcar involves the poem in intertextuality. The retrieval of Eve, Cain, and Abel as types infuses the poem with connotations funded by biblical mythology: That Eve, the mother of humankind, is the boxcar's scribe emphasizes its claim upon all who are her children; that Abel is the boxcar's child names that which threatens its passengers as unprecedented fratricide. Still, if these echoes place values in the text, the intertextual relations work no less to displace other connotations.[20] In particular, Pagis keeps the boxcar free of any confinement within the schemes of biblical salvation history or covenantal logic of national destruction and rebirth.[21] When Pagis puts Abel in the boxcar, he displaces, for example, the nearly sacrificed Isaac (or a crucified Christ) from the role of paradigmatic victim, a displacement that resists any surrender of the Holocaust to frames of theological rescue or nationalistic empowerment.[22] For Pagis, too much coherence lurks in the biblical historical scheme. When he fills the boxcar with the personae of myth, his intertextuality functions critically; that is, it displaces historical or theological schemes that would fix the boxcar's meaning and conscript its service within religious, cultural, or national agenda. His use of myth guards against closure and its companion, the ideological purchase of history.[23] Eve's boxcar remains uncoupled.

The deictic "here" and the mythic displacement prepare the way for the culminating expression of difference: Eve's final silence. We do not know what accounts for this silence. In mid-scrawl has the door been thrown open with harsh, male shouts to hurry, to make a line, to march to this side or that? Or has Eve crouched for days in the fetid chamber, pencil ready to inscribe words that simply do not come to language? Whether the silence of interruption or of inexpressibility, Eve's message remains fundamentally enigmatic. We know only the profundity of its effect.

All lines converge in the intractable blank of Eve's silence. At the poem's conclusion, when the reader most wants to bring Eve's message under the control of some perspective, the poem exposes an unbridgeable gap. The blank guards Eve's difference by rendering her message as an empty space, effectively negating any ideological impulse. No reader can co-opt the otherness of Eve's fragment, for it refuses to express itself in terms that one could subordinate to other controlling interests or could govern by analogy to anything other than its own emptiness. Silent, it refuses to express itself in terms at all, an effacement of language that hushes the reader's inclination to speak before the difference of this boxcar. What Eve does not say, the poem forbids the reader to utter in her behalf. Any language would be only the reader's, not hers.[24]

From Difference to Connection

Eve's silence enforces the distance between the boxcar and those who would speak of it. It dramatizes the chasm between HERE and THERE. Still, in the midst of this discontinuity, the poem shows undeniable concern for connection. If Eve's silence stifles the pretense of language, her word to "tell [Cain]" affords no refuge in the absence of speech. The poem obliges the continuity it has rendered so problematic. It insists upon the meeting of HERE and THERE.

The second half of the poem shifts the grammatical mood from the indicative to the conditional imperative:

> if you see my other son
> cain son of man
> tell him that i[25]

This turn reshapes the theme of closure. If, in one sense, the poem moves from the closure of the boxcar to the open silence of Eve, in another, it moves from the statement of Eve's closed isolation to an expression of her will not to be thus sealed. Eve's imperative, like the gesture of the mother in Lodz, reaches out to another self. Her command implicates a reader—the poem's "you"—whose attention frees the mother's voice from the confines of the boxcar and becomes the channel through which it connects with the world beyond. Through the reader, the voice addresses Cain, Eve's other son, who roams outside the chamber walls.

The poem summons the reader to perform a dual role. He or she receives Eve's empty message, but also her mandate to "tell" the "other son." The poem tangles these roles intricately. As the poem's "you," the reader receives Eve's imperative and the devastating blank that follows. Accordingly, the reader must both hear and transmit the message of the silence. However, transmitting the message to Cain is ironic, for the poem identifies him not only as Eve's "other son" but as "ben adam." Literally, the phrase names Cain as "Adam's son," but the same words also bear the meaning of "son of man," or simply, "a human being."[26] Thus, at least in one sense, the poem compels the readers to transmit Eve's legacy to themselves, to address themselves as Cain, the figure who lurks outside the boxcar.[27]

Returning to the spatial grid of the poem, both the reader and Cain are not "here" in Eve's sealed chamber. While their status as outsiders to the boxcar may imply simply a different fate, the mythic identity of Cain suggests a stronger over-againstness. Not to be present with the victims is to stand with their executioners, guilty of a distance that, at least, imposes detachment and may escalate from indifference to violence. If the reader is to avoid remaining Cain, he or she must somehow move from outside to inside the boxcar. Eve's imperative demands more than simple contact with Cain: To "tell him" is to transform him so the weight of the heavy emptiness becomes his own, so he becomes present among the sufferers as their witness instead of their oppressor, so Eve's isolation comes to an end.

The poem's linking of Cain and the reader underscores the importance of Eve's fragment as text. She writes her lines within and likely on the walls of the sealed chamber, an act that endues her text as an artifact of the boxcar. The text belongs to and emanates from Eve's "here" such that to encounter the artifact is to connect with its source. The textual artifact makes available to some other time and place a vestige of that "here," creating a channel through which the reader, although "not here," is yet touched by its presence. Reading does not empower one either to overcome the difference of the boxcar or to say with confidence that one has "here" arrived. The moment of listening to the text, however, does prod the one who has heard to a point no longer so clearly on the outside. It is then that the reader turns away from the role of Cain and begins to unseal the chamber that has enclosed Eve.

SILENT LEGACY

"Written in Pencil in the Sealed Railway-Car" does not describe events of the Holocaust as much as it inscribes the dilemma they pose for those who would speak of them. A poetic icon of the aftermath, these lines re-create something of the ordeal of the witness caught between the moral demand to testify and the impossibility of finding language with which to do so. The radical difference of the victim's experience, inscribed in Eve's blank, leaves one in silence. The victim's struggle against oblivion, heard in her imperative, compels one to find a language and a way not to stand apart. With what language can one respect Eve's otherness and yet fulfill her imperative? Here we are brought back to the questions raised by Primo Levi's trope.

Continuity and Difference

Pagis's poem sustains a stubborn dissonance. In its competing directions toward difference and connection, it preserves a tension that does not resolve. Such dissonance impedes the path of ideological reading, of seizing some one direction in the poem as absolute and using it to suppress any other claim. Read as a dissonantal whole, this icon of the Holocaust allows the reader neither to mystify nor control its meaning. It forbids the reader either to ignore the artifacts or to reduce the Holocaust's legacy to their mere accounting.[28] Still, the poem involves the relation between more than the simple juxtaposition of clashing tones.

As the poem's readers approach the boxcar's "here," the connection enables a continuity of silence. The frustration of the readers' language, when standing before the empty blank, yokes them with Eve in a moment's "raid on the articulate." The poem hosts a connection between artifact and reader that joins to the difference itself. The poem's "you" stands, in Paul Celan's words, "*Davor das Fremde, des Gast du hier bist*"—as a guest of the [boxcar's] strangeness.[29] He or she stands in relation to that which is other and receives the full expression of its difference. Before any such connection allows the reader to claim "here" as his or her own, it displaces the reader's world and subjects it to the incursion of *das Fremde*. The reader does not claim, but is claimed by the profound difference, a connection forged from the other side. The same discontinuity that robs the reader of speech offers a continuity of silence.

The path of connection exists, but runs one way. A pronounced asymmetry governs the relation between the artifact and the reader who must defer to its difference.[30] To honor Eve's difference means *not* regarding the boxcar from the outside, a vantage that yields only the view of Cain. That view, however, persists. When Claude Lanzmann interviews a Mrs. Michelsohn, the wife of a Nazi schoolteacher in Chelmno, he asks: "'Did you see the gas vans?'" She replies, "'No. . . . Yes, from the outside. They shuttled back and forth. I never looked inside; I didn't see Jews in them. I only saw things from the outside.'"[31]

Mrs. Michelsohn's response reveals more than simple information regarding her observations during the war. Hers is the Cain hermeneutic that can witness the traffic of gas vans, but see no Jews in them, no human faces to haunt the scene, no sign of *das Fremde* to claim her humanity. Viewed from the outside, the event of Chelmno remains in captivity to her reflexive self-interest and banality. She speaks of a site indescribably primitive—"You can't imagine such places exist"—but refers not to the death camp, but to the privies in a town short on sanitary facilities. She recalls the "delousing [of] the Poles" and must be corrected that it was Jews who were here "deloused," a confusion that could only be maintained from the outside and with a German indifference to the fate of either group. When asked about the Jewish work squads that went through the village in chains, she responds: ". . . people wanted nothing to do with all that. Do you see? Gets on your nerves, seeing that every day. You can't force a whole village to watch such distress!" Without any awareness of irony, this Cainlike outsider assumes the primitivity and distress to be hers, a perception scandalous in its refusal to see the real surpassing horror emerging from the inside, where Jews populate gas vans and chained work squads march in exhaustion to their death. Her refusal to look inside condemns Mrs. Michelsohn to her own banality. She has neither knowledge nor the ability to be disturbed by its absence. In a final question, Lanzmann asks her: "'Do you know how many Jews were exterminated [in Chelmno]?'" She answers: "'Four something. Four hundred thousand, forty thousand.'" Lanzmann corrects her: "'Four hundred thousand.'" She answers again, "'Four hundred thousand, yes. I knew it had a four in it.'"[32]

To escape Cain and his heirs, the boxcar must be maintained in its difference. It must not be integrated into the reader's familiar world as if its categories had not been cracked already by Eve's silent scream. Against every Mrs. Michelsohn, it must not be rendered as a cipher of an outsider's self-interest and projection. The alternative to Cain's hermeneutic confers on the boxcar a fundamental status, the freedom to express its own "*Lager* language," itself generating metaphors and types: in this case, the mother in the boxcar with pencil in hand and a message rendered with silence.[33] Such a type, unavailable to the outside, yet interprets the reader's world, reversing the direction of Cain. The hermeneutic of the witness, that reader who touches the silent inside of the boxcar, leads him or her to see the world through the now cracked openings of the train's panels, instead of seeing the sealed car through the seemingly unbroken glass of the world. The boxcar, as fundamental, provides the lens through which the witness sees and the ground from which he or she must speak.

What can the witness say? The poem bequeaths Eve's intention to "tell," to forge the connection that breaks her enclosure. A witness might speak of this but must guard from betraying that intention by reenclosing Eve in categories not her own. To transmit Eve's message may finally occur less through word than through the speaking of silence. The witness's silence, in contrast to the outsider's speech, expresses the willful refusal to any longer say certain things: "I know" and "You are." As such, the witness's silence becomes a mode of listening to the difference of Eve and crafts a vessel through which its resonance may be heard in the world of Cain. The language of continuity and difference is the language of silence; the testimony, a transmission of the gap.

Intertextuality and the Bible

The presence of Eve in the boxcar exposes an intertextual relation in Pagis's poem. As a textual strategy, intertextuality emphasizes the relation between texts and thus may threaten the perception of difference in any one text.[34] Moreover, where difference is radical, the strength of a precursor text may be called upon to suppress its threat. Pagis's use of biblical types—Eve, Abel, and Cain—avoids this ideological temptation in three ways. First, the mythic types function not to displace the boxcar as the center of the poem's meaning, but to frustrate any retrieval of other types, theological or historical, whose presence would run in an ideological direction. Second, the poem's primary type, Eve, is itself anti-ideological in its self-consuming character.

Shaped by the blank of Eve's message, the type empties rather than asserts itself in any form that could be fixed or used to oppress. It expresses rather than obscures difference. And third, in that very respect, the biblical types are themselves interpreted by the boxcar, taking on the features of its enclosure, isolation, and separation.

While serving to express the boxcar's difference, do these biblical types manifest sufficient continuity to justify Levi's category of "stories of a new Bible"? Such continuity, in this case, would show a tendency in the precursor text to manifest its own "simple and irreducible" difference and to demand a connection with that difference. The biblical account of the murder of Abel by Cain (Gen. 4:1–16) narrates an unprecedented act, a deed for which there is no available language. It is not for fear alone that Cain fails to answer YHWH's question, "What have you done?" (4:10). To answer, he cannot reduce the fratricide to anything else, for it is its own first instance and thus, in its moment, filled with difference. A blank exists in the text at the point when Cain is called to confess or be a witness to his brother's absence. He has once evaded and now YHWH talks on, but never does Cain utter what there is no language for: "I killed my brother."[35]

This silence, hidden in the noise of the text, only underscores the deeper silence of another. The murdered Abel has no voice: Separated from the world of the living, he cannot speak and his brother has no words to say. As a story of a victim whose unprecedented fate forms silence and demands testimony, the biblical text finds common ground with the boxcar. Like his mother in the boxcar, this silent victim is not silenced. Absence leaves its trace in both texts: the stain of blood crying out from the earth (Gen. 4:10) and pencil marks in a sealed chamber. These artifacts of difference speak their imperative and claim their Cain. The silence of "the simple and incomprehensible" again seeks connection. If this feature of the ancient narrative invites us to find in *Lager* tales the "stories of a new Bible," the more recent chronicle of our poem suggests that we search scripture for signs of a former Holocaust; that is, that we read it from the vantage of the boxcar, listening for the moment when this Eve claims her precursor and calls forth text and silence to link the voices of HERE and THERE.

NOTES

1. David G. Roskies, *Against the Apocalypse* (Cambridge, Mass.: Harvard University Press, 1984), 202.

2. David Grossman, *See Under: Love*, trans. Betsy Rosenberg (New York: Washington Square Press, 1989), 99.

3. On the incurability of memory after profound victimization, see Mieke Bal,

Death and Dissymmetry (Chicago: University of Chicago Press, 1988), 124. Consider also the testimony of Frieda W. Aaron: "As a girl in the ghetto and camps, I knew certain truths that only the immediacy of experience could yield. As a woman, I still know many of these truths. But total recall is neither always possible nor perhaps even desirable, for contrary to contemporary psychology, to remember certain events might be worse than the vacuous spaces memory both recoils from and strains to fill." ("A Handful of Memories: Two Levels of Recollection," in *Burning Memory: Times of Testing & Reckoning*, ed. Alice L. Eckardt [New York: Pergamon Press, 1993], 169).

4. "THERE" or "Over There" renders the Hebrew of Grossman's "*eretzsam*," literally "land of there."

5. *See Under: Love*, 29.

6. Martin Gilbert writes of the fate of Italian Jewry during the end of 1943: "Of the 1,015 Jews deported from Rome on October 18, only 16 survived the war. Within two months, a further 7,345 Jews had been seized throughout northern Italy. Of these, 6,746 were gassed on arrival at Auschwitz, or died soon afterwards" (Martin Gilbert, *The Holocaust: A History of the Jews of Europe During the Second World War* [New York: Holt, Rinehart & Winston, 1985], 223). Levi was deported in February 1944. Between February and December of 1944 another 4,056 Jews were deported to the east, of whom 2,425 were known to have died. See Meir Michaelis, "Italy: General Survey," in *Encyclopedia of the Holocaust*, ed. Israel Gutman (New York: Macmillan Publishing Co., 1990), 2:725. On the history of the writing of *Survival in Auschwitz*, Levi's first memoir, see his own comments in Primo Levi, *The Reawakening*, trans. S. Woolf (New York: Collier Books, 1986), 195.

7. Primo Levi, *Survival in Auschwitz*, trans. S. Woolf (New York: Collier Books, 1961), 112–13.

8. See Franz Kafka's parable, "My Destination," in Franz Kafka, *Parables and Paradoxes* (New York: Schocken Books, 1961), 189.

9. *Survival in Auschwitz*, 59. Emphasis is mine.

10. In particular, note the discussions of writing, type, and genre in the works of Roskies, *Against the Apocalypse*, and James E. Young, *Writing and Rewriting the Holocaust: Narrative and the Consequences of Interpretation* (Bloomington, Ind.: Indiana University Press, 1988).

11. On the breaking of analogy, see Lawrence L. Langer, *Versions of Survival: The Holocaust and the Human Spirit* (Albany, N.Y.: SUNY, 1982).

12. On the notion of "*caesura*" and its theological implications, see Arthur A. Cohen, *The Tremendum* (New York: Crossroad Publishing Co., 1981), 27–58. Note, too, the various writings of Emil Fackenheim on the uniqueness of the Holocaust, a uniqueness that presupposes an unbroachable gap between the world of the death camps and the interpreter's world. See, for example, *The Jewish Thought of Emil Fackenheim: A Reader*, ed. M. L. Morgan (Detroit: Wayne State University Press, 1987), 119–56.

13. In addition, Pagis became an important scholar of Medieval Hebrew poetry, teaching at Hebrew University from the early 1960s until his death in 1986.

14. Sidra Ezrahi, "Dan Pagis and the poetics of incoherence," in *Remembering for the Future*, ed. Y. Bauer et al. (New York: Pergamon Press, 1989), 2418.

15. The poems that involve personifications of Cain and Abel are "Autobiography," "Brothers," and "Written in Pencil in the Sealed Railway-Car"; the last of these

personifies Eve as well. Each of these poems appears in Dan Pagis, *Variable Directions*, trans. Stephen Mitchell (San Francisco: North Point Press, 1989).

16. Note Shoshana Felman's comparable use of the categories "inside" and "outside" to interpret Claude Lanzmann's important film, *Shoah*. See S. Felman and D. Laub, *Testimony: Crises of Witnessing in Literature, Psychoanalysis, and History* (New York: Routledge, 1992). Reading the film as an inquiry into the "particularity of difference" that separates insiders and outsiders (222), Felman probes the work of art's capability to "create a *connection* that did not exist during the war and does not exist today *between the inside and the outside*—to set them both in motion and in dialogue with one another" (232).

17. For one description see Claude Lanzmann's interview of Franz Suchomel, SS *Unterscharfuehrer* at Treblinka, in *Shoah: An Oral History of the Holocaust* (New York: Pantheon Books, 1985), 53 (hereafter referred to as *Shoah*). Lanzmann's mammoth film amply shows the potent iconography of trains, or even their suggestion, by abandoned tracks.

18. In Hebrew the title reads: "*Katub be ipparon baqqaron hechatum*." Naomi Sokoloff analyzes the form of the title as an icon of its semantic content. She writes, "The form of the title puts into relief its semantic content, as a striking symmetry of pattern divides the line quite neatly in two; the number of syllables in each half is an even six, and this balance is strengthened by the close assonantal and consonantal rhyme (*a-u*, *ron* + *ron*, *a-u*) that depends on the chiasmic pattern of *pa'ul* + (preposition and noun) / (preposition and noun) + *pa'ul*. This conscious fashioning of simple vocabulary into strict design, which brings the two adjectives to frame the two nouns clearly, thereby encloses them and so dramatizes the meaning of *chatum*." See "Transformations: Holocaust Poems in Dan Pagis' *Gilgul*," in *Hebrew Annual Review* 8 (1984): 216 (hereafter referred to as "Transformations").

19. "Here" and "there" are relative terms, although absolute in their opposition to one another. David Grossman's Momik, for example, sees the Holocaust from a present vantage that looks back on the events that occurred at some other time and at some other place. His "here" is a 1959 Jerusalem suburb; the Holocaust, for him, is always and ever THERE or "Over There." The vantage of Pagis's Eve in the boxcar is just the reverse. She writes from within the contemporaneity of the boxcar, her "here." Those who live outside its bounds or come to it only in the aftermath are not "here," but "there." Read in terms of the Lodz photograph, Eve writes from the young boy's side of the fence; Momik writes from the mother's side. The opposition, although not the vantage, is constant.

20. On intertextuality and displacement, see Vincent B. Leitch, *Deconstructive Criticism* (New York: Columbia University Press, 1983). In discussing Roland Barthes, Leitch notes: ". . . the theory of intertextuality works less as a positive notion about social-historical determinations in [of] language and more as a tactical instrument to arrest the extensions and continued expansions of ideological repressions. That is to say, intertextuality, as a critical instrument, combats the 'law of context,' which always attempts to set borders on dissemination" (109–10).

21. David Penchansky notes a comparable use of the book of Job's legendary, or at least dehistoricized setting, to displace any efforts to infuse that text with the explanations of catastrophe offered by the Deuteronomistic history. See David Penchansky, *The Betrayal of God: Ideological Conflict in Job* (Louisville: Westminster John Knox Press, 1990), 32–34.

22. On the dynamic of displacement in Pagis's poetry, especially with regard to the displacement of politically constructed theologies of history, see Sidra Ezrahi, "Dan Pagis: The Holocaust and the Poetics of Incoherence," in *Remembering for the Future*, 2415–24. On the displacement of Isaac as the Jewish victim archetype, see Ezrahi's review of Pagis's *Variable Directions* in *The New Republic* 204 (Feb. 25, 1991): 36–39. The use of Abel and Cain typology in Holocaust literature is rare, but note Michel Tournier's *Le roi des aulnes* as one such instance; see the discussion of R. Quinones in *The Changes of Cain* (Princeton, N.J.: Princeton University Press, 1991), 231. The Isaac type, however, is common, especially in its association with the writings of Elie Wiesel, and may underlie the very tendency to speak of the death camps as a "Holocaust." See Zev Garber and Bruce Zuckerman, "Why Do We Call the Holocaust 'the Holocaust'?" in *Modern Judaism* 9 (1989): 197–211.

23. As Ezrahi's articles remind, Pagis's poetics of displacement involve a significant departure from Zionist ideology and render him controversial within Israel. For significant critiques of the logic of destruction and rebirth and its ideological use, see Marc H. Ellis, *Beyond Innocence and Redemption: Confronting the Holocaust and Israeli Power* (New York: Harper & Row, 1990); and James E. Young, *Writing and Rewriting the Holocaust*, 185. Young interestingly pursues the semiotic connections of political and religious commemoration in Israel, connections that depend upon a scheme of nationalistic history. Of *Yom Hasho'ah* he notes: "Now falling on the Hebrew calendar in the same month as Passover, seven days before *Yom Hazikkaron* (remembrance day for Israel's war dead) and eight days before *Yom Hatzma'ut* (Israeli Independence Day), Holocaust Remembrance Day in Israel simultaneously recalls—and thereby links— biblical and recent historical liberation, modern resistance and national independence" (185).

24. The presentation of Eve's message as an essentially empty space functions similarly to the negative space in Mendel Grossman's photograph of the Lodz mother of the wire fence (see chapter 1). Grossman's depiction of the young boy about to be deported utilizes the dynamics of negative space to destabilize any sense of static order that the photograph might otherwise bear. The boy behind the wire fence cannot be turned into the poster child for an ideology, for he never appears face forward or with assertion of identifiable features. He is a blank in the photograph—a tear in the wholeness of its fabric—that resists any viewer's appropriation of his image. So, too, the emptiness of Eve's message can only frustrate a reader's desire to commandeer it for an ulterior purpose.

25. For one development of this shift, see Sokoloff, "Transformations," 218–21.

26. For Pagis's own use of *"bene-adam"* to denote "human beings," see the opening two lines of his poem "Testimony," in *Variable Directions*, 33.

27. In this regard, a certain parallel exists with Mendel Grossman's photograph of the mother of the wire fence (see chapter 1). If Pagis's Eve addresses a complex figure that is both the reader and Cain, who jointly are outside the domain of the boxcar, the mother of the wire fence reaches for an other side wherein sits not only the son, but the viewer. That is, Grossman takes the photograph from the vantage of being behind the fence with the young son who is about to be deported. Accordingly, the viewer, too, although not with the same vulnerability, sits opposite the mother and faces the compelling power of her gesture.

28. The most obvious case of "ignoring the artifacts," the concrete history of the Jewish ordeal, occurs among revisionists who challenge the historicity of the Holo-

caust. Note the discussion of this literature, s.v., "Holocaust, Denial of the" by Israel Gutman in *Encyclopedia of the Holocaust* (New York: Macmillan Publishing Co., 1990) 2:681–87; and in N. Kampe, "Normalizing the Holocaust? The Recent Historians' Debate in the Federal Republic of Germany," *Holocaust and Genocide Studies* 2 (1987): 61–80. The flaw, however, may also take the form of habits of interpretation that abstract the Jew from his or her concrete history for the sake of universalizing the Holocaust or pressing it into service of a theoretical perspective. On this issue, note Langer's criticism of Victor Frankl and Bruno Bettelheim in *Versions of Survival*, 1–129. On the other end of the spectrum, one finds discussions that reduce the event to its brute, historical base, a vulnerability, for example, of social scientific discourse. Note the protest of this tendency by Emil Fackenheim, *God's Presence in History* (New York: New York University Press, 1970), 72; and eloquently in Elie Wiesel's "A Plea for the Dead," in *Legends of Our Time* (New York: Schocken Books, 1982), 174–97. Note also, however, Lucy S. Dawidowicz in *The Holocaust and the Historians* (Cambridge, Mass.: Harvard University Press, 1981), 4–21. Fictional and artistic styles that emphasize "concentrationary realism" may also manifest a comparable rhetoric or poetic of fact that finally undermines its own historical base and must work hard not to reduce that which it would portray. On this matter, see the discussion of James E. Young in *Writing and Rewriting the Holocaust*, 16–18, 51–80.

29. See Celan, "*Stilleben*," in *Von Schwelle zu Schwelle* (Stuttgart: Deutsche Verlags-Anstalt, 1961), 38

30. This notion is informed by the writings of Emmanuel Levinas, whose perspective structures the moral relation in terms of an other-centeredness or a decentering of the self. See, for example, *Totality and Infinity*, trans. A. Lingis (Pittsburgh: Duquesne University Press, 1969), 215.

31. *Shoah*, 82.

32. For the quotations of Mrs. Michelsohn, see *Shoah*, 80–83 and 92–94. In her lack of self-cognizance, Mrs. Michelsohn approximates the banality of evil discussed by Hannah Arendt. See her *Eichmann in Jerusalem* (New York: Viking, 1963). For discussion of her controversial thesis, see Karl A. Plank, "Thomas Merton and Hannah Arendt: Contemplation after Eichmann," in *The Merton Annual* 3 (1990): 121–50.

33. To confer on the boxcar a fundamental status is to allow it to function, in Fackenheim's terms, as a "root event" or to have a "commanding voice." See *God's Presence in History*, 8–14 and 67–104.

34. In current discussion "intertextuality" appears both as a constitutive feature of language (a property of texts as such) and as a textual strategy. The latter takes the form of an author's deliberate choice to construct a relation to some other text or discourse through quotation, allusion, typology, or other literary means.

35. Pagis accents the unprecedentedness of Cain's deed in his poem "Autobiography." Here, a murdered Abel says: "My brother invented murder, / my parents invented grief, / I invented silence." In the poem's opening verse, a raven has to teach Abel's parents what to do with his body: It had never before been necessary to bury a human corpse.

3 LEAVES FROM A NEWER TESTAMENT: A FATHER'S POEM

You have come to an evening of the Bible
Broken in spirit
And beaten in body
With darkness in your hearts
You are full of sorrow, of sorrow
　　　. . . .
Come, you unbelieving Jews,
Come and by your own Bible, you shall become believers!

Yitzhak Katzenelson
(November 1940)[1]

AN EVENING OF THE BIBLE

"You have come to an evening of the Bible." So began the poet Yitzhak Katzenelson as he introduced a public reading of scripture to a group of Warsaw Jews. "Beaten" and "broken," as Katzenelson noted, this group faced on the next day the sealing of the Warsaw ghetto.[2] Only a few weeks earlier, Chaim Kaplan, a Hebrew teacher in Warsaw, had written of his gnawing fear: "Will it be a closed ghetto? There are signs in both directions, and we hope for a miracle—which doesn't always happen in time of need. *A closed ghetto means gradual death.*"[3] Two days after the sealing, Kaplan's diary records the transition:

> What we dreaded most has come to us. We had a premonition that a ghetto life awaited us, a life of sorrow and poverty, of shame and degradation, but no one believed that the fateful hour would come so soon. And suddenly—a frightful surprise! On the eve of the Sabbath of Parashat Vayera, the fourteenth of Marheshvan, 5701, we went to bed in the Jewish quarter, and the next morning we awoke in a closed Jewish ghetto, a ghetto in every detail.[4]

Dreaded, the confinement of some 400,000 Jews, nearly a third of the Warsaw population, in an area less than 2.5 percent of the total city, meant not only disorientation, immobility, and shameful poverty but, as Kaplan had noted, "gradual death."[5] Given this ominous transition, Katzenelson's Sabbath eve reading is remarkable in several respects. First, at a point of critical and threatening change this group of Warsaw Jews gives attention to the reading

58

of texts. Arguably a task for an idler time, the presentation and hearing of Katzenelson's words nevertheless assume here the quality of decisive action and pertinence. In his intention, this reading responds precisely to the broken spirit and the beaten body, the dark heart, and the full sorrow.

Second, the document from which Katzenelson, a Zionist intellectual, begins to read is no modernist tract, but the Bible, a book whose literary tradition Katzenelson claims for the nonfaithful as well as for the devout. Without forfeiting secular canons, Katzenelson turns to scripture to express his concern for Jewish survival and to empower it with a sense of continuity and historic challenge. As Roskies notes:

> Ghetto writings, in contrast to postwar literary responses, were over-whelmingly secular, never more so than when couched in scriptural terms. . . . Not God or His covenant but the Bible itself, that timeless document, established a higher reality than that of the ghetto. The Bi-ble's message was survival, even to those who had lost their faith, for the Jewish people was as eternal as its literary creativity. . . . Katzenelson argued for the continuities—of the ghetto as a link in the chain of Jewish suffering and as an actualization of parts of the biblical past—by omit-ting God from the line of authority: the truth of the Book derived from the people, even as the people's survival was mirrored in the Book.[6]

Third, as his prologue indicates, Katzenelson understood the "evening of the Bible" to offer a transformation: "unbelieving Jews . . . shall become be-lievers!" No idle text, the power of the Book was sufficient to change its readers and provide them with a sense not only of identity, but of hope, as they awaited the events of the morrow. Still, Katzenelson hawked no theologi-cal wares to accompany his language of belief. The reader's belief was in the eternity of the Book and the continuity of experience it exposed in the Jew's ordeal of suffering and survival. No Jewish readers would enter the crucible of history alone. Katzenelson's reader would recognize, on the one hand, that the current experience shared in the eternal history of the Book and was thus survivable. On the other hand, the reader would hear the challenge to bring to that history the chronicle of the contemporary, a mandate to survive and make of eternity a present reality.

The poet's reading was no facile exercise of piety. This "evening of the Bible" involved reading the Book in tandem with the secular experience of contemporary Jews as they faced the transition to the ghetto, itself a way station in a still bleaker passage. Katzenelson's sense of the Book's eternity suggests the prospect of integrating ghetto and *Lager* into the larger frame of the biblical narrative. At the same time, however, the grounding of that eter-nity in the people's survival warrants a counterreading that considers the current history as fundamental, if not surpassing.[7] Here, the biblical story becomes read through the focus of the contemporary experience, instead of itself providing the lens through which all else is seen.

Already implicit in his 1940 reading, this counterdirection emerges forcefully three years later in Katzenelson's "Song of the Murdered Jewish People." In lamenting "the millions of [his] murdered ones" he notes:

> It's they. . . . They suffered more and greater pains, each one.
> The little, simple, ordinary Jew from Poland of today—
> Compared with him, what are the great men of a past bygone?
> A wailing Jeremiah, Job afflicted, Kings despairing, all in one—it's they![8]

For Katzenelson, the biblical language remains pertinent, if not inescapable; he asserts its continuity but now within the frame of "the little, simple, ordinary Jew from Poland" whose experience rewrites the wail, affliction, and despair of biblical tradition. The experience of this ordinary Jew calls forth, as Primo Levi put it, "stories of a new Bible."[9]

If an "evening of the Bible" in a Nazi ghetto retrieves a past text, it no less rewrites the text it retrieves.[10] The juxtaposition of biblical story and contemporary scene establishes a dynamic intertextuality that qualifies the reading of either instance and marks the genesis of new scripture. To understand this intertextual rewriting, we turn to a case in point: the poem "Lekh-Lekho" by Simkhe Bunem Shayevitsh.[11] In certain respects, Shayevitsh, a self-educated mitten-maker in Lodz, is that "little, simple, ordinary Jew" from Katzenelson's Poland. Yet more, as a poet, he describes his experience with ample biblical allusion, appropriating traditional types to describe the deportations in his ghetto. If Katzenelson held a public "evening of the Bible," Shayevitsh depicts its private counterpart. "Lekh-Lekho" shows a father teaching his daughter a "terrible chapter" (line 340) of scripture on the last night within their home. As with Katzenelson's audience, the next day will bring father and daughter threatening change, now radicalized as the deportation from ghetto to Lager. On their last night they too turn to the Book: What they will endure they will understand in biblical terms. But what they suffer will also transfigure that biblical legacy, adding to it the query of contemporary experience. If, in turning to the Bible, they assert its continuity, their reading also rewrites the scripture, struggling with its difference and discontinuity.

"LEKH-LEKHO"—POEM OF A FINAL SABBATH

Setting and Structure

Like Grossman's photograph of the Lodz family at the wire fence, "Lekh-Lekho" portrays a domestic scene. Here a father speaks to his young daughter within the familiar setting of home and its steadying rituals. But like the moment captured in the photograph, the poem's world is anything but secure. It, too, stands at a point of laden passage as this family prepares to journey to a destination unknown, yet imagined in horror. Although a weekday, this last night the family marks as a Sabbath, reciting its prayers and singing its joyful songs. It is precisely this Sabbath world that deportation will suspend and put out of time. The poem, a witness to the interruption, brings together daughter and parents in a final *Havdalah*, a foreboding reckoning of sacred and profane, light and dark.[12]

Completed on February 23, 1942, "*Lekh-Lekho*" anticipates the Grossman photograph taken some seven months later in Lodz, where both photographer and poet lived. Shayevitsh, only thirty-five at the time, had been known before the war for his prose, but now he turns increasingly to poetry to contend with the realities of ghetto life. In the ghetto, he writes two poems of epic stature and style, both of which dramatize the contemporary crisis: "*Lekh-Lekho*" and, later, on Passover eve, "Spring 5702 [1942]."[13] If the Grossman photograph captures its moment, so do Shayevitsh's poems reflect their own season, sharing in the swirl of chaotic transition and uncertainty. Unlike survivor testimony, which has both the clarity and construction of retrospect, "*Lekh-Lekho*" stands in the midst of a historical process under way and, in this case, scarcely imaginable.[14] On the one hand, the poet has witnessed the trains leaving the ghetto but cannot know their destination to be Chelmno, a death camp.[15] On the other hand, life in the ghetto and the simple fact of the community's deportation have already blocked his retreat to any prewar perspectives, either traditional or modernist. Shayevitsh writes from a vantage between the times, between knowing and not-yet-knowing the full reality of his situation. "*Lekh-Lekho*" concerns itself with transition. Between the times, the poem is also between perspectives, giving voice both to tradition and dissent.

No narrational or poetic distance detaches "*Lekh-Lekho*" from the circumstance of its writing. Addressing his daughter, the father in "*Lekh-Lekho*" bids Blimele to "Look outside, how the second group / Is already wandering into Exile. / Soon we'll have to set out, too."[16]

On February 23, 1942, as Shayevitsh finished writing the poem, he might have said these very words to his own daughter. Her name, too, was Blimele.[17] During the preceding month, between January 16 and 29, some ten thousand Jews had been deported from Lodz. Now, starting on February 22, a second, more severe round of deportations had begun, forcing more than seven thousand Jews to board the trains before the week was out.[18] In addition, as if to inaugurate the resumption, German authorities had gathered some eight thousand Jews on the morning of February 21 and compelled them to witness the spectacle of an execution, the first public hanging in the ghetto.[19] Although Shayevitsh writes of a father's words to his daughter in order to personify the plight of his community, the exercise is no mere poetic figure. In writing of them—father and daughter, the Jews of Lodz—he ultimately writes of himself.

If *"Lekh-Lekho"* mirrors Shayevitsh's world, it yet submits to the tight structure of poetic craft. Set as a father's continuing address to his daughter, the poem's rhyming quatrains fall into five main sections.[20] Each section begins with a vocative address, "And now, Blimele, dear child," followed by an imperative peculiar to each section. The father calls his daughter by name and, with kind authority, instructs. The constant repetition of the address gives way to a sequence within the imperatives, as Blimele's instructions require her initially to suppress childish ways of joy (see 2) and play (106) and culminate in her adult preparation to join the deportees: "let's go" (414). Further, the imperatives move Blimele from a position within the boundary of the house, where the family yet celebrates Sabbath and knows the support of familiar artifacts, to an encounter with the outside and its danger. At the outset, though she stifles childish joy and stops her playing, she remains within the refuge of the house. The poem's progression, however, takes her to the threshold as she must "look outside" (330) and then, finally, take her place among those who no longer have a home (414). For Blimele, deportation surrenders the "here" of home to an alien "there," even as her childhood yields to the call for an extraordinary maturity.

Each section provides an image or scene that makes concrete the crisis brought by ghettoization and deportation. No abstraction, the threat to the community approaches as a scorching frost (33), a silver-snowy web spun by a spider of frost (84). Vulnerable, the deportees have no Jeremiah to accompany, lament, and comfort (120–24). The artifacts that have identified and sustained their personal lives they must abandon (185–89) and forfeit to desecration and destruction (293–98; 325–26). Cast out from their homes, pregnant women go forth on the arduous journey, ice underfoot, only to writhe and abort in the snow (385–400): a new and bloody Moriah (424).

Shayevitsh, however, does not leave these concrete images on their own. Within each section, images of crisis combine with closing affirmations that bring the challenge of the contemporary into ironic, if not dissonantal, relation with the claims of tradition. Thus, the snaring frost coexists with the sustaining dream, a "sun-bronzed honey-cake" (99–100); the absence of a Jeremiah with the presence of Blimele's comforting mother (179–80); and destroyed artifacts with the flame of a bed used for firewood to cook a ghetto soup (325–26). The story of life aborted, the imperilment of a family's future, claims the hearing of grandfather Abraham and forges a link with a persisting past (409–12). Climbing the new Moriah, Blimele and her father yet affirm

God's oneness and invoke the protecting presence of his angels who guard human lives at the fall of night and slumber (441–48). Neither words of traditional affirmation nor of crisis sound apart from the other in Shayevitsh's poem. Each section of the poem insists upon their interaction and self-exposure as the text wends its way between the rejected extremes of cynicism and naivete.

To be effective, the interaction of tradition and contemporary voice requires more than their simple juxtaposition. The poet must find or create a common structure that relates the juxtaposed items and shows their point of mutual concern. In Shayevitsh's poem, the use of biblical and liturgical types functions to link the affirmative and the critical in precisely this way. It generates a syntax within the poem through which traditional images not only express themselves but seek and include their contemporary analogy, even in the latter's expression of dissent or dissonance. Thus, each section of the poem offers a controlling image that at once reflects the claim of scripture and liturgy while also building a bridge over which the reader passes back and forth between the demands of past and present.[21]

The first three sections take their controlling images from Sabbath liturgy, which itself reflects biblical themes of exodus and creation. Woven within the narrative fabric of the poem, Sabbath liturgy surfaces as Blimele and her father celebrate their final evening at home as a Sabbath. Thus, in section one, the father recites the Sabbath *kiddush*, a blessing that inaugurates the Sabbath meal and acknowledges the Sabbath's sanctity. In section two, he portrays Blimele's mother and underscores the significance of her role, even as in Sabbath liturgy a husband will praise his wife through the recitation of Prov. 31:10–31. The third section finds father and daughter bidding the house good-bye, a parting not only from its artifacts but from the Sabbath preserved within the house. Accordingly, the third section parallels the movement of *havdalah* in which one parts from the ending Sabbath and takes seriously the return of profane time.

Sections four and five are not peculiarly sabbatical, reflecting that Sabbath effectively comes to a halt when Blimele confronts the outside in section four (330). Instead, the dominant image here centers on the father's instruction of the daughter in a portion of Torah, a reading of "the terrible chapter 'Lekh-Lekho'" (340) in which God commands Abraham, the deportees' precursor, to "Go!" (Gen. 12:1). As the crisis of deportation reshapes the meaning of Sabbath (and is itself nuanced by that meaning), so does it rewrite the biblical chapter (and is itself written by that text). Finally, section five, while prolonging the Abraham imagery, drives toward an ultimate repetition of a prayer traditionally recited before sleep, a prayer now offered before yielding to a more ominous night. We will discuss these five sections—Shayevitsh's pentateuch—under the headings suggested by their liturgical and biblical typology: (1) *Kiddush*—Sanctification; (2) *Asheth Chayil*—The Woman of Valor; (3) *Havdalah*—Separation; (4) *Parasha*—Torah Lesson; and (5) *al Hamitah*—Night Prayer.

1. *KIDDUSH*—SANCTIFICATION (1–104)

Allusion

"*Lekh-Lekho*" teems with allusion. As the title itself suggests, the language of the poem involves more than one level of reference. When Shayevitsh writes the words "*Lekh-Lekho*"—"Go!"—he refers to the pending deportation of Blimele and her father but, also, quotes God's first command to Abraham (Gen. 12:1). Thus, the title creates a double system of reference wherein the reader hears the echo of an earlier text (the Abraham story) within the setting of the poem's own narrative context. The poem expresses its own situation but, in doing so, alludes to another horizon, an antecedent situation whose reference shapes any perception of the poem's concern. Something in the poet's "here" calls to mind Abraham's "there" and the poem forges a connection between them, forbidding the reader to see the poem on any single horizon of meaning.[22]

In its habit of allusion, "*Lekh-Lekho*" manifests a rich and overt intertextuality.[23] Its language reaches for and brings into play the meanings of other texts whose relation to the poem deepen and define the poetic situation. In turn, those texts themselves are reinterpreted through their relation to the poem. The poem's allusive title prompts the reader to search for the intertextual connections, disposing him or her to listen for echoes of precursor texts resonating within the portrayal of Blimele and her father. The reader's task is Midrashic: to seek the connections of texts and the whole of which they are part; and to pursue the meaning of the whole, what the texts say together that they cannot say alone.

If an author plants the echoes of allusion in a text, the intertextuality yet depends on the reader to perceive the connection and bring to bear a fuller awareness of what the allusion only suggests or provides in fragments. Allusion leaves much unsaid. It relies upon the hint to stimulate the reader's supply of connotations drawn from the precursor text. For instance, the poem's title alludes to the Abraham saga, specifically its opening command, but it does not provide more than a pointer to YHWH's instructions and promise. From the little that the text explicitly says, however, the reader calls to mind additional associations, filling the gap of the unsaid. The reader, if biblically literate, sees "*Lekh-Lekho*" and supplies not only the tie to the Abraham story, but the command's separation of Abraham from homeland and family and its promised culmination in the blessing of land and progeny. As such, the allusion is a bit of text that summons awareness of a larger, implied network of association, a jot of the said that calls to mind dimensions of the greater unsaid.

From Kiddush to Exodus

The poem's first section is intertextually intricate. Unsurprising, given the mechanics of the poem's title, the initial section fashions a complex chain of allusion that links the contemporary and the biblical. It does so largely through the mediation of liturgical allusions that, on the one hand, evoke biblical tradition and, on the other, point to a present reenactment of its legacy. The clearest and most important instance of liturgical allusion involves the father's recitation of the Sabbath *kiddush*. On this last evening at home, a weekday Wednesday, the father marks the moment as a Sabbath, offering the traditional benediction over wine that inaugurates the Sabbath meal. The poem reports his words to Blimele:

> Do not gaze in wonder at me
> With your great brown eyes, surprised
> That on a weekday Wednesday
> I recite the Sabbath *kiddush*.
> I recite the *kiddush*, "*Yoym hashishi*,"
> over the nest of our home (61–66).

The poem only alludes to the benediction, providing just a small fragment of its text: "'*Yoym hashishi*'"—"the sixth day." Still, the mention of these opening words of the blessing stimulates the reader to call to mind its remainder, to supply the unsaid. In this case, the reader's imagined hearing of the *kiddush* brings to the poem reminders of the biblical narratives of Creation and Exodus. In hearing Blimele's father, the reader overhears the words of the benediction:

> Blessed are you, Lord our God, King of the universe, . . . who has graciously given us your holy Sabbath as a heritage, in remembrance of the creation. The Sabbath is the first among the holy festivals which recall the exodus from Egypt. Indeed, you have chosen us and hallowed us above all nations, and have graciously given us your holy Sabbath as a heritage. Blessed are you, O Lord, who hallows the Sabbath.[24]

The liturgical allusion itself alludes to aspects of the biblical narrative and gives them a presence in the poem. Moreover, the allusion alerts the reader to look further for other signs of biblical reference.

Once alerted, the reader can detect a peculiar interest in the Exodus that pervades this section. Like deportation and the journey of Abraham, the Exodus is a going forth.[25] The poem, however, unsettles this analogy and recollects the Exodus primarily to show its difference: What Blimele and her father face is no Exodus, but an anti-Exodus—a journey into bondage and death.[26] The father's repeated demand thus takes on new meaning. At the outset and soon again, he tells Blimele: "Do not gaze in wonder at me / With your great brown eyes / And do not ask any questions why / We have to leave our home" (5–8 and 41–44). No simple impatience, the father's prohibitions distance Blimele from the traditional, inquiring role of the youngest child at a Passover seder, the ritual meal that commemorates the Exodus. On Passover the youngest child asks, "Why does this night differ from all other nights?" and provokes the telling of the Exodus narrative that answers "any questions why / We have to leave our home."[27] By restraining Blimele's questions, the father makes clear that, although the ghetto oppresses, deportation is not deliverance. The evening's meal is no seder, for on this night it is *not* again "as if [each person] came forth out of Egypt."[28] The father confesses:

> Dear lovely child, I am
> An adult, already grown,
> And I don't know why they're driving
> The bird out of its nest (9–12).

That he has no answer for the child means already that, in this context, the Exodus story has forfeited the self-evidency of its authority.[29]

Read in this way, the father's recital of the *kiddush* evokes the Exodus so that the reader may not miss its subversion. This eve of deportation differs from the earlier going forth and cannot be subsumed under the Exodus paradigm of divine power and human liberation. Read another way, however, this section of the poem moves from subversion to a counter-assertion of the Exodus tradition. Although challenged, its authority has not been completely overcome.

Shayevitsh uses images of stinging frost (25–40, 84) to convey the deathly conditions of the ghetto and the danger of the "foreign cold" (28) beyond its bounds. The ghetto is "a silver-snowy web / . . . spun by the spider of frost" (83–84) and within "its cold eerie gleam" (88) one finds hunger (89), terror (91), and darkness (78–80). Still, as the father reminds the daughter:

> . . . in our hearts the fire burns,
> The dream flaps its wings—of hope—
>
> Like the full golden kernel
> In the beak of a bird;
> The dream is our sustainer,
> A sun-bronzed honey-cake
>
> Which, although more than once
> We've been disappointed, bitterly duped,
> Yet it has given strength
> And we have waited for better things (95–104).

The image of the "sun-bronzed honey-cake" directly contrasts with that of the cold, the dark, and the hunger of the ghetto. That portion, the dream of hope, sustains and strengthens, enabling one to endure the bitter, disappointing hardship of history. The poet leaves vague what constitutes the dream of hope, but offers a clue in his likening it to the "sun-bronzed honey-cake." With this image he retrieves the notion that the God of the Exodus yet provides in the wilderness, sending manna, the taste of which "was like wafers made with honey" (Ex. 16:31). "Sun-bronzed honey-cake," the deportees' manna, comes to the barrens of the ghetto as a sign that "it was YHWH who brought [them] out of the land of Egypt" (Ex. 16:6) and remains their Lord to provide and deliver. In that conviction, a return of the Exodus perspective, Blimele and her father "[wait] for better things."[30]

From "the nest of our home" to Psalm 91

Avian imagery recurs throughout section one. In speaking of the demand to leave home, the father confesses that he does not "know why they're driving / the bird out of its nest" (11–12). To Blimele he declares, "I recite the *kiddush* . . . / Over the nest of our home" (65–66). And when speaking of the sustaining dream, he notes that it "flaps its wings—of hope— / Like the full golden kernel / In the beak of a bird" (95–97). Shayevitsh's likening of "home" to a bird's nest seems common upon first reading, but gains interest in light of the poem's intertextuality. In reciting the *kiddush*, the father acknowledges and claims the sanctity of the home, affirming it as a sanctuary where the Sabbath comes to bring joy and peace. When he then describes that home as a nest, he alludes to Psalm 91 (a psalm belonging to Sabbath liturgy) and introduces its theological dimension.[31]

The home, itself a metonym of the Sabbath world, is that nest where God covers with "his pinions" and offers refuge under "his wings" (Ps. 91:4).

Where there is home, there is sanctuary and Sabbath, the signs of God's protection. But what, then, when the bird is driven from the nest (11–12)? Unlike those who dwell safely "in the shelter of the Most High" (Ps. 91:1), the exiled deportee must beware of the "snare of the fowler" and fear "the arrow that flies by day [and] the pestilence that stalks in darkness" (Ps. 91:3, 5–6). Homelessness stirs a theological crisis. If consoling in the Sabbath moment, the allusion turns and devastates in its implication for Blimele's next scene: to be driven from the nest casts one away from the haven of divine protection. The danger of deportation thus coincides with a deep threat of estrangement, of living as a stranger in a world where one can rely on neither divine nor human hospitality. In its death-dealing condition, homelessness expresses the onset of an alienation that renders one finally isolated in history, exposed vulnerably to face its hazard alone as if somehow the God of the Exodus were not still Lord to deliver and save.[32]

As with Shayevitsh's allusions to the Exodus, so does his intertextuality with Psalm 91 show a critical edge that unsettles the biblical claim. The psalmist's confidence culminates in his conviction that

> Because you have made the LORD your refuge,
>   the Most High your dwelling place,
> no evil shall befall you,
>   no scourge come near your tent (Ps. 91:9–10).

Yet the poem depicts a situation where Blimele's family is being driven from the safe dwelling place, the bird from its nest. Shayevitsh does not paint a scene of theological antagonism. God is neither the one who drives them from the nest nor the fowler that pursues them. But neither is God one who protects and rescues. The nest is violable. Evil will befall those who there had made their dwelling place. Already the scourge has neared their tent.

The poem's use of Psalm 91, however, does more than subvert the biblical text. Again, as in the allusions to the Exodus story, the intertextuality conserves elements of the same text or traditions that it brings into question. Once more Sabbath liturgy provides the key. On this weekday Sabbath eve, Blimele's father not only recites the *kiddush* over the nest of their home, but "sing[s] with joy "*Sholem-aleikhem*" / To the two angel guests" (67–68). This hymn, sung immediately before the *kiddush*, welcomes the angels of peace whose presence accompanies Sabbath.[33] At the hymn's conclusion, the liturgy quotes from Psalm 91: "He will command his angels concerning you / to guard you in all your ways" (91:11).

The intersection of liturgy and text (the former stimulating the reader's recall of the latter) addresses the plight of the bird driven from its nest. If homelessness portends isolation, the father's hymn yet celebrates the presence of the accompanying angels

> Who stay by [him], go everywhere
> With [him], side by side (69–70).

Something of the nest endures in this accompaniment and, with it, a hint of the psalm's affirmation that the people are not finally alone in their ways (Ps. 91:11). The affirmation is in no way meager, especially given the later emphasis Shayevitsh will place on the role of accompaniment (for example, 179–80, 441–44). It does, however, remain skeptical of divine rescue. The father asks the daughter:

> These two angel guests—who are they?
> Now guess, quick as arrow from bow.
> They are: you, Blimele, beautiful child
> And your mother, the woman of valor (73–76).

If God is to be "with [God's people] in trouble" (Ps. 91:15), God will do so through angels, now understood by the father to be none other than his wife and daughter. It is to them he looks for the decisive act of accompaniment and enduring signs of the nest. Upon them he relies.

The Weekday Sabbath

The *kiddush* recognizes God's hallowing of the Sabbath in creation. When he recites it, Blimele's father himself sanctifies the time in imitation of the Creator's distinguishing of the seventh day. The *kiddush* reminds: time is not of one piece. Time arrives at points of threshold where what follows may differ fundamentally from what has preceded. Such difference makes possible and summons a marking of time, a noticing of the boundaries that separate one day from another, one season from the next, and affords a valuing of the distinction. Increments of time not only differ, but they bear particular meaning and value. To sanctify time, as does Blimele's father, imparts a certain significance to the hallowed interval. At its core, such sanctification recognizes the threshold and attends to the moment's difference and meaning. Not to do so surrenders time to a profane blur, to an unmarked chaos of days wherein the past cannot identify and the future cannot claim.[34]

Though it is only a weekday Wednesday, Blimele's father stands at a temporal threshold, a turn that separates sacred and profane, light and dark, this midweek evening from those that will follow. His recitation of the *kiddush* reckons the time. As Sabbath interrupts the ongoing profanity of time, so now the father summons this Wednesday evening to stand apart from the dulling procession of ghetto days and to call forth blessing while blessing remains to be found. In pronouncing the *kiddush*, the father recognizes the preciousness of life together in this nest of family and names the moment as Sabbath. But with that same benediction comes a sad awareness that this is a passing moment. Already shadowed, its time will soon end, yielding to a darker season that eclipses Sabbath light "as the sun rests behind clouds / On a rainy day when the sky is darkened" (79–80).

As with the biblical intertextuality, Shayevitsh's use of the Sabbath moves the poem in two directions, both conserving the meaning of Sabbath and offering a challenge to it. Read from the vantage of Sabbath, a vantage that looks to its liturgical and biblical pattern as fundamental, the poem sounds a traditional tone in its defiance of deportation despair. Read from the vantage of deportation, however, the poem questions precisely that tone so sounded with hope.

On the one hand, through the father's *kiddush*, Shayevitsh allows the rhythm of Sabbath to frame the crisis of deportation. Facing the darkness of deportation on a Wednesday eve, the father's words, in essence, assert: "let there be Sabbath." Bringing Sabbath to this midweek void, the father protests the dimming of light and, at once, tries to order the imminent chaos. He checks the profanity of time by bringing to bear the Sabbath interruption. Read from its own vantage, the hallowing of Sabbath, even at midweek, implies that darkness is not absolute, but vulnerable to the return of light. Seen as provisional, the world of deportation is subordinated to Sabbath's cycle and thus countered with a dream of hope (96) that sustains like the "sun-bronzed honey-cake" of manna (100). The incursion of Sabbath, itself an icon of the Exodus, reminds that servitude is limited and that angels yet accompany this people's journey.

On the other hand, although the father's *kiddush* is compelling, the poem reinterprets the Sabbath as much as looks to it as a fundamental category. If the pattern of Sabbath frames the deportation, that present crisis yet constrains how Sabbath appears in this world of frost and hunger. On Wednesday eve, Sabbath is outside its proper time, an oddity that extends to other connotations that do not fit the hallowing of joy and peace. Read from the vantage of deportation, this is a final Sabbath. No expectation of Sabbath's return denies that the house has heard the mother's "last happy laughter" (21–22); although Sabbath rests in the mother's spirit, no candle lightens her darkened face (77–78). Where the marking of Sabbath calls one to anticipate an Exodus, here the father contemplates a going forth that leads not to freedom, but "to [being] thrust alive, alive / Into a common grave, scattered with

earth" (59–60). Finally, the Sabbath of Blimele's father is a Sabbath that challenges transcendence: Facing the absence of God's Sabbath, the father fills the
void with the Sabbath of his own consecration, the weekday Sabbath. The
Sabbath messengers who come to protect and accompany are his daughter
and wife. This, the final Sabbath of household angels, is nonetheless sacred,
yet sober in tone and traumatic in its awareness of divine eclipse.

2. *ASHETH CHAYIL*—THE WOMAN OF VALOR (105–180)

The beginning of the Sabbath liturgy involves not only the *kiddush* and
the hymn "*Sholem-aleikhem*," but the reciting or chanting of Prov. 31:10–31.
Traditionally, just before the *kiddush*, the gathered family hears these words
that describe the "woman of valor" (*asheth chayil*, Prov. 31:10) whose children
bless her and whose husband praises her (Prov. 31:28). This praise "*Lekh-
Lekho*" has already expressed when the father names the Sabbath angels "you,
Blimele, beautiful child / And your mother, the woman of valor" (75–76). The
poem says little about this mother, however, in the opening section. We know
that she has mended Blimele's clothes (17–18) and is presented sacrificially in
her "last happy laughter" (22–24). She embodies the spirit of the Sabbath, but
"her face is darkened" (77–78). We thus see the effect of the pending deportation upon her but not yet the action that conveys her valor. Section two turns
to that action as its culminating scene and shows the significance of Blimele's
mother in terms far different from the "good wife" of Proverbs 31.

The valor of Blimele's mother emerges over against a focused image of the
deportation crisis. This going forth is still no moment of Passover or Exodus,
as the father reminds Blimele to curtail her play (106) and again to "not gaze
at [him] . . . / With questioning wondering eyes" (125–26). Neither, however, is this trek of heavily burdened old people and children (115–16) an
Exile whose ordeal knows a prophecy of return. The father describes the look
of the first groups: "In their eyes, their death sentence" (120).[35] He then adds:

> But there is no Jeremiah
> To lament the Destruction.
> He does not go with them into Exile
> To comfort them by Babylon's streams (121–24).

Asserting the difference, the father makes clear that if this is an Exile, it is one
that proceeds without prophetic accompaniment, and thus also without lament and comfort.

The allusion to Jeremiah evokes the reader's awareness of the Exile as a
point of analogy only to show the inadequacy of its likeness. The difference

focuses the plight of the deportees. Unaccompanied by a Jeremiah, they are isolated from the prospect of prophecy, left on their own without guidance to interpret the contemporary signs or to sustain them in the current catastrophe. Cut off from the prophetic gaze, their suffering takes place without witness.[36] Unnoticed, their plight evokes no sound of lament or protest or cherishing. Thus unseen and unrecognized, the deportees are left without consolation, bereft of the comfort that connects their affliction to a past and to a future. Their situation differs from that of the past, reflecting a discontinuity that is also the underlying symptom of their plight. Isolated in time, they experience the breaking of connections—an existential discontinuity—that otherwise would express meaning, value, and hope.

As the poem focuses upon the plight of discontinuity, it also begins to counter its threat. The father repeats an adage: "You know, child: *oylem* means world and it means eternal" (129), or "the world is always the same."[37] To illustrate, he refers to the story of the Cantonists, wherein there were "Poor children, kidnapped, / Torn away from father and mother" (133–34) and forced to serve in the army of Nicholas I.[38] Blimele need not be surprised, he suggests, that such times as these have returned to "greet the ghetto" (136). The continuity that emerges in his example is strange, an ironic continuity of discontinuity. The severing of connections between children and parents, itself a stark image of discontinuity, does not provide Blimele with the whole cloth of tradition, but with a point of its tearing. It is the rupture that returns and is continuous.[39]

To ease Blimele's tears, the father next speaks words that would assure. They seem, however, too conventional to meet the girl's fear of the stark scene he has portrayed. He speaks of the persistence of life's beauty (154–56) and of the human need to prepare for both life and death (157–60). However, such beauty lies "beyond the ghetto" (156), and such preparation gives little comfort to one ready for life's color and not death's bleakness (159–60). Greater power attaches itself to his concrete gesture:

> Look I'm packing the *tallis*
> And the *kitl* for a shroud
> And also the small red Bible
> And Leivick's poems for a time of rest (161–64).

Here the father wagers that even the continuity of rupture obliges a retrieval of the past and makes possible the continued pertinence of certain artifacts. With him, they journey from "here" to "there." Whatever the future will be, his gesture suggests, it will include the demand for reverence and the chance to rest. Thus, he gathers the prayer shawl and the white linen robe; he packs his books. He brings to the future tokens of his past, not out of any nostalgia, but from anticipation that the future may require them, as does his present—a continuity of obligation and need.[40]

The father's packing, his wager of continuity, claims the daughter. Her tears end, not because there is no reason to weep but because she has a task. She must "bring the bar of soap" (165) and "the white nit-comb" (170). As the father stows white garments of symbolic purity, so the daughter must bear the tools of simple cleanliness. If the future obliges the father's worship, so does it compel the daughter's cleanliness, a venture that, in this pending morrow, it will be possible for her to live cleanly, as a human being, and significant that she does so: "One must keep clean at home / And still more in a strange, strange land" (167–68).[41]

As the father calls the daughter to remain clean, so does he begin to relate the mother's role in a way that expresses her valor. Earlier in this section, the signs of discontinuity had attached themselves to an absent Jeremiah. Without his presence, the deportees lost the prophetic connection that rooted them in time and made possible lament and comfort. Discontinuity, if unchecked, erodes value and races toward cynicism. Such discontinuity would strip the past of its power to oblige and the future of its power to claim, thereby making empty such acts as packing the *tallis* and *kitl* or the intention to remain clean. If the present has lost its connection to the past and to the future, why must one keep the habits of a former day or, with the concern to be clean, struggle to retain the visible sign of humanness? Only with an eye to some continuity do these gestures have meaning. Precisely here, the mother's role emerges forcefully. She is the new Jeremiah (179), present and connecting, the agent of continuity.

The mother reappears in the poem with Blimele's white nit-comb:

And don't forget to bring
The white nit-comb, that we talked about before;
Every night mother will use it
To straighten out your hair

And take good care of you
Lest, God forbid, you get lousy,
And sing to you "Bibl, bibl
Little louse . . . " (169–76).

Where no Jeremiah goes with the deportees in this exile (121–24), Blimele's mother accompanies her daughter, as indicated in these lines. Present in the deportation, she is there "every night" to comb Blimele's hair and take care of her lest she become lousy.[42] In the father's rendering of the scene, the mother's presence counters the prophetic absence and brings to bear a constancy that humanizes, in this case through the maintenance of a cleanliness and basic purity. What mother and daughter did at home, they will do in the "strange, strange land" (168), effecting a continuity warranted by the mother's ongoing accompaniment.[43]

More than the guardian of cleanliness, the accompanying mother assumes the prophetic mantle. Her being there by the streams of a new Babylon (124) provides the comfort (180) that Jeremiah's absence fails to deliver. The nature of that comfort shows itself as the forging of connections that her presence and words enable. Holding Blimele on her lap, she will

> tell [her] stories
> Of the past that is like today
> And she herself will be Jeremiah
> Who comforts all, though the heart fears and weeps (176–80).

As she tells her stories, the mother situates the episodic present as part of a history and fulfills her prophetic office. She interprets the time, forbidding its escape into unbounded discontinuity and limiting the isolation that such would threaten to inflict. Isolation ever wounds, whether through the fragmentation of a people's history or through the severance of human ties. Blimele's mother consoles those wounded, with the comfort of human presence and the integration of human stories. With child in lap, she is *asheth chayil*; and more, the prophetess of the deportees.

Similar to the poem's initial section, the second section has moved in two directions, each qualifying the other. As the first groups of deportees gather, the scene displays signs of discontinuity. Theirs is no exile like the Babylonian captivity, for no Jeremiah accompanies them and no prophet witnesses so as to lament and comfort. At the same time, Blimele's father speaks of the present as a season such as that known by the Cantonists, averring that the world, somehow, is always the same. Wagering that continuity, he packs *tallis* and *kitl* for the deportation and insists that the child bring her soap for, if "one must keep clean at home" (167), it will be all the more important to do so in the "strange, strange land" of the morrow (168). Finally, the father portrays the mother's constant presence, her care and her words that knit the present crisis into the stories of the past. An agent of continuity, she replaces the missing Jeremiah.

By the section's sequence, Shayevitsh tempts the reader to focus on the assertions of continuity. Following the scene of discontinuity, they seem to answer its crisis. Indeed, they do check the growth of deportation despair, that its journey dislocates the traveler not only from home but from history and the prospect of witness, lament, and comfort. In the poem, what Jeremiah fails to supply, the mother provides. Still, the mother's continuity does not mark a return to an unbroken circle of faith and tradition; nor is the father's wager without reservation. Catastrophic times may have returned to "greet the ghetto" (136), but that it is the reappearance of catastrophe marks any continuity as a line of rupture. In these echoing times, the father has no confidence of a place of rest (142) and, as a "sick [bird]" likely to "fall / Dead in a field, in a valley somewhere" (145–46), he cannot himself nest in the safe refuge of God's wing (Psalm 91). Riddled by a sense of catastrophe, such continuity cannot secure access to the Sabbath world. Nor does it expect any future festivity: the *kitl* that the father packs he designates for a shroud and not for a Passover seder or marriage canopy.

But neither does discontinuity reign. As previously mother and daughter became the Sabbath angels (73–76), so now the mother stands as the prophet's surrogate. The prophet's continuity with heaven has been broken by the departing trains. In the void, Shayevitsh emphasizes the power of the human connection: The mother's presence "comforts all, though the heart fears and weeps" (180). She steps into the void of Jeremiah and holds her child. Such comfort comes but seemingly from no other.

3. *HAVDALAH*—SEPARATION (181–328)

The coming of Sabbath evokes greetings from those who would receive its blessing. Thus, they sing "*Sholem-aleikhem*" and recite the *kiddush*. Similarly, as Sabbath nears its end, they offer words of parting that, in the liturgy, recall the distinctions that have ordered their lives. The *Havdalah*, marking the end of Sabbath, blesses God for the separation of sacred and profane, light and darkness, Israel and the other nations, and Sabbath and the six working days.[44] Honoring these distinctions, the *Havdalah* is recited at the point of threshold between them and anticipates the transition from one to another. It bids farewell to the Sabbath and prepares for the different morrow.

The third section of "*Lekh-Lekho*" approximates such a parting from the Sabbath world. Constructed as a "goodbye to the house" (184), this section alludes to the *Havdalah* as the father says: "Let us take leave of each tiny thing / Just like old grandmothers / Piously taking leave at dusk / Of the holy Sabbath day" (197–200).[45] Moreover, as in the poem's first section, the house symbolizes the Sabbath world. Thus, when Blimele and her father say goodbye to the house, they also offer farewell to the Sabbath preserved within that house and to the world in which Sabbath revealed the edge of sacred and profane, light and dark. Like Sabbath, the house is both refuge and boundary. To part from it is sad and, here, dangerous.

Concrete items fill the house. If father and child say good-bye to the Sabbath world, they do so not abstractly, but through the given artifacts of the household. The father understands the artifacts—the table, the wardrobe, the cupboard—to have witnessed the blessing of the family's life.[46] What they have witnessed, these artifacts now call to mind in the father's sight. For the one who beholds them with familiarity, they evoke memory as tangible signs of those who have peered into their mirrors, wept upon their surfaces, and taken into hand their worn texture. They stir the imagination to picture the world in which they have had a distinctive place. Artifacts are vessels for remembrance and vision. They bear the freight of human lives and make visible a world in which those lives have known blessing and struggle. To part from these is, in the father's words, to "say goodbye / To all that we hold dear" (185–86). It is to surrender the vestige of this family's life and the evocation of their Sabbath days.[47]

Saying good-bye to the house makes its objects unusually precious and persistent in their claim. The father notes,

> every little thing we leave
> . . . runs after us like fire,
> With the longing that my lung
> Breathed into each thing—
> And bounds up like a puppy
> Everywhere, faithful yet and swift (187–92).

Abandoned, the artifacts of a past life yet haunt. Still, the farewell separates the family from more than the legacy of the past. It severs them from a future that cannot be realized in this place of table and bed, from the "unsung songs / That flutter about the house" (193–94) making perceptible the dream forfeited and the hope unfulfilled. The family's good-bye to the house marks no local transition, no move within a continuing world. On this final Sabbath, the yielding of the artifacts signal a world-ending. Farewell must contend with a momentous discontinuity, the rupture of a family's history in a hallowed place.[48]

The surrendered artifacts cannot easily sustain their same value. Set at distance from those who have used them or cherished them, they face a new limit to their power to evoke personal memory or to bring into view the world of which they have been a part. Sadly useless to the deportees in their transition, or simply impossible to retain, the same precious objects may have no connection with and, thus, no real significance for others. Elie Wiesel, in describing a deportation scene, points to a sudden obsolescence of a people's belongings:

> The street was like a market place that had suddenly been abandoned. Everything could be found there: suitcases, portfolios, briefcases, knives, plates, banknotes, papers, faded portraits. All those things that people had thought of taking with them, and which in the end they had left behind. They had lost all value.[49]

Put out of date by the deportation and left ownerless in their discard, the treasury of artifacts becomes vulnerable to decay or to other forms of destruction. Even the appropriation of these old objects for new functions will alter their value and may finally consume them so they no longer are of symbolic meaning or of practical use. In his final good-byes, the father contends with the likely deformation of those things he has held precious, particularly his books and "the bed where the power / Of the first Adam was revealed" (301–2).

The father's library stands out among the other items of this house. One sees his reluctance to part from the books in his detailed naming of their authors and playful sporting with their combinations:

> Isaiah hobnobs with Goethe . . .
> And Yesenin wants to get drunk
> And urinate in public
> But suddenly he sees Abraham
> Leading Isaac to Mount Moriah (259–64).

His comments show not only intimacy and fondness, but identification. Among these holy books and worldly books lie the father's own manuscripts, poems, and stories (257–58; 281–82). Thus, in parting from these "sacred books" and "dreams of geniuses" (293–94), he takes leave of the marks of his own vocation and must contemplate its futility. What he envisions, however, concerns more than the pride of his own voice, the sacredness of holy texts, or in his wide canon, the genius of the creative. The fate of literature as such appears in his ghetto scene:

> Tremble, tremble, sacred books,
> Tremble, tremble, dreams of geniuses—
> Some dawn, someone will get up
> And, dressed only in underpants,
>
> Will cut squares out of you
> For toilet-paper (293–98).

He contemplates no less than the final subversion of the literary artifact, here pressed in exigency to serve the most transient of purposes.

Last of all, the father says good-bye to the bed, the "gracious, holy bed" (325) upon which he learned sexuality's power of "a new Genesis" (304) and found dreams

that lifted [him]
Like a magic rocket
And over all fences and wires
Carried [him] out of the ghetto (309–12).

The bed's sanctity emerges in these categories that consider it a site where one touches the power of creation and transcends the stricture of the ghetto. Yet, like the books and all else, the bed can maintain neither its sanctity nor even its existence. The father concludes:

Groan, groan—gracious, holy bed,
You're being sold now by the kilo.
To cook by your flame a ghetto soup
Is not, God forbid, a sin (325–28).

The worldly artifact of creation and transcendence is consumed as firewood.

The father, however, does not see such a destruction, a profanation of the holy bed, to be sinful. He understands the point to be inevitable: Where the ghetto afflicts with frost and hunger (84–90), the bed remains a luxury of Sabbath days now gone. To meet elemental human need takes priority over preservation of the artifact, although, as we have seen, the destruction of a people's objects is not without consequence. The father's judgment does not surprise, in part because the need is urgent and the bed, heightened description notwithstanding, may appear in the reader's mind as an ordinary object. When applied to the case of the books, however, the father's concession appears more radical.

Read within a Jewish tradition that has understood certain texts to be sacred, the poem draws upon the reader's cultural disposition to prize books and privilege them as artifacts.[50] A pious reader, encouraged to take tradition seriously, already would be inclined to maintain written texts that preserve its legacy and to share the poem's sense that a book's destruction is a trembling matter (293–94). A secular reader, too, would share this textual sensibility, differing only on what texts are significant.[51] The devotion to texts as artifacts, striking under any condition of hardship, takes on extraordinary power in the context of the *Lager*, that is, in the time after deportation when the books have already been burned, left behind, or commandeered for Nazi purpose.

In writing of David Weiss Halivni, the noted Talmud scholar, one journalist portrays such devotion:

> From Auschwitz, the 15–year-old Weiss [Halivni] was shipped to Wolfs-berg, a camp in the Gross Rosen complex. Once, he saw an S.S. auxiliary about to eat a sandwich wrapped in what Weiss recognized as chapter 442, torn from the Lemberg edition of the Code of Jewish Law. Falling to his knees, Weiss begged to be given the wrapping, which he then read over and over and passed around to fellow Jews. The last one to have the chapter was a prisoner who collapsed and died during forced labor; the chapter went with him into the crematorium.[52]

Halivni's rescue of the text assumes no interest in this single page as a relic. Rather, one sees the deep conviction that even the smallest fragment of text may be precious for what it discloses and thus warrants great risks to preserve its existence. The loss of the artifact would not be that of a relic, but of the voice speaking through the words on a printed page, the loss of what the text reveals and enables when read.

Devotion to the textual artifact appears in the Halivni example as a rare vestige of Sabbath days. Set in the context of Jewish life before the intrusion of wire fence and ghetto, the passion to preserve a text would draw little attention, for such would be expected in that world of Sabbath and sanctity. What strikes one, instead, is its utter incongruity with the environment of the *Lager* where desperate physical need and near-total jeopardy overwhelm claims of the precious and the trace of Sabbath days. Blimele's father, a writer and a reader, might well have acted as Halivni, if given the chance, but he expects this of no one, not even in the ghetto, because the time of Sabbath days has neared its end. Now is the time of elemental want: A bed may be burned to heat the ghetto soup; pages, even sacred pages, may be cut into squares for toilet paper and discarded with the muck of human waste.

The father's concession involves more than the reckoning of desperate times. Of the burning of the bed he judges, it "is not, God forbid, a sin" (328). Is the same true for the profanation of the books? Halivni's extraordinary act can only be righteous, but had an inmate of ghetto or *Lager* used for toilet paper that "chapter 442, torn from the Lemberg edition of the Code of Jewish Law," would he or she be less than just? The poem vindicates that person in two ways. First, as the father has already told his daughter, "One must keep clean at home / And still more in a strange, strange land" (167–68). No prudish sentiment, the instruction reflects the pressure of an "excremental assault" upon the humanity of those victimized by the ghetto's poverty and filth.[53] If used to resist degradation and to retain human dignity, surely the scrapping of printed pages "is not, God forbid, a sin."

Second, the deformation of the artifacts is a symptom of a larger disorder that has fractured the boundary of sacred and profane and obscured the clarity of religious and moral categories. Where beds are burned for firewood and books mutilated for toilet paper, the artifacts become "matter out of place."[54] The resulting chaos tempts one to speak of the sin, for instance, of profaning sacred books, but profanity itself makes sense only against the foil of apparent sacredness. It is this that is missing from the world of Blimele and her father: not the sacred as such, but the evidence of its distinction, its separation from the unholy and the profane. In the poem's context of desperate need, the odd use of the artifacts does not finally appear so strange, but somehow appropriate, and even obliged. It is the world of ghetto and *Lager* that is "out of place" and ever incapable of sustaining the religious distinction.

Havdalah, this section's focusing image, traditionally took note of that religious distinction as its celebrant moved from the light of Sabbath to its darker complement. The ghetto ritual of Blimele and her father, however, has marked a different transition, as they enter a realm where no such distinction can be discerned or entertained. What in other contexts would have appeared profane and "out of place" may now well serve the human cause and resist its oppression, but even this lacks authority. The end of Sabbath that prompts this family's gesture of farewell sets them in no secure pattern of order, only its abrogation—a darkness without contrasting light, the end of a final Sabbath.

4. *PARASHA*—TORAH LESSON (329–412)

When Chaim Kaplan wrote about the closing of the Warsaw ghetto, he dated it by the synagogue lectionary. November 15, 1940, in his account, was the Sabbath of *Parashat Vayera*, the particular Sabbath when one read the biblical portion (*parasha*) of Gen. 18:1–22:24.[55] A day has its text. This connection, seen in lectionary cycles that structure seasons of devotion, reflects more immediately the textual sensibility of persons like Kaplan. For them, the progress of days is punctuated by texts; transitions are read, accompanied by the testimony of written words.

The day of the final Sabbath has its portion. Like Kaplan, Blimele's father conjoins moment and text: "The evil hour has come, / When I must teach you, a little girl, / The terrible chapter (*parasha*) 'Lekh-lekho'" (338–40). If the poem's third section marked a blurring of boundaries and distinctions, the fourth witnesses to the change. What formerly was "an unworthy sin" (336), the teaching of Torah to the daughter, now appears as *a must*. The ghetto's exigency claimed books for unholy purposes. Now deportation claims scripture in a reading that events have made strange and unfamiliar. Unfettered by any impulse to sequester the text in sacred tradition, Blimele's father rereads the story of Abraham's going forth in terms of his own family's imminent deportation. At first look, the text's intertextuality appears uncomplicated. The father identifies the *parasha* by its initial keyword (*Lekh-lekho*) and quotes the opening sentence: "And God said to Abram: / Go forth (*lekh-lekho*) from your land / And from the place of your birth / And from your father's house / To a land that I will show you / And there make of you a great people" (343–48; Gen. 12:1–2).[56] The quotation, although only a small bit of text, embodies a pattern that structures the Genesis saga of Abraham and his descendants. Therefore, when the father quotes the opening sentence, he effectively alludes to features of the greater story, in this case the pattern of imperative, disjunction, journey and blessing. God commands Abraham to leave behind his own home, journey to an as yet undisclosed place, and there receive the blessing of progeny.[57]

Although the poem makes apparent which text the father has in mind, it leaves the purpose of his reading more enigmatic. The father announces the *parasha*, but then introduces the quotation with a demurral: "how can one compare it [that is, the *parasha*] / To the bloody "*Lekh-lekho*" of today?" (341– 42). His question reflects an ironic perception of the text and his own situation. On the one hand, he begins his reading with a sense of difference between the biblical narrative and his own pending event. The two, he suggests, cannot be compared, a conviction that paves the way for his exposure of the difference in verse after verse. On the other hand, the very term he has used cannot escape the continuity of likeness. The deportation, for all its difference, is yet a "*Lekh-lekho*." Something persists from the biblical narrative in the midst of an otherwise uncompromising discontinuity.

The father can speak of the deportation as the "'*Lekh-lekho*' of today" (342) because of the common pattern that underlies both Abraham's going forth and his own. With continuity, both involve the sequence of imperative, disjunction, and journey and understand the journey to have consequence for the traveler's children, either establishing blessing or its lack. At the same time, the father must assert the deportation's incomparability because of the different connotations that this event forces upon each movement of the sequence. Within a common pattern, the deportation rewrites the Abraham story, bringing to it the forceful challenge of the contemporary woe.[58]

Both Abraham and the Lodz family come under the command of a power that forces their departure from home. In Abraham's case, the command comes from YHWH (Gen. 12:1), to whom the patriarch will build an altar (12:7) and upon whose name he will call (13:4). The biblical narrative understands the commanding voice to be Abraham's God. Shayevitsh, however, does not name the source that compels Blimele's family to "Go!" Concerned with what this family must endure, he scarcely refers to its oppressors as such, letting their profile emerge obliquely through the suffering they inflict.[59] One needs to know little else. The voice that commands in the ghetto is not God, but that of an enemy; or if God, a deity now manifesting an enmity at odds with the voice that leads Abraham to worship and to call upon the divine. In either case, the voice of the enemy, human or divine, has unqualified power, but no allegiance to the cause of Jewish life or human life. As "someone in the forest waste / Who lies in ambush for your step" (405–6), the enemy appears in the *parasha* of the new "*Lekh-lekho*," incomparable to the voice Abraham initially hears and obeys.[60]

The command that both Abraham and Blimele's family hear involves two steps: a separation from one place and a movement toward another; disjunction and journey. The biblical narrative emphasizes Abraham's disjunction as a separation from place and kin (12:1), although the company of his wife and nephew qualify the extent of his isolation. Blimele's family faces a comparable break as they take leave from their house and the community of which it has been a part. They do not leave alone, but as part of larger groups (330 and 415). The mass deportation, however, itself becomes radically isolating, as within it "Families will get lost / And never find themselves" (367–68). Moreover, the deportation of large numbers, ominous in its own right, accents the rupture of any one person's relation to a particular place. Unlike the situation of Abraham, here no one remains in the familiar place to make return imaginable or desirable. No constant face appears to identify the place as one of personal connection.

The disjunctions differ in one other respect. When Abraham leaves Haran, he takes with him "all the possessions that [he] had gathered" (12:5) and travels with the empowerment that wealth provides (13:2). Taking with him the possessions of one place, he brings tokens of continuity to the new land and meets its challenge with minimal vulnerability. Blimele's family, by contrast, has bid farewell to the artifacts of its household, an act that we have read as tantamount to a world-ending. No items from their former place will establish continuity elsewhere. No wealth will protect or advantage them. Already impoverished by ghetto life, they set out "sick and weary" (351) and "faint with hunger" (353). Their vulnerability, unlike Abraham's, is near-total.

YHWH guarantees Abraham's journey, or at least allows his promise and protection to mediate its ordeal. At the outset, YHWH assures Abraham that the journey will end in a land that will belong to his offspring and, by implication, will sustain their lives as they multiply and become a great nation (12:2,7; 13:14–17). Further, YHWH will protect their passage, blessing those who bless the travelers and cursing those who curse them (12:3; 15:1). No promise shields Blimele's family. No Canaan beckons. Deportation forces their trek down an "unknown distant road" (350); they travel as "broken ships / That do not reach a shore" (351–52). Without sight of any destination, Blimele's father anticipates only that the journey itself will kill: The one who is hungry will faint in the snow to die quietly like a hurt puppy (353–56); the heartstring of the terrified will suddenly snap, sending him to the ground heavy as a stone (357–60); and "someone's shivering child / Will freeze to death in the frost-fire" (361–62).[61]

If God's command separated Abraham from his past, its accompanying promise claims his future. The continuity of progeny and the gift of the land upon which offspring will live make Abraham's journey a source of blessing. Shayevitsh's poem, however, riddles precisely these assurances. In the most sustained portion of the father's vision, the poem details the sight of pregnant women, collapsing and aborting in the snow:

> And women, pregnant, will collapse,
> Fainting, to their knees.
> Soon they will fall behind
> And the snow will glow for them like coals.
>
> And from their fiery faces
> Death-cold sweat will pour
> And the doggish howl and cry
> They'll bite back with their lips
>
> And vomit and writhe
> On the painful, snowy birthing stool
> Against heaven, against sun, against God,
> Against all who merrily played (377–88).

The "'Lekh-lekho' of today" moves not toward the generation of offspring but to their painful miscarriage; not toward the fulfillment of the future but to its annihilation.

Further, the abortion of life climaxes in the anguishing revolt of nature in the struggle to survive. If Canaan's land was to sustain the life of Abraham's descendants, the new "Lekh-lekho" finds the field's golden sheaves to rise red from the aborting blood (391–93). The night shudders a thousand terrors and the glitter of stars hunt with fear, like rifle bullets (394–96). Here, the ice crackles like shrapnel exploding underfoot and the snow offers "'Shrouds for all!'" (397–400). Every shrub, twig, and little tree provide the landscape for ambush (401–6). Here there is no flowing of milk and honey, only "the flow of [one's] own warm blood" (408).

The father's reading of the story of Abraham's going forth in tandem with the "*Lekh-lekho*" of his present brings to bear the connotations of the contemporary upon the ancient narrative. Yoked to the contemporary through a common pattern, the Abraham story cannot escape the challenge of Blimele's family. What they experience now infuses the story's sequence with a rival meaning, a rewritten script. The voice that commands "Go!" may be an enemy's voice, sounding to bring about one's downfall. Disjunction, the separation from place and kin, may be a form of near-total vulnerability in the presence of one's enemy. The journey, unmediated by promise or protection, may itself be murderous and lead not to blessing but to its opposite: the aborting of life and the anguishing of nature. Abraham's story does not disappear in the juxtaposition, but it can no longer be read innocently. What the chapter "*Lekh-lekho*" means may belong as much to the suffering of Blimele's family as to the promise of Abraham's.

The father's awareness of the deportation forces him to see in the pattern of Abraham's going forth an emerging horror that subverts the security of promise and blessing. In his detailed vision of the "'*Lekh-lekho*' of today," he appears to drive a wedge between the contemporary event and the biblical text. The poem's intertextuality, however, resists simple discontinuity, even as it establishes the difference so apparent to the father and the reader of the poem. When the poem proposes a rival reading of the pattern, it imitates scripture's own counter-commentary.[62] Thus, as we will show, even the manifestation of discontinuity stands within a biblical line of tradition. "*Lekh-lekho*" perpetuates scripture's own self-critique.

The words "*lekh-lekho*" allude not only to the beginning of the Abraham saga, but to the opening imperative of the *Akedah*. There God commands Abraham: "Take your son . . . and go (*lekh-lekha*) to the land of Moriah, and offer him there as a burnt offering on one of the mountains that I shall show you" (Gen. 22:2). The same pattern is at stake in both episodes as Abraham receives the command to leave one place and go to another in a journey involving his offspring. This second biblical "*lekh-lekho*," however, creates a tension comparable to that of the poem. It, too, unsettles any connotation of blessing that may have become attached to the pattern through the language of promise. In the *Akedah*, the commanding voice is divine, but reveals itself as hostile in its demand. It shows no allegiance to the human life promised to Abraham and vouchsafed as his blessing. On the contrary, Abraham's obedience to the divine voice endangers the life of his child, jeopardizing not only Isaac but the future of his descendants and the continuity of blessing. Fulfillment of this command is world-ending.[63] That the story ends in rescue is, to a certain extent, beside the point. The voicing of the command already disrupts confidence in any promise and makes of going forth a dreadful prospect.[64]

With this second layer of allusion, the end point of the deportee's "*Lekh-*

lekho" appears as a Mount Moriah, not Canaan. The poem makes explicit this connection in its final section (424), thereby exposing a continuity with the biblical text, albeit a continuity that subverts as well as conserves. As the poem distances itself from the story of Abraham's call, it turns back and retrieves through its own difference a likeness to the *Akedah*. The poem's intertextual continuity with scripture thus persists in two ways: first, in the continuity of the pattern of "*lekh-lekho*," a narrative grid of imperative, disjunction, journey, and consequence that the poem recognizes in Genesis 12 and for which it provides rival connotation; and second, in the continuity of connotation established by the poem's affinity with the *Akedah* (Genesis 22), itself a counterreading of the "*lekh-lekho*" pattern. The second way shows scripture furnishing the precedent for its own subversion and attesting a continuity of interruption.

The continuity of interruption shows how the contemporary experience of various generations, including that of ancient Israel, challenges the connotations of scripture, for example, the yoking of a necessary journey with promise and blessing. The dissent from those connotations, such as we have found in the *Akedah* and in Shayevitsh's poem, itself constitutes a tradition. When Shayevitsh writes "*Lekh-Lekho*," he inflects not only the biblical allusions, but voices the echo of their appropriation by other texts that share the same complex intertextuality. One such appropriation of "*lekh-lekho*" that precurses Shayevitsh's poem is Bialik's "In the City of Slaughter."[65] Writing in the aftermath of the 1903 Kishinev pogrom, Bialik begins his poem with a reference to Gen. 12:1. The poet commands: "Arise and go now [*lekh-lekha*] to the city of slaughter." His detail of the landscape of ruin builds into an indictment of the theological traditions that have failed to protect human victims and have encouraged passivity in the face of suffering. Bialik's point differs from Shayevitsh's. "In the City of Slaughter" expresses a vengeful anger and accusation that would be out of place in the sensitive pathos of "*Lekh-Lekho*." However, a common thread runs between them. Bialik's poem precurses "*Lekh-Lekho*" by unmooring the biblical reference from its given association. In dissent, Bialik turned scripture back on itself. He held up to the promise of Canaan the ruin of the slaughtered city and thereby opened further the gate through which Shayevitsh was soon to pass.

Not even the ire of Bialik, however, escapes a certain affirmation of the biblical narrative. In his most furious rejection of tradition he yet refers to Abraham. He quotes the command "*lekh-lekha*" and contends with its legacy. Whatever challenge the contemporary chronicle brings to bear upon the ancient text, it remains connected to it as to a source. The modern anguish of pogrom and deportation, with all its difference intact, still occurs within the ongoing history of Abraham, and from that neither Bialik nor Shayevitsh attempt to flee. They speak within that history and to its anguishing turn. In concluding this section of "*Lekh-lekho*," Shayevitsh has Blimele's father move from description to direct address:

> So greetings to you, grandfather Abraham!
> We go on your hard journey
> But won't you be ashamed
> Of your grandchildren's bloody tears? (409–12)

Teaching his daughter the terrible *parasha*, the father himself stands as grandchild in the presence of an ancient grandfather—one whose journey he resumes, one whose journey he will surpass in horror.

5. *AL HAMITAH*—NIGHT PRAYER (413–48)

The fall of night has its own alarm. As darkness blankets familiar terrain, one enters a time of heightened vulnerability, surrendering control of one's life to the rhythm of sleep, the haunt of dreams, and the shadow of the unseen. The night prayer that the Jew recites upon retiring (*al hamitah*) warns: "Solomon's bed—sixty heroes are around it, heroes of Israel. All of them are armed with swords, and are trained in war; each has his sword on his hip, because of danger at night."[66] The night prayer confronts peril with the call for divine protection and company. Blimele's family now stands at the threshold of a descending night. Before the onset of deportation they have marked not only a final Sabbath, but perhaps a last day. The poem's concluding section thus aptly utters the beckoning of the night prayer as its ultimate expression.

Blimele's journey is no longer in prospect. Her father tells her to put on her little coat and announces a shared command: "let's go" (414–15). He adds, "let us not weep. / Let us not lament" (417–18). With these words the poem sounds a tone that seems to accept what cannot be changed and what has happened before (433–35). The father's voice shows determination as it repeats the exhortation and encourages the child's smile (419 and 439), but it offers no rancor or accusation. Solemn confidence stands in place of anguish; prayer in place of protest.

Assertions of continuity dominate this section, contrasting with the incomparability of the terrible *parasha*. The shift toward continuity and confidence, accented by being the poem's final statement, provides a marker of the work's intention. Shayevitsh does not aim to subvert the perspectives of scripture and tradition; still less does he intend to be intertextually clever or theologically provocative, although he is all of these, in effect. Rather, as this section shows, the poet's task is more immediate: to address, as a father would a child, the need of one who has heard the daunting words "let's go." The poem moves toward the exhortation "let us not weep." It requires the poet, on the one hand, to be a mender of experience and, on the other, a seer of the irreparable that is beyond tears.

Facing his community's deportation, Shayevitsh tries to maintain a sense of continuity lest those near him perish in their own despair. But he will neither comfort cheaply nor dry Blimele's eyes with deception. He will not purchase faith at the expense of fidelity to his contemporaries, whose experience must be recognized as well as consoled. Therefore, soberly, he shades any continuity with the account of its coincident rupture. Throughout the poem, Shayevitsh has refused to separate continuity and discontinuity. Still, the poem's first sections, as we have read them, have documented the breaking of Blimele's world and thus emphasized the discontinuity of the experience. Now, in the departure, the poet must respond to connections already broken and speak of what cannot be self-evident: the persisting continuity that discontinuity has not overcome.[67]

The continuity that Blimele's father claims here takes two forms. First, echoing the last verse of the previous section, he points to "the power of our grandfathers / Who in all generations / Climbed atop so many Moriahs" (422–24). Something of the grandfathers endures in the deportees—flows in their blood (421)—as they embark up the Moriah that waits beyond Lodz. With this language, the poet points to a continuity of human experience manifest in Jewish history, a history of "so many Moriahs" that have jeopardized the future's promise and interrupted the realization of blessing. The continuity does not derive from the smooth line of Genesis 12, but from the recurring ordeal of the *Akedah's* "*lekh-lekho.*" The image of "so many Moriahs" unifies Jewish history in terms of the human experiences of crisis that have endangered children and shattered the lens through which they otherwise have appeared whole and safe. But if, in its narration of jeopardy, the *Akedah* interrupts the security of Abraham's going forth, it no less preserves a rival meaning by telling of Isaac's survival. The interruption is itself interrupted and, with it, a survivor's story begun. The continuity of "so many Moriahs" warns of danger, yet prompts the struggle to survive.[68]

If the first form traced the constant of Jewish history, a human connection, the second expresses a transcendent continuity. The poem's closing lines find the father repeating a portion of the night prayer, introduced by his claim of continuity:

The same angels go with us as before:
On the right Michael, on the left Gabriel
Uriel in front and Raphael in the rear (442–44).[69]

Earlier in the poem, the father had identified the Sabbath angels with his wife and daughter (73–76). Now he boldly names the angels that guard the night as the divine messengers sent to protect and attend. The angels that had stood the watch of other nights still accompany the present moment of *lekh-lekho.* The father's words, as prayer, both declare and call. As testimony, they bear witness to the journey of the angels; as petition, they summon the angels' presence.

This fragment of the night prayer does not end with the company of the angels. As the angels come to surround on the right and left, before and behind, so does the divine presence hover overhead. The prayer, in its liturgical form, moves directly from the angels to the *Shekinah,* but Blimele's father introduces a striking concession that precedes the theological recognition. He notes: "And although beneath our feet is death / Over our head is God's Presence" (445–46). Again, the words bear witness to and summon an accompaniment; this time not of the angels, but of God. The concession does not obstruct the path of divine accompaniment, but makes clear the context in which God's presence must be sought and called for. On the father's lips, the night prayer's transcendence finds the pull of a disturbing gravity, the weight of deportation and death.

"So child, let us go with devotion renewed / And our old proclamation of Oneness" (447–48). These closing lines of the poem warrant Roskies' judgment that Shayevitsh's "transcendent faith only intensified during the renewed deportations from the Lodz ghetto."[70] Roskies continues his comment, however, to note the workings of irony in this same poetry. Where irony brings together diverging perspectives, the father's affirmation of transcendent continuity cannot deny or overwhelm the signs of discontinuity. The father cannot confess that divine presence hovers overhead without also granting the heavy pull of what is occurring in human experience: the mire of death beneath their feet. The ironic undertow yokes the poet's religious assertion with wariness. As the last verse reminds, deportation has made him skeptical, not of transcendence, but of any language that would separate it from its human context of suffering and anguished embodiment. Any proclamation of Oneness must include Blimele's hearing of the fateful "*lekh-lekho,* " if it is to be a serious word in the scene of bundled children and deporting trains.

The ironic shadowing of the poem's transcendent continuity means as well that the recognition of divine presence does not trivialize the significance of human acts of connection and accompaniment. The poem culminates in the *Shema's* proclamation of Oneness and affirms divine presence in the descent of night (Deut. 5:4–9). More than confession, however, the poem all along has been shaping a perception of how God is present in the world of deportation. Throughout, its verses have been struggling to identify channels of connection that would enable one to speak of unity or of God's Oneness. When death mires the steps of human children, the poem suggests, divine presence depends upon the human surrogate to make transcendence immediate and of avail. In this way the power of the human deed to stand for and embody the divine presence fills the poem's conclusion with both irony and faithfulness. Ironically, transcendent continuity reveals itself here as no unbroken autonomy but emerges in the more fragile freight of a mother's words as the new Jeremiah, of a daughter's welcome as the Sabbath angel, of a father's enactment of a weekday *kiddush* and *havdalah*, and of a grandfather's trek up "so many Moriahs." These vulnerable human deeds faithfully allude beyond themselves to the history of which they are a part and forge connection to the voices, divine and human, that speak within that history. For the moment, they transcend the walls of ghetto and boxcar; they unify and sustain. They proclaim a Oneness.[71]

In the world of "*Lekh-Lekho*," unity does not simply descend from above but arises from below, in and through the thick of human experience. God is One in no abstract way. Rather, God becomes One through the people's stubborn expression of tradition that, even in ironic parody, alludes to and summons divine presence. In its capacity to allude and call, the human deed of Blimele's father voices the prayer that God be One. Moreover, in the season of dark rupture, such deeds themselves unify, refusing to surrender the link between past and present, between *Shekinah* and the ordeal of human history. Discontinuity, although evident and severe, is not yet all. The night prayer, recited at this moment past Sabbath's glow, utters both hope and demand. Spoken to heaven in the presence of a departing child, this human word stretches for a glimmer of light and a touch that waits to join.

GHETTO SCRIPTURE

Just as Katzenelson in Warsaw, the Lodz poet has held his "evening of the Bible." Shayevitsh, speaking through Blimele's father, has both proclaimed an ancient story and rewritten its script. When he speaks of deportation, his words resonate with the Abraham saga and draw to themselves tones of Sabbath liturgy and readings. When he sounds the chords of tradition, however, the tenor echoes his contemporary anguish and modulates revered testimony into a new key. The command "*lekh-lekho*" no longer means what it did before the spider of frost had spun its silver-snowy web and tangled all life in the wire netting of ghetto and *Lager*. Shayevitsh's poem narrates the ancient story and enacts the established ritual, but all within the transposed frame of Lodz in the winter of 1942. What the poem conserves, it no less comments

upon and fills with rival connotation. Undetached from its precursing traditions, the poem yet provides the leaves of a newer testament. Such ghetto
scripture writes, in Levi's phrase, the "stories of a new Bible."

As Shayevitsh contends with the Bible, the poem situates him as part of a
Midrashic tradition, both pious and not, that wrestled with contemporary
claims in tandem with the legacy of antecedent texts.[72] Shayevitsh, like
Blimele's father, writes, yet remains a reader even and especially as he puts
pen to paper. Sixteen years earlier, Martin Buber had insisted that the task of
every Jewish generation was, in some way, to become such a reader. Of the
Bible, he wrote:

> Since this book came into being, it has confronted generation after gen-
> eration. Each generation must struggle with the Bible in its turn, and
> come to terms with it. The generations are by no means always ready to
> listen to what the book has to say, and to obey it; they are often vexed
> and defiant; nevertheless, the preoccupation with this book is part of
> their life and they face it in the realm of reality. Even when generations
> negated the Book, the very negation confirmed the Book's claim upon
> them; they bore witness to the Book in the very act of denying it.[73]

In 1926 Buber could not have known the context in which his generation
would be forced to "struggle with the Bible." As seen with Shayevitsh, that
context only intensified what Buber had envisioned as the encounter with the
Bible: The words "vexation" and "preoccupation" seem too tame to describe
Blimele's father and the poet he personifies.[74] Nevertheless, the truth of
Buber's statement upwells in the example of Shayevitsh as one who was
compelled to "face [the 'terrible chapter'] in the realm of reality."

Shayevitsh, although an individual talent, belongs to his generation.[75]
Buber's observation helps the reader of "*Lekh-Lekho* " raise further questions of
the poet and his generation. Writing the scripture of the ghetto, how does this
generation come to terms with the Book? How does it listen and obey? What
is its vexation and defiance? One finds several aspects of a response to these
questions in Shayevitsh's poem. First, the poem clearly shows an intent, in
Buber's language, to struggle with the Bible and come to terms with it. Read
on a continuum of responses to catastrophe that includes various apocalyptic
and secularist perspectives, the poem's trenchant use of biblical and liturgical
types seems far from inevitable. Shayevitsh's allusions to tradition reflect his
choice to pursue a line of writing that understands past and present to be
intimately related. Where apocalyptic and secularist writings antiquate history, poetic midrash such as Shayevitsh's grants it continued pertinence and
looks to the documents of tradition for its vector. The modern poet as
midrashist may not revere that tradition, but he or she will be its reader.

Shayevitsh willingly accepts a relation to the Bible and refuses to ignore or deny its claim.[76]

Second, as Shayevitsh accepts a relation to the Book, he claims a freedom to read it openly in light of its contemporary challenge. Accordingly, coming to terms with the Book, in this case, includes providing a counter-commentary that exposes biblical claims to the present's rival assertions. If the Book functions in Shayevitsh's poem as an accepted given, it yet bears no self-evident connotation or necessary meaning that binds the poet to read in some prescribed way. Joined to an ongoing present, the Book's meaning can have no specified closure. With an irony born of his current anguish, the poet's reading may, in effect, rewrite the ancient text and transform the value it offers to the contemporary reader.

Third, coming to terms with the Book, in Shayevitsh's instance, also includes allowing biblical narrative (and its liturgical expression) to furnish a frame for the reading of contemporary experience. At the minimum, this means empowering the language of tradition to focus the current situation and to provide the language for its interpretation. Thus, for example, while Shayevitsh fills "Sabbath" and "lekh-lekho" with rival connotations, he nevertheless sees his world in their terms. This third aspect, however, implies more than an openness to traditional vocabulary. Allowing the Book to frame the contemporary experience grants an authority to its connotations to challenge, in turn, those of the present critique. If, in light of present experience, Shayevitsh offers a rival reading of the "lekh-lekho" pattern, he then allows the biblical text—itself a connotation-creating performance or reading of the pattern—to rival the challenge.[77] He exposes the discontinuity of the deportation to the continuity of the Akedah's precedent in dissent, the new parasha's dissolution of unities, to the night prayer's resisting claim of the angels' return and the presence of God's Oneness.

As we have seen, the poem's intertextuality exposes a precursor Book that is itself complex. The phrase "lekh-lekho" leads both to Canaan and to Mount Moriah, to affirmation and to dissent. When the Bible frames the contemporary situation with this complexity, it upends any enthusiasm of the present to finalize its own despair or confidence. Thus, the poem's movement between discontinuity and continuity may be no idiosyncrasy, but a pressure exerted by the biblical frame. Precisely in its allegiance to the Bible, the ghetto scripture counters naive affirmation of divine promise with the detail of discontinuity; and, conversely, it resists despair with the stubborn assertion of connection.

Both this complexity and the poem's emphasized counter-commentary preclude certain styles of reading that depend on closure. When Shayevitsh "listen[s] to what the book has to say, and obey[s] it," he gleans neither a code of moral conduct nor a theological belief. Rather, he listens for a resonance, a resounding of the ancient pattern in his current context. He obeys no dictum, but follows a line of allusion that insists upon the interrelatedness of the Book and his time. Faithful reading, in Shayevitsh's generation, derives not from affirmation or dissent, but from the response itself: the recognition that the words of the Book claim and await their meaning in the reader's "realm of reality."

Ghetto scripture does not *quote* the Book, as much as comment upon and rewrite it in the reader's "realm of reality." It presupposes perplexity or tension by its very attempt to challenge, supplement, or simply read anew. "Vexed and defiant," Shayevitsh protests the Book's connotations of promise and protection, because these efface what he has learned in the real realm of Lodz's ghetto. However, the protest does not aim at the Book as such, for the poet goes on to claim the Book's own countermovement in the *Akedah* as a precedent for his vexation. No smooth dialectic eases the tension between ghetto and Book, a tension heightening into dissonance in ghetto scripture. Precursed in the Book's own movement between protection and endangerment, the vexing difference leaves the reader caught between fragments, suspended in an unresolvable chord. Defiance follows no Hegelian path to transcend the gaps of experience and text, of chapter and chapter, but instead, remains stubbornly in the contradiction. Shayevitsh forcefully expresses both continuity and discontinuity, and can tangle them with significant irony. Still, he cannot draw an unbroken line that leads from one to another. He defies not the Book, but its own effort to construct a unity or elevate any one set of its connotations as a norm. In the ghetto generation, vexation and defiance become obligatory. To become at ease in scripture purchases comfort with bad faith toward the Book's dissonance and, unthinkably, toward its living intertext: the experience of Blimele's abandonment and accompaniment.

The rich intertextuality of ghetto scripture illumines not only Shayevitsh and his generation, but finally something of the legacy of their Book. Like the wire fence at Lodz and the wall of Pagis's boxcar, their Book is two-sided. Shown by poems such as "*Lekh-Lekho*" to witness to its own rupture, the Bible preserves or joins to an alien quality of difference that disrupts attempts to make it whole. Like the world of the Lodz mother and Eve of the boxcar, the Book shows the signs of its breaking into fragments, an icon of the experience of ghetto and *Lager*. Accordingly, to read scripture "here," in the manner of the ghetto poet, may enable one to touch something of the other side, "there." Difference remains. The Bible is not that other side but, as Shayevitsh's poem attests, a gate to it. Passing through that gate, one does not leave behind the breaking, but enters a realm where fragments themselves invite connection.

POSTSCRIPT

Shayevitsh's family was to know an ordeal that surpassed the agonies envisioned in "*Lekh-Lekho*." As documented in the diary of Jozef Zelkowicz, the *Gehsperre* of September 1942 struck the poet's home severely and at its most vulnerable moment. Shayevitsh's wife prematurely gave birth to Blimele's little sister on September 4, the day before the curfew was to begin. Ghetto flies swarmed around the baby, leading her father to shoo them from her face. But, as Zelkowicz hauntingly put it: "He chased the flies away and the wolves came." On the first evening of the *Gehsperre*, September 5, police barged in to take away the poet's precious Blimele in the massive round up of children. The next morning, at 9:30, the German commission came and claimed the fever-weakened mother and the newborn infant, now only 33 hours old. Unlike the poem in which the father accompanies, Shayevitsh's fate was to face alone in Lodz the overwhelming loss of his Sabbath angels and the newborn. Zelkowicz's entry ends with a picture of the poet wandering the streets "with his extraordinary woe in his heart, compelled to believe that he will once again see his weak and feverish wife, who will bring back his most beautiful song—Blimele—and his beautiful, tremulous little infant—the newborn who will then have a name."[78] Shayevitsh was deported to Auschwitz in 1944 and from there to the Kaufering camp. He died only days before its liberation.[79]

NOTES

1. On the eve of the sealing of the Warsaw ghetto, Yitzhak Katzenelson organized a public reading of the Bible. The words here cited are from the rhymed prologue with which he began the program. Translation and discussion are in David Roskies, *Against the Apocalypse* (Cambridge, Mass.: Harvard University Press, 1984), 208–9.

2. Ibid., 208. The sealing of the ghetto occurred on November 15, 1940.

3. Diary entry of October 24, 1940, in *The Warsaw Diary of Chaim A. Kaplan*, trans. and ed. Abraham I. Katsh (New York: Collier Books, 1973), 213–14. Emphasis is mine.

4. Diary entry of November 17, 1940, in Ibid., 225.

5. For a statistical account of the ghetto's boundaries and population see *Encyclopedia of the Holocaust*, s.v. "Warsaw: Jews during the Holocaust," ed., I. Gutman (New York: Macmillan Publishing Co., 1990), 4:1608–11. The census of death shows Kaplan's estimation to be unexaggerated. 445 deaths occurred in November 1940, rising in the summer to between 4,000 and 5,500 deaths a month, a mortality rate virtually constant throughout the remainder of the ghetto's existence (its final liquidation began in April 1943). This does not include those whose deaths would come through deportation.

6. *Against the Apocalypse*, 208–9.

7. Regarding the centrality of the people's continuity and survival, the people's eternity, note Katzenelson's imperative and description in the evening's prologue: "Believe: you who have created eternity on this earth / Are yourselves eternal." Quoted in Ibid., 209.

8. Translated from the Yiddish by Noah H. Rosenbloom, in David Roskies, *Literature of Destruction* (Philadelphia: Jewish Publication Society, 1989), 542. This section of Katzenelson's poem was written between November 23 and 26, 1943.

9. Primo Levi, *Survival in Auschwitz*, trans. S. Woolf (New York: Collier Books, 1961), 59.

10. By thinking of reading as "rewriting," I want to emphasize (a) the constructive nature of these activities and (b) their intertextual basis. Rewriting, for example, is a mode of reading that not only conserves the text read, but comments upon it or reframes it in such a way that it takes on new or additional meaning, even unto dissonance. As such, rewriting necessarily involves relations of both continuity and discontinuity with its precursor text. These relations may be highly explicit, as when a text is read in an "evening of the Bible" or quoted within a new text; but they may also be implicit, veiled in attempts to write with alleged originality or to read innocently. The category "rewriting" reminds that no act of reading or writing can escape the tangle of tradition. For a comparable use of the category see James E. Young, *Writing and Rewriting the Holocaust: Narrative and the Consequences of Interpretation* (Bloomington, Ind.: Indiana University Press, 1988) (hereafter referred to as *Writing and Rewriting the Holocaust*).

11. Elinor Robinson's translation of "*Lekh-Lekho*" is included in *Literature of Destruction*, 520–30. The title—literally "Go!"—alludes to God's opening command for Abraham to leave his home (Gen. 12:1) and again for him to *go* to Mount Moriah to sacrifice his son Isaac (Gen. 22:2).

12. The *Havdalah* service concludes the Sabbath and, as the name indicates, involves a series of blessings for the distinctions God has made: the sacred and the profane, light and darkness, Israel and the nations, the seventh day and the six days of work. For discussion of the *Havdalah* service see Isaac Klein, *A Guide to Jewish Religious Practice* (New York: Jewish Theological Seminary, 1979), 73–75; and Lawrence A. Hoffman, *Beyond the Text: A Holistic Approach to Liturgy* (Bloomington, Ind.: Indiana University Press, 1989), 20–45.

13. We do not know what else Shayevitsh may have written during the war years: These are the only two works of his that are known to have survived the ghetto. The Yiddish texts were published by the Central Jewish Historical Commission in Lodz in 1946. In addition to Elinor Robinson's translation of "*Lekh-Lekho*" (see n. 11), another translation is published in *Lodz Ghetto: Inside a Community Under Siege*, ed. Alan Adelson and Robert Lapides (New York: Viking, 1989), 216–30 (hereafter referred to as *Lodz Ghetto*). A translation of "Spring 5702 [1942]" is printed in the same volume, 250–62. For biographical sketches of Shayevitsh, see *Literature of Destruction*, 630 and *Lodz Ghetto*, 504.

14. Not all Holocaust literature is alike. In the same way that distinctions in genre call for particular styles of reading, so do differences in vantage and context. As James Young has shown, the difference between the present recollection of a survivor and a diary or document contemporary with the Holocaust does not privilege one over the other, but makes one sensitive to the way in which both construct their meanings (see

Writing and Rewriting the Holocaust, 15–39). In the case of survivor testimony, the Holocaust is constructed out of memory and cannot be separated from the past's ongoing claims upon the speaker's present, a present at once distinct from yet tied to the remembered past. In the case of contemporary documents, the Holocaust cannot fully be seen as such for it manifests itself as a present coming to pass. Not memory as much as the imagined future shapes the contemporary construction of the Holocaust, an imagining of the future inseparable from the speaker's or writer's ongoing experience of the present. The survivor's distance from the event brings the breadth of retrospect, but its very gift of perspective may also be a limitation if it assumes for the past a comparable clarity of situation. The contemporary's proximity brings the vitality of immediacy—the freshness of a view not yet over-interpreted by intervening schemes—but its nearness to the event may lack the perspective gained only in hindsight. On the distinctiveness of survivor's testimony, see Lawrence L. Langer, *Holocaust Testimonies: The Ruins of Memory* (New Haven, Conn.: Yale University Press, 1991) and Shoshana Felman and Dori Laub, *Testimony: Crises of Witnessing in Literature, Psychoanalysis, and History* (New York: Routledge, 1992); note too the review of Langer's book by David Roskies in *Commentary* (November 1991): 57–59. One can see readily the contrast between retrospective and contemporary vantages by comparing Alan Adelson's film *Lodz Ghetto* and Claude Lanzmann's *Shoah.* The former employs photographic stills and voice-over readings from contemporary documents; the latter, present recollections of survivors and those who shared their landscape.

15. On the isolation of the ghetto and, consequently, the virtual impossibility of its knowing of the nearby Chelmno, see chapter 1, n. 9. Not until the summer of 1942 does this situation seem to change.

16. "*Lekh-Lekho,*" in *Literature of Destruction,* 528 (lines 330–32). All subsequent references to the poem will be to this translation and publication and specified parenthetically by line number.

17. Jozef Zelkowicz's diary entry for September 6, 1942, provides a description of Shayevitsh's family, including the daughter's name, Blimele. See *Lodz Ghetto,* 342.

18. On these deportations from Lodz, see *The Chronicle of the Lodz Ghetto, 1941–44,* ed. Lucjan Dobroszycki (New Haven, Conn.: Yale University Press, 1984), 123–74 (hereafter referred to as *Chronicle*); *Lodz Ghetto,* 197–265; and *Encyclopedia of the Holocaust* 3, s.v. "Lodz."

19. On the public execution, see the record of the *Chronicle,* 129–30.

20. The sections are as follows designated by line numbers: (1) 1–104; (2) 105–180; (3) 181–328; (4) 329–412; and (5) 413–48. The quatrain structure is maintained throughout the poem. In the Yiddish original the endings of the second and fourth lines of the quatrains tend to rhyme (although not without exception).

21. On the necessary self-exposure of tradition to the claims of the contemporary—an act required by the affirmation of God's presence in history—see Emil Fackenheim, *God's Presence in History* (New York: New York University Press, 1970), 30–31 and 45–46; also "On the Self-Exposure of Faith to the Modern-Secular World: Philosophical Reflections in the Light of Jewish Experience," in Emil Fackenheim, *Quest for Past and Future* (Boston: Beacon Press, 1968), 278–305.

22. The double system of reference created by allusion differs from simple ambiguity. The meaning of the words "*Lekh-Lekho*" is not uncertain, but rather has (at least) two certain dimensions whose involved relation the poet wants to emphasize.

23. At this point, it may be helpful to distinguish between philosophical and

rhetorical notions of intertextuality. The former understands intertextuality to be an inescapable feature of language and textuality as such. It refers to the inability of one to speak or write and *not*, at the same time, refer to a precursing tradition and system of language. The latter notion, rhetorical intertextuality, does not refer to properties of textuality per se, but to particular rhetorical strategies by which an author links one text with another and leads a reader to perceive their connection, for example, through the use of allusion, quotation, and typology. Shayevitsh's overt use of allusion accents the rhetorical intertextuality of the poem.

24. From *Daily Prayer Book. Ha-Siddur Ha-Shalem*, trans. Philip Birnbaum (New York: Hebrew Publishing Company, 1949), 289–90; alt.

25. In the Exodus story, the Hebrew terminology for "going forth" (יצא, e.g., Ex. 13:3) and being "let go" (שלח, e.g., Ex. 11:10) differs from the הלך root of Abraham's command (Gen. 12:1). Each, however, shares an obvious sense of disjunction and departure.

26. Note that in the next section the deportees meet a fate not unlike that of the Egyptian soldiers. Instead of crossing the sea on dry ground (Ex. 14:22), the deportees are "hurled into the midst / Of a naked furious sea" (111–12).

27. On the child's questions at Passover, see *The Passover Haggadah*, ed. Nahum Glatzer (New York: Schocken Books, 1953), 20–21. On the child's role generally, note the interesting discussion of Ruth G. Fredman, *The Passover Seder: Afikoman in Exile* (Philadelphia: University of Pennsylvania Press, 1981), 115–27.

28. *The Passover Haggadah*, 48–49.

29. Within the Exodus paradigm, the signature of God's presence in history is the manifestation of power to liberate and rescue the people. Facing deportation, the father's unknowing silence suggests that, at this moment of history, the liberating presence of God is not so apparent. Shayevitsh's assertion of discontinuity between the Exodus and the current "going forth" does afford, however, an ironic continuity with the Passover *haggadah* in its own affirmation of the difference of "this night." The poet and the haggadist stand together in the assertion of the singularity of their given moments. Each would say: "this night is different."

30. The image of the honey-cake may also be metatextual, drawing on the association of Torah and honey (for example, Ps. 19:10; Prov. 24:13; 25:16). As the God of the Exodus provided manna in the wilderness, so does the same God sustain with the Torah whose written words narrate the Exodus story, mediating its presence to readers who, in their own contexts, regard themselves as going forth from Egypt. On the association of Torah and honey, note the custom of some Jewish communities that initiate a child to traditional studies by writing the letters of the Hebrew alphabet on a slate and covering them with honey. The child, encouraged to taste the honey, then approaches the words of Torah as something sweet and nourishing. The ceremony is accompanied with the serving of honey-cakes. See *Encyclopedia Judaica* 8, s.v. "Honey."

31. Psalm 91 is recited in the morning service for Sabbath and festivals (*Daily Prayer Book*, 309–12) and in the liturgy for the conclusion of Sabbath (Ibid., 537–38). As we will subsequently discuss, Ps. 91:11 is cited just prior to the *kiddush* on Sabbath eve (Ibid., 283–84). Pertinent to our context, the recitation of Psalm 91 also accompanies the prayer for a safe journey (Ibid., 731–32).

32. On the theme of homelessness and the Holocaust, see chapter 5 following, "The Survivor's Return: Reflections on Memory and Place." On alien existence and the experience of the stranger, note Karl A. Plank, "The Human Face of Otherness," in

Faith and History: Essays in Honor of Paul W. Meyer, ed. J. Carroll, C. Cosgrove, and E. Johnson (Atlanta: Scholars Press, 1990), 55–73; and John B. Mathews, "Hospitality and the New Testament Church: An Historical and Exegetical Study" (Th.D. dissertation, Princeton Theological Seminary, 1965), 105–18.

33. See *Daily Prayer Book,* 283–84. The tradition derives from a Talmudic passage indicating that two angels accompany every Jew when he returns home from the Sabbath eve services (b. Shabb. 119b).

34. On the profanity of homogeneous time and, conversely, the sacrality of demarcated time, see Mircea Eliade, *The Sacred and the Profane: The Nature of Religion* (New York: Harvest Books, 1959), 68–113.

35. As translated in *Lodz Ghetto,* 221.

36. As Martin Buber keenly saw, unwitnessed affliction suffers the erosion of its own capability to testify or to become a testimony. In a critical letter to Mohandas K. Gandhi (February 24, 1939), he writes: "Testimony without acknowledgement, ineffective, unobserved martyrdom [is] a martyrdom cast to the winds." *The Letters of Martin Buber: A Life of Dialogue,* ed. N. Glatzer and P. Mendes-Flohr (New York: Schocken Books, 1991), 478.

37. Thus the paraphrasing translation of line 129 in *Lodz Ghetto,* 221.

38. On the Cantonists, see S. Ettinger, "The Modern Period," in *A History of the Jewish People,* ed. H.H. Ben-Sasson (Cambridge, Mass.: Harvard University Press, 1976), 814–15.

39. Note, for example, that the father's assertion of continuity does not protect the world of Sabbath or rehabilitate it as a place of refuge. Immediately after speaking of the Cantonists, the father inverts Sabbath imagery, reminding Blimele that they may not "reach a place of rest" (142) and, unlike those under the refuge of God's wings (Psalm 91), may be "like sick birds that fall / Dead in a field" to "perish on the road" and "not be buried as Jews" (145–48).

40. The father's packing, although it anticipates a continuity in the future, yet distances him from the confidence of the traditionalist. Significantly, he understands the *kitl* as a burial shroud and not as a festive garment that one might wear on Passover or at one's marriage. The books that he takes enable him to study the tradition but also to move in another direction with the poems of H. Leivick (1886–1962), a Russian-Yiddish poet and dramatist. On Leivick, see *Against the Apocalypse,* 101–4.

41. The issue of cleanliness gains in importance when seen from the vantage of the *Lager.* There, the impossibility of remaining clean becomes an engineered mechanism for dehumanization. Terrence Des Pres aptly describes the *Lager* strategy as an "excremental assault" and goes on to show how even an inmate's futile efforts to remain clean take on the character of resistance. See Terrence Des Pres, *The Survivor: An Anatomy of Life in the Death Camps* (New York: Oxford University Press, 1976), 51–71 (hereafter referred to as *The Survivor*). Note, too, the comparable point of Primo Levi. In writing of the *Lager's* washroom, he declares: "In this place it is practically pointless to wash every day in the turbid water of the filthy washbasins for purposes of cleanliness and health; but it is most important as a symptom of remaining vitality, and necessary as an instrument of moral survival" (*Survival in Auschwitz,* 35). Both Des Pres and Levi, however, should be read in light of Lawrence Langer's caution regarding theories of survival. It would be misleading to elevate cleanliness into a criterion for survival or to locate it unqualifiedly in the realm of choice. See Lawrence L. Langer, *Versions of Survival* (Albany: SUNY Series, State Univ. of New York, 1982), 53–65.

42. Unwittingly, Shayevitsh's focus on the importance of Blimele's not being "lousy" expresses a cruel irony and foreshadowing. The mother's loving act of combing out lice will later give way to the death camp's use of the scenario of delousing as a stage for extermination of the Jews. On delousing, Langer writes: "Delousing is a vital controlling image for the deathcamp experience, not as metaphor but as literal reflection of a place where men and women did not choose heroic death and were not even killed like human beings, but were *exterminated*" (Ibid., 107).

43. On the significance of accompaniment, see chapter one, "The Mother of the Wire Fence," 23–25 and 34–36.

44. *Daily Prayer Book*, 551–52.

45. Here Shayevitsh refers to the "*Gott fun Abrohom*" prayer recited or sung by women as an introduction to the *Havdalah* service at the end of the Sabbath. For its text, see Abraham E. Millgram, *Sabbath: The Day of Delight* (Philadelphia: Jewish Publication Society, 5725–1965), 415.

46. The personification of the artifacts as witnesses can be seen in their attributed capacity for observation: the table's wooden heart hears (215) and the damp bowed walls also lend an ear (221–22); the wardrobe mirror sees everything (230–31) and, like a phonograph record (237), preserves the sounds of household life.

47. On the phrase "Sabbath days," see Chaim Grade, *My Mother's Sabbath Days*, trans. C. Goldstein and I. Grade (New York: Schocken Books, 1987). As Grade in his memoir uses "Sabbath days" to evoke the Jewish world of Vilna between the wars, so do I intend it with breadth. At stake in the phrase is more than simply the weekly celebration of Sabbath. "Sabbath days" includes that whole life-world within which a family would keep the Sabbath and for which the Sabbath furnishes the central symbol.

48. As Hannah Arendt has shown, the objectivity of artifacts makes it possible for a "world" to exist and to manifest durability. See Hannah Arendt, *The Human Condition* (Chicago: University of Chicago Press, 1958), 93–96 and 136–44. As artifacts endure, so does the human world know a sense of constancy and place; in temporal terms, the prospect of continuity. The converse, depicted in the poem, must also be taken seriously. Without one's artifacts, one's sense of a "world" is jeopardized, left without signs of recognizability or permanence. Without that constancy of place, continuity in time becomes, at best, a tenuous matter, a fragmented history of episodes. In addition to Arendt's writing, note the plentiful discussion of artifact and world in Elaine Scarry, *The Body in Pain* (New York: Oxford University Press, 1985), esp. 38–45.

49. Elie Wiesel, *Night*, trans. S. Rodway (New York: Avon Books, 1969), 27.

50. The disposition does not depend solely on the religious or cultural environment of the reader. The poem itself sets up this affinity through its reference to "sacred books" (257 and 293) and identification of the narrator as a writer (258).

51. I do not here assume that the poem's reader necessarily is either pious or secular. Rather, I want to suggest that the religious convictions about sacred texts have a cultural corollary identifiable as a seriousness about books themselves. The religious and the secular Jew may differ as to what texts are sacred or significant, but they will share an affinity for thinking in terms of texts, for understanding writing and reading to be important activities, and thus for considering books to be precious. Moreover, within the Yiddish culture of Shayevitsh, the literacy may overlap in extensive ways, for there even the Jew who wishes to revolt against tradition may well know and refer to its texts in order to reject its meaning. The textual sensibility seems inescapable.

52. Israel Shenker, "A Life in the Talmud," in *New York Times Magazine* (September 11, 1977), 77.

53. The phrase "excremental assault" is taken from *The Survivor*, 51–71. See above, note 41.

54. Here I allude to Mary Douglas's well-known dictum that dirt or impurity is "matter out of place" and thus a symbol of disorder. See Mary Douglas, *Purity and Danger: An Analysis of Concepts of Pollution and Taboo* (London: Routledge & Kegan Paul, 1966), 2.

55. See *The Warsaw Diary of Chaim A. Kaplan*, 225.

56. "*Lekh-lekho*" vocalizes the Hebrew imperative and pleonastic pronoun, from לֶךְ, meaning "Go!" On the construction, see *Gesenius' Hebrew Grammar*, ed. E. Kautzsch and rev. by A.E. Cowley (London: Oxford, 1910), #119s. Shayevitsh draws on the convention of identifying biblical readings by their first words or their first key words. Thus, he refers to the story of Abraham's journey in Genesis 12 through its keyword heading, "*Lekh-lekho*" (for example, lines 340 and 342; both, לֶךְ לְךָ). The quotation itself, however, is given in Yiddish.

57. For the use of "Go" imagery (לֶךְ) in the more intricate pattern of Genesis as a whole, see Devorah Steinmetz, *From Father to Son: Kinship, Conflict, and Continuity in Genesis* (Louisville: Westminster/John Knox Press, 1991), 50–85.

58. On the connotative or symbolic value of texts, see Daniel Patte and Aline Patte, *Structural Exegesis: From Theory to Practice* (Philadelphia: Fortress Press, 1978), 3 and Daniel Patte, *What Is Structural Exegesis?* (Philadelphia: Fortress Press, 1976), 28–29. Following Patte, I understand a text's connotation in ways comparable to de Saussure's concept of the "value" of a sign. For de Saussure, "value" is determined by the correlation or opposition of a sign with other signs in a given system. Thus, in our instance, the common pattern of "*lekh-lekho*" may take on different values or connotations through its juxtaposition or correlation with other textual elements, including the language of the contemporary situation.

59. At the one point where Shayevitsh points to the ghetto's external opposition, his language remains metaphorical: the ghetto's "silver-snowy web / Has been spun by the spider of frost" (83–84). The poem's relative silence regarding the oppressors allows them to be defined, as they are in Grossman's photograph of the "Mother of the Wire Fence," strictly in terms of what they have done. This silence refuses to surrender the situation to the vantage of the oppressor or to distract from the deed done.

60. I have no interest in any theological laundering of deity. Divine antagonism is too unavoidable in both Jewish and Christian scriptures to permit the apologetic and the texts too individualized to allow generalization. A caution is still venturable: to note that divine enmity occurs in scripture does not warrant the conclusion that it is manifest necessarily in any and all instances of human suffering or jeopardy. I do not think that Shayevitsh presupposes a divine enmity, although his relative silence makes the point inconclusive. At one instance, however, the aborting women's writhing "against God" (387) does make explicit a theological opposition, but this is singular in the poem and itself surrounded by other objects of their rage: heaven, the sun, all who merrily played (387–88). Neither do I see a divinely commanding antagonism in the opening episode of the Abraham saga. In principle, divine enmity could be in either situation, but I do not see any emphasis of its signs. On the question of divine antagonism in biblical texts, see James L. Crenshaw, *A Whirlpool of Torment: Israelite Traditions of God as an Oppressive Presence* (Philadelphia: Fortress Press, 1984) and Karl

A. Plank, "Raging Wisdom: A Banner of Defiance Unfurled," in *Judaism* 36 (1987): 323–30. With regard to pogromic settings, the issue is powerfully raised by Elie Wiesel's drama, *The Trial of God*, trans. Marion Wiesel (New York: Random House, 1979).

61. One must remember Shayevitsh's vantage. He writes, in all likelihood, without knowledge of the death-camps as the destination of the deportees. His vision is of the murderous journey itself. One can scarcely imagine how this *parasha* might have read had Shayevitsh known what awaited beyond the journey.

62. On counter-commentary, see *Against the Apocalypse*, 19–20.

63. In this regard, note Mishnah Sanhedrin 4.5: Any man who has caused a single Jewish soul to perish, the Torah considers it as if he has caused a whole world to perish. On child endangerment, note that the biblical text prepares and emphasizes this theme in the *Akedah* through the parallel with the near death of Abraham's other son, Ishmael, in the preceding chapter. See Gen. 21:15–16.

64. On the challenge of the *Akedah*, see Emil Fackenheim, *Encounters Between Judaism and Modern Philosophy* (New York: Basic Books, 1973), 53–77.

65. See Hayyim Nahman Bialik, "In the City of Slaughter," in *The Literature of Destruction*, 160–68. Shayevitsh's familiarity with the poem can be seen in his specific allusion to it in "Spring 5702 [1942]." See section 9 of Shayevitsh's poem, published in *Lodz Ghetto*, 260; and *Against the Apocalypse*, 213–14. For discussion of Bialik's poetry responding to the Kishinev pogrom, see David Aberbach, *Bialik* (New York: Grove Press, 1988), 60–69.

66. A quotation from Song of Songs 3:7–8 incorporated within the night prayer. See *Daily Prayer Book*, 784.

67. Given the dialectic relation of continuity and discontinuity that pervades the poem, the shift in emphasis may be explained in terms of the poem's changing rhetorical situation. Where, at the outset, the still perceptible realities of home, ritual, and artifacts tempt a reliance on continuity, the poem must guard against illusion and thus must make apparent the growing discontinuity. At the work's end, when deportation seems to allow no continuity, the poem must guard against despair and make apparent the surviving thread of connection. At no point can the poet speak of one without the other. That he emphasizes one or the other seems to follow from the rhetorical need of the poem and the dialectical demand to supply the hidden complement that the situation might otherwise obscure.

68. On Isaac as the first survivor, see Elie Wiesel, *Messengers of God*, trans. M. Wiesel (New York: Random House, 1976), xiii and 69–97; also "Freedom of Conscience—A Jewish Commentary," *Journal of Ecumenical Studies* 14 (1977): 638–49.

69. See *Daily Prayer Book*, 783–84.

70. *Against the Apocalypse*, 213.

71. The theological perspective suggested here finds its fullest articulation in the writing of Abraham Joshua Heschel. For Heschel, the divine presence may be manifest in human deeds (*mitzvot*), even as in the natural world of creation, or in the revelation of the Bible. As such, deeds may bear sublimity, a "silent allusion . . . to a meaning greater than themselves" that provokes amazement and wonder or a religious recognition. The actor, in performing *mitzvot*, may not only imitate God, but *represent* God in history. She or he, as a bearer of the divine image, lives as a symbol of God and thus shares guardianship of divine unity, preserved in acts of human connection. For Heschel, God *needs* the deeds and solidarity of human community in order to be One in

the world. On the sublimity of human deeds and their capacity to represent God's pathos, see Abraham Joshua Heschel, *Between God and Man*, ed. Fritz Rothschild (New York: Free Press, 1959), 36–39 and 79–87; on the divine need of human community, see 140–45; on the human self as bearer of the divine image, thus symbolizing God, see Abraham Joshua Heschel, *Quest for God* (New York: Crossroad Publishing Co., 1954), 124–27.

72. For discussion and appropriation of a "midrashic framework," see *God's Presence in History*, 3–34. Note also David Jacobson's study of recent Hebrew fiction and poetry under the rubric of "modern midrash." See David Jacobson, *Modern Midrash* (Albany, N.Y.: SUNY, 1987).

73. Martin Buber, "The Man of Today and the Jewish Bible," trans. O. Marx, in *Israel and the World* (New York: Schocken Books, 1963), 89–90; the essay is also published in the Buber anthology, *On the Bible: Eighteen Studies*, ed. N. Glatzer (New York: Schocken Books, 1968), 1–13. On Buber's biblical hermeneutic generally, see Michael Fishbane, *The Garments of Torah: Essays in Biblical Hermeneutics* (Bloomington, Ind.: Indiana University Press, 1992), 81–98, and Steven Kepnes, *The Text as Thou: Martin Buber's Dialogical Hermeneutics and Narrative Theology* (Bloomington, Ind.: Indiana University Press, 1992), 41–60 and 120–43.

74. Note Fackenheim's qualification of Buber's continuity of generations. See Emil Fackenheim, *The Jewish Bible after the Holocaust* (Bloomington, Ind.: Indiana University Press, 1990), 16–17.

75. Note, for instance, Roskies' discussion of Shayevitsh in the context of "scribes of the ghetto." See *Against the Apocalypse*, 196–224. Shayevitsh stands inseparable from the concerted effort of diarists, chroniclers, and poets in the various ghettos to fulfill the mandate attributed to the dying words of Simon Dubnov: "*Schreibt un farschreibt!*" (Write and record!). On the reports of Dubnov's death and his final words, see Sophie Dubnov-Erlich, *The Life and Work of S.M. Dubnov: Diaspora Nationalism and Jewish History*, trans. J. Vowles (Bloomington, Ind.: Indiana University Press, 1991), 245–47.

76. Note how Fackenheim similarly argues for the Midrashic scheme of God's commanding and saving presence in history over against apocalyptic and secularist perspectives that detach God from history, in the first instance, and history from God, in the latter. See, in their totality, his Deems lectures, published as *God's Presence in History*. Although writing in a different mode, Roskies' *Against the Apocalypse* shares Fackenheim's dialectical concern to maintain a connection between the Shoah and antecedent Jewish history, while yet taking seriously the Holocaust's distinctive dimensions. Roskies writes: "The Jewish people are at the point of turning the tables on themselves, of allowing the Holocaust to become the crucible of their culture. I have set out to challenge this apocalyptic tendency by arguing for the vitality of traditions of Jewish response to catastrophe, never as great as in the last hundred years" (9). Roskies opposes any mythic displacement of history that leaves pre- and post-Shoah worlds unconnected, a discontinuity that would render Buber's Bible, for example, obsolete. Using Fackenheim's own language, Roskies notes that this constitutes "a posthumous victory for the murderers if there ever was one" (7). If Shayevitsh's relation to the Bible resonates with the writings of Fackenheim and Roskies, it stands at odds with the general tendency of Richard L. Rubenstein's rejection of the traditional scheme, although Rubenstein's is neither a mythic displacement nor one without nuance. See his essays collected in Richard L. Rubenstein, *After Auschwitz* (Indianapo-

lis: Bobbs-Merrill, 1966). Rubenstein's example serves to remind that Shayevitsh's use of scripture and tradition is not simply inevitable, but it is a choice; if it is a given in his culture, it nevertheless is one that the poet accepts.

77. The biblical text, like Shayevitsh's poem, is also a reading of the story, a version that presents narrative with certain associations and oppositions, creating connotation or value.

78. Zelkowicz's entry for Sunday, September 6, 1942, is published in *Lodz Ghetto*, 342–46

79. Thus *Literature of Destruction*, 630.

PART 2. CONNECTION

4 UNBROKEN TRAINS

That the way not be lost
That the world once common to all of us
Might be recalled and restored
                                        Michael Martin[1]

It makes no difference where one starts. The tear is always present. The silo of a farm in Brown County no less than the towering column at Yad Vashem can evoke the chimneys of Hitler's Europe. The night's clatter of a train in Bristol can lead the mind onto tracks that penetrate dark woods and follow ramps to the gates of Chelmno and Treblinka and Auschwitz. After the time of savagery, no symbol is safe, no icon is innocent. All may allude to the rupture caused by wire fence, boxcar walls, and vanishing daughters. Nowhere is secure from the need for repair, for a mending of a deep chasm that draws to itself the fragments of human experience, here and there.

The images of the mother of the wire fence, Eve of the boxcar, and Blimele's father have documented both the breaking of vital continuities and the struggle to maintain a line of connection that would preserve and sustain. These photographic and textual images witness the power of gesture, word, and artifact to approach the other side of history where ghetto and *Lager* manifest their scandalous difference. Two of the images have been expressed in poems: Dan Pagis's evocation of Eve in "Written in Pencil in the Sealed Railway-Car" and Simkhe Bunem Shayevitsh's portrait of Blimele's father in "*Lekh-Lekho.*" Our readings of these poems have focused primarily on the implication of the scenes, imagery, and dynamics of the poems themselves. We turn now to consider more explicitly the task of the poet and the role of a poem in mending broken continuities. To do so, we begin a reading of Michael Martin's "Mountain-City," a cycle of poems that not only brings a poignant world into view, but makes a keen statement on the poet's vocation.[2] Unlike the other texts, it does not begin in the realm of Holocaust, but in the landscape of the Blue Ridge. From this place, the poet approaches the history of his life and also of his lifetime that includes the sound of the trains running to "Buchenwald / Belsen / Birkenau" (*IMR*, 5). Here, it makes no difference where one starts.

POETIC MENDING

A discarded spoon, unearthed from a lump of dead creeper leaves: To us it is trash, insufficiently thrown away; to the poet, a relic of a lost world remembered and revered. A train vibrates on the rails, its hum rising from some distant freight yard: To us it is clatter; to the poet, a message linking us to the nightmare of other trains in other times. While we live dully among the signs that even ordinary moments provide, the poet tunes echoes that may burden memory or quicken hope. Where we have thinned the resounding of history to a tinny thud, the poet discovers a resonant depth in the connections of lived experience, connections forged in the fusion of memory and imagination. To that poet, then, belongs the vision of universe that perceives continuity and, where broken, discontinuity.

To describe the poet's vocation in this way attributes to it a mythic dimension that involves basic patterns of life—the relations between things lost and things found, the interweaving of presence and absence. Such poetry, for example, follows the rhythm of the Lurianic cosmogony as it moves from presence to absence, and from fragmentation to repair. Within this kabbalistic tradition God withdraws into Godself, an absenting that makes room for the creation of the world (*tzimtzum*). The withdrawal, however, shatters the wholeness of creation (*shevirat hakelim*) and breaks the connections between the fragments and their divine source. Thereby men and women are called to mend the fragments (*tikkun*), to restore connections that reunify what has been broken and give presence to what is absent. This task of repair summons the poet as an emergency. In its fulfillment, poetry would redeem.[3]

Michael Martin's epic poem "Mountain-City" well exemplifies the poetic mending whose dimensions this essay pursues. Fred Chappell has placed Martin's work in the tradition of the modernist long poem, an admittedly "ambitious mode" here reflected in the poem's size and mythic scope.[4] The modernist epic, as Chappell notes, characteristically concerns itself with the relation of an individual's identity to the larger culture. It asks: "What constant qualities of history (if any) are exemplified or illustrated by our isolated modern biographies?" and complicates that question with keen awareness of the "disintegrated chaos" which that history imposes.[5] Or, in terms already suggested, the modernist epic raises the question of the possibility of a mending between a self and the tangle of its severed contexts, its antecedents that paralyze with guilt and its prospects that promote anxiety. Is it possible to forge a connection between a self and the history in which it is ever implicated without, at the same time, being simply devastated by the connection that is made?[6] Can poetry's repair finally redeem?

The theological tone of the question underscores the ambitiousness of the modernist epic, and also its importance. The alternative to pursuing the epic's question would seem to be a surrender of the self, or for that matter, history, to ultimate fragmentation and loss;[7] or worse, to the banality that would feebly supplant the pain of that fragmentation.[8] Martin's poem challenges this surrender, although not in the abstract. Rather, it reflects the poet's own attempt to repair a life fraying in one particular history and to enlist the poem in the very process of a mending that is both ominous and holy. The poem affirms, but not without a shudder.

CONNECTION

"—whatcha do it for then / why throw yr life away" (*IMR*, 17). To these questions, themselves intimating great sacrifice, the poet responds with an answer that can only be partial before a larger unknowing. Still, the response exposes a path that wends its way under and through Martin's poem:

—whatcha do it for then
why throw yr life away
. . . to believe in the connections (*IMR*, 17).

A reading of "Mountain-City" that focuses upon "the connections" clarifies the idea of poetic mending and provides a vantage for considering Martin's poem.

"Connection" describes a coincident perception of the separateness of something and of an underlying relation between the perceiver and that separate thing. One lives in a world that hosts persons and objects other than oneself; but in that world of difference one experiences a claim that to the other one still belongs, as a father yet belongs to his children even "when their Mother / bent down with the cutters / & severed the conductors" (*IMR*, 16). Connection is this persistent sense of belonging to something that is other than oneself, of being claimed near and far by its kinship in a common world.[9]

The connections in a person's history, however, are neither obvious nor secure. We experience more commonly the anguish of separation brought by the passage of time, if not by more willful estrangement. We readily know the loss of connected relation that obscures the face of precious others:

Now I can't see my children enough—
can't find their eyes
for the shadow
for the glare of a twelve-year winter (*IMR*, 16).

Or we find in human affairs only the accented difference of the other whose strength may emerge as "the underlying menace, in any peace" ("Mtn-City," 60). And where there is only difference, hostility ensues, drawing upon fear and resentment to drive connections underground. Whether by history's inevitable displacements or by more intentional evasions, the connections have lost their immediacy. Elusive in human experience, the connections must be found again, discovered with attention and surprise.

For Martin, the discovery of connection involves concrete realities: artifacts, such as an old discarded spoon or the rearview mirror from a '46 Ford; sounds, such as the hum of a freight train vibrating on its rail; encounters, such as meeting with a stranger in an elevator above Riverside Drive; and words—words spoken by others and words made into poems. The epic hero may be cut off from the connections that harbor belief, but the world of concrete realities offers signs that point to a path of return and repair.

Artifact

We remember in particular places. As pilgrims, we may journey to a site where once life was won or lost and, amid the echoes in some ruined choir, recite a litany of deeds attempted and deeds done. There the markers of place, stone cairns of history, prompt recollection. Here something happened, the weatherworn stones insist; and here, in response, we remember. Yet what we remember is always less than the land itself knows. It bears within its storied layers not only the deposit of the honored name, but the impress of those "who have no memorial, who have perished as though they had not lived" (Sirach 44:9). The pilgrim, in seeking memory of the saint, may discover the anonymous trace of other souls whose steps, imprinted in soft earth, entered history. Simply to live *in situ*—to stand in a particular place—renders one vulnerable to the surprising intrusion of memory unexpected, recollection unaware.

The particularity of a place extends from the lives of those who have there resided. What their hands have done and their eyes witnessed shape the perceptible topography of a place—how it is envisioned in memory and imagination that makes it unlike any other. Still, particularity transcends simple personal construal through artifacts, precious and common, that human activity leaves behind. Although they crumble and rust, artifacts may yet survive their makers and users. Eloquent, they testify where voices have been silenced. Even if there were no witnesses, the storehouses of abandoned luggage, the mounds of heaped eyeglasses, the tracks that run near crumbled chimneys would all declare that here, in the place where they remain, something ominous happened, leaving an indelible scar that can be masked but not forgotten so long as the objects exist to prompt question and recollection.

Certain objects endure, enabling remembrance to persist beyond the scope of any one generation's reach and shaping the memory that follows.[10] In their objectivity, artifacts may resist conscription in our desire to remember in a given way or to forget that which is not to our advantage. Where we may have known of nothing to remember, the artifact comes into our presence with a tugging to consider and to recollect. As reifications of human activity—tangible signs that here something happened—artifacts may surprise with the presence of a memory unsought. The discarded object, no less than the designated marker, may afford unexpected connection.

In the afternoon section of Martin's "Iron Mountain Day" ("Mtn-City," 13–17), the narrator joins Beulah, a mountain potter, and her sister, Flo, who have set out before supper to find a place for twenty-eight fresh sweet potato plants. There, in the tangled clutter between potato patch and driveway, the three work with hatchet, mattock, and poke. After a few minutes,

> Flo, with the mattock,
> gives a little cry, startled, curious, by the oak stump;
> bends down, fishes; lifts up something—long, curved, thin,
> mud-covered, rusty underneath—and dangles it
> toward Beulah, twenty feet away: "Beulie, what's this?"
>
> Her find shimmers dully under the mud.
> It glints and shortens, as the dirt drops from it,
> lumped with dead creeper leaves.
>
> Beulah's face brightens, as she looks up, piercingly,
> at Flo's new-found thing, *into* its murky sheath.
>
> "Oh," she says instantly, "that's poor Meg's spoon."
> "Poor old Meg, she lived right over there," Beulah points. . . .
>
> "Bless her heart."
>
> . . . Meg.
> . . . Flo puts the spoon down on the oak stump; picks up the mattock:
> "I'm gonna save me that spoon" Flo says, "since it was Meg's. Poor old
> Meg."
>
> "Yep. Poor old Meg," agrees Beulah, soberly,
> and after a moment: "It got hard for her to keep up in boy friends."
> I laugh; Flo smiles, and goes on working ("Mtn-City," 14–16).

The actions Martin describes transcend their simplicity; they trace a powerful sequence: an object not sought is found; the object gives rise to narrative, both a remembrance and a marking of place; and the object, now invested as symbol, issues in benediction and the human sound of laughter.

Not seeking culminates in finding. This progression, common in treasure stories, locates Beulah, Flo, and the narrator in an act of discovery.[11] They do not find what they seek—only a spot for the sweet potato plants—as much as that which they somehow need but could not know to seek, the treasure of Meg's spoon. No intention provokes the discovery; rather, the three are simply claimed by that which is given serendipitously in the particularity of this patch of Virginia mountain.

Flo upholds more than she realizes. The mud-covered object in her hand reveals itself more fully as it calls forth Beulah's narrative word: ". . . that's poor Meg's spoon / . . . she lived right over there." Beulah identifies the spoon and situates it in an implied narrative context, the story of its owner who "lived right over there." Between Flo's held treasure and Beulah's identifying word a twofold dynamic occurs: on the one hand, the object summons a narrative recollection that otherwise would have had no occasion to emerge; on the other, the narrative identifies the object, enabling it to reveal itself as no unrelated thing, but as an artifact of a person and a world whose place these three now share.[12]

Together, narrative and object forge the connection that is the real treasure of Meg's spoon. As object, the spoon exposes an absence, an awareness of something past and displaced (and for this reason, if for no other, the treasure could not be sought prior to its absence becoming manifest). The spoon, rusty and muddy, testifies to the absence of Meg. Yet, as artifact gives way to remembrance, a narrative presence qualifies that absence, connecting the past with the word of the present. Present in her story, mediated through her artifact, Meg lives again in the world of Beulah, Flo, and the narrator, evoking from them blessing and laughter. Moreover, as she becomes present in their memory, that presence re-marks this place with a new or, at least, forgotten particularity.[13] This is no nameless potato patch, but the place where one can envision Meg's "last room on earth" ("Mtn-City," 15), an identification of place that, in turn, identifies those who share its location as heirs of a legacy. With poignance Flo says, "I'm gonna save me that spoon since it was Meg's." And well she should, for the spoon that was Meg's has become the symbol that is theirs, giving to their here and now a link of relation that affords a sense of home and belonging amid the vagaries of time and the threatening anonymity of place.[14]

Trains

The particularity of a place claims us not only with its own legacy, but with the echoes of something more. What an anonymous landscape denies, particularity affords: an echoing resonance in human affairs that links the legacy of one place with that of another; an underlying connection that ties the history of one person to that of many others, known and unknown.

In a haunting section of Martin's epic, the poet narrates an intense act of remembering occasioned by the vibrations of a moving train. Something in "the trains' cries, & the ubiquitous hum / of the rails," he says, comes to him as a resounding, an echo that makes of the present hearing a hearing again of earlier experience. Thus, he once more knows "the locomotives, working the yards, in Bristol" and hears in their recollected din "a signal of connection"; thus, he knows the vibrations of the trains that moved "from the chimneys' red fires over Bessemer," giving to the signal of every train a resonance that links it with an undercurrent running on tracks from Bristol and Birmingham, to "Buchenwald / Belsen / Birkenau" and to "the scorched & tangled neurons / in the brain of [his] father"; "from the time to come . . . from Everywhere / nowhere" (IMR, 5–6). And to make unavoidable the connection between the poet's individual memory and the broader historical experience of his time, Martin frames this section of his poem with an inclusio from Paul Celan's "Todesfuge": "wir schaufeln ein Grab in den Luften da liegt man nicht eng; we'reshovelingagrave in the air. plentywide / you'llresteasy."[15]

Like the discovery of the artifact, listening to the train's vibration occasions recollection. Here, however, the retrieval does not stay put within the contours of one place, but roams history's diverse regions, personal and collective, drawing to itself the vibrations of other experiences that sound a common chord. The poem instances a familiar phenomenon: something in the concreteness of the here and now—a patch of color, a gesture, the fragment of a song's refrain—calls to mind another place, a different time, and makes them available to memory. Even so, the remembering does not move the subject into some accessible past time, but rather, fills the present with connections from "Everywhere [and] / nowhere" that claim the subject and allow no escape from the given moment's tangle in history. Such memory denies innocence. To hear the vibrations of the train is to make of Celan's Shoah-wrenched words a present confession: We are those who shovel graves in the air.

"These Trains cannot be broken," (IMR, 23) Martin contends. No simple free association or arbitrary maneuver of memory makes the trains one. Memory can establish presence, because it admits finally of no absence, of no ultimate fragmentation in the imagination's capability to bring together separate entities—in short, to make connections. Still, memory can make connections because there are connections to be made. The poet acknowledges that an undercurrent links the trains and freights them with a common signal to which memory and imagination respond. That signal may be deeply hidden, or it may be more overt. But, in either case, an underlying signal—a common signifying—chains together moments and places and charges the present with their depth.[16] The trains at Bristol and Bessemer cannot be separated from those that led to Buchenwald, Belsen, and Birkenau, *not* just because they sound alike to the imaginative ear, but because, in a common history, they *are* alike as vehicles of "warning / & of mourning" (*IMR*, 5); alike as bearers of the human cry that pursue some destination as yet not fully known, but whose tracks trace lines that have witnessed graves dug in the air over a smoke-filled Europe and observed the assault of Alzheimer's on a father's brain. Although "broken in our separations"—our fearful evasions of implication—"these *Trains* cannot be broken" (*IMR*, 23), because their signal echoes in the history of this poet's life as compellingly one.

As in the sustained iconography of Claude Lanzmann's film, *Shoah*, Martin's poem emphasizes the unity of the trains.[17] However, he does not blur the distinctions between the trains: connection remains a relation between separate items. His concern is not to equate the particularities of different historical experiences, but to stress the lines of implication that pass between them and issue in a common claim. Although unique, both the trains of the Holocaust and of Bristol and Bessemer call the poet to respond to a mysterious human difference that concerns him decisively. Martin would take seriously cautions that one not domesticate the unprecedented character of the Holocaust with inadequate analogy.[18] Indeed, the movement of the poem shows a concern not to tame the memory of the Holocaust, but to radicalize the more local memory by allowing it no distance from the larger ominousness. The distinct cry from the Holocaust reverberates within history, drawing other vibrations to itself with connections that implicate and haunt.[19]

If the artifact gives rise to narrative, the train's vibrations yield resonance, that which is "repeated, in [the] memory" (*IMR*, 5). Resonance, as a physical property, describes the intensification and prolonging of tone by sympathetic vibration. Thus, the accumulation of sound waves in a cavity approximates a resounding of the initial tone that enriches and deepens its quality. So, too, signals of historical experience may overlap in such a way as to allow one instance to resound in the recollection of another, each being deepened by the connotations brought into play by the other. The vibrations sounding near "the chimneys' red fires over Bessemer" (*IMR*, 5) prolong the tone of boxcars that ran toward other chimneys and bring to the present the deeper resonance of its urgent cry. The present, no thin moment, thus thickens with the texture of history, the proliferation of connections.

The deepening resonance draws upon the increased connections to express a larger wholeness or unity. The connection couples not only the trains, but the symbolic worlds of which they are a part.[20] As such, the unity of the trains relates more than simply the humming locomotives: the trains link the mechanized *Umwelt* of the death camps with the culture of American industrialism; the "chimneys' red fires over Bessemer" (*IMR*, 5) with the soul-spewing chimneys of Birkenau and the fiery flames at Nagasaki; the current that drives the engines with the charge that scorches the neurons in a father's brain; and the freight yards of Bristol, mountain town, with "the horizon of the City," where the vibrations sound "on the crumbling facades, downtown: / on the windowless north wall / of the psychiatric wing" (*IMR*, 5). The part signifies the whole. Through the coupling of the trains we glimpse a larger convergence of worlds and, in their rushing signal, doppplering to a point of intensity, we hear intoned the deep resonance of history, lived and remembered.

Das Fremde

The vibrations of the trains sound overtones of mystery. As connections reveal the tangence of separate things, they render strange our familiar worlds and surprise us with unexpected signals. Unforeseen memory may make habitable a place foreign to us, or may alienate us from our assumed home, but it does so in either case by manifesting an unfamiliar or strange connection. The strangeness of connections disrupts our attempts to know what meaning a place or moment may hold. That alterity leaves one less secure in any daily attempt to manage history; but it also brings novelty to situations whose constancies oppress and whose familiarities deaden. The trauma of unknowing has as its complement the prospect of hope, the recognition of mystery.

Martin opens his "City" section with an epigraph from Paul Celan's "*Stilleben*": "*Davor das Fremde, des Gast du hier bist*" ("Before it [the eye], the strange thing, whose guest you are here").[21] This quotation presides over the epic while allowing no connection to escape mystery:

> What is the lifetime
>
> but the space we can see
> encrypted by those tracks
> which disappear
>
> into the trackless Fields
> long trains of unknown ones
> traverse on their way
>
> toward Those
> who labor beyond us
> at the end of their supplies (*IMR*, 22–23).

In this lifetime encrypted by disappearing tracks, we meet the "unknown ones" and their mystery. Before our eyes appear not only strange things, the muddy spoon in the potato patch, but *das Fremde*, the strange thing itself, which imparts otherness to the alien items of our connection. Other things—the objects, persons, and experiences that effect a world of difference—connect us to a larger Otherness before which we stand in need of hospitality.[22]

Hospitality, as a receiving of strangers in their otherness, provides a metaphor for Martin's sense of connection. Yet, as the Celan quotation indicates, hospitality here involves an ironic twist. In welcoming connection, we host *das Fremde*, only to discover that we are ultimately *its* guest. Accordingly, to resist connection estranges doubly: on the one hand, it turns away the stranger and thereby levels the world of its resonant difference and depth; on the other, it leaves us finally alone, adrift without relation to a place, a time, an other. In contrast, hospitality, in the integrity of its giving and receiving, makes the world a human home, an arena of connection in which we belong.

An elevator above Riverside Drive provides Martin's poem with a setting for hospitality. The narrator, "a country-boy, born and bred / in the face of a civilization— / and a city— / embattled" (*IMR*, 4), identifies himself as the stranger but also, by virtue of his claim on the elevator, shows himself to be the *de facto* resident of this particular chamber. Left for a long moment by his friend to hold the elevator—"Whatever you do, Mike *don't* let that elevator go down" (*IMR*, 3)—the clarity of his task becomes challenged by the sudden appearance of a stranger, the philosopher Hannah Arendt.

Arendt, although more properly at home in this elevator, enters as a stranger:

> She seemed out of place, *abstracted*,
> indefinite—as to age, caste, status—undefinable:
>
> she might have been a noblewoman,
> a doudy Latvian princess, from another era:
> she might, almost, have been a cleaning woman—
> fresh off the boat, and Ellis Island—from Warsaw, or Vilna.
> Almost but for the eyes (*IMR*, 3).[23]

Moreover, Arendt is the stranger because someone else has appropriated her territory. It is Mike, the narrator, who controls the "Down" button and, for the moment, Arendt's own freedom: "So there she stood / in her makeshift cell / captivated, by its unkempt, / part-beatnik Keeper" (*IMR*, 4). Here, the issue of difference loses all abstraction. To receive this stranger into the world of "the close little *Kammer*" means concretely the assent to her freedom, her will that runs contrary to the host's charged task: It means letting the elevator go down. In connection, the host must surrender autonomy to *das Fremde*.

Mike mumbles some explanation, an awkward effort reminding that he is kept by his own keeping. The dis-ease, like the bondage, is his. The stranger's steady gaze contrasts with his "shaggy bent neck, trembling with tiny, / uncontrollable spasms" (*IMR*, 4); her speech that "render[s] each word its due" throws into relief his "smiling mumble" (*IMR*, 4). Finally, the elevator *is* the stranger's world, not because of any prior claim or innate power, but because of this host's own connection to her freedom: He cannot be free and, at the same time, her keeper, a connection that bids him open this place to her own intention. As hospitality accords the stranger freedom to come near, so must it recognize the freedom to depart, the freedom of the stranger to be *das Fremde*. "With a faint bur of the *Muttersprache*," Arendt speaks, "—I think you'd better let me go now." The narrator responds, "I hesitated. I dropped my hand. I let her descend" (*IMR*, 4).

As he does so, the host becomes guest of *das Fremde*. Immediately, he is liberated by the stranger's freedom. But he soon finds that in his meeting her otherness—her appearance that he could not expect, her will that he could not control—he comes into the presence of a reality that does not either cast *him* aside or itself deny connection. Connection sustained here leaves behind a gift binding host to stranger:

> I was left with her voice,
> with its echo . . . and even now,
> when I read her books—
> or those she celebrated—
> I remember the steady eyes, beneath the shawl,
> and the iron bur in the voice
>
> in its demand for freedom (*IMR*, 4).

What memory knows, encounter with the other first brought: recognition as one who has been seen and addressed; acknowledgment as one from whom something has been asked. We remember the other and, in doing so, find the reflection of ourselves as persons who have belonged to a world, as persons who appear before the mysterious eye of *das Fremde*.

Poem

Recollection, resonance, and mystery—we receive these gifts in distinct places only to lose them as habit blurs particularity or as time banishes us from their points of origin and renewal. Even were we to stay put, history would yet alter our landscape. The same place on some other day can never be simply the same place. Flo saves Meg's spoon, but it will again be discarded; trains will continue to sound their cry, but will become dull with repetition; strangers will come and depart, and we will learn to tame their surprise to avoid their dare. This is a "melancholy lot."[24] The selves who have known the gift of connection will keenly experience this falling off, for only those who have perceived continuity can recognize its breaking. But therein lies the compelling call: Only those who see discontinuity can begin the mending repair and they must do so as surely as faint echoes sound somewhere from a distance within them and beyond them.

In Birmingham, the poet first listened to the trains. Under Vulcan, he shared the night with their low, mournful cries while he ran through Agee's "'hard flat incurable sore'" (*Shen*, 79). As he entered the city, so the city entered him, leaving an image, a sound, and a precedent to shape the work and life that would follow. In "Return Letter" (*Shen*, 79–86) the poet turns to that moment as it defined his vocation as writer.

The city, resonant in its nighttime desertion, hosts the poet in a moment of rich presence. Within the sounds of "a child's bare feet on dry clinkers, / . . . a screen door closing, a sudden wail," all mingling with the longer cries of the trains' monotonous melody (*Shen*, 79)—within these sounds the poet finds or, rather, is found by an enduring image:

> . . . it left me a precedent,
> a standard for want and fear as well as fulfillment
> which I could never put into words, or even approach with them,
> but whose energies have never ceased to supply me. . . .

> The image was of a sound: a call which became a vibration, distributed
>   there also:
> a stillness which, like sound, was everywhere, yet nowhere,
> and, yet, which *passed* through the thousand rooms
> and the roomers in them . . .
> inseparable from the beat of my heart: from the pulse of my wrist on the
>   windowsill. . . .

> the source-image, which collects my thoughts
> under the memory I relate to you
> and reach out with, toward you,
> is of a wide floor, and of voices

> which become inaudible
> as they descend, and yet remain

buried yet *still* in us,
without an end (*Shen*, 80–83).

Where the source-image reflects a city of voices that descend to sound within and beneath human history, the poet's call can only be to echo that vibration, "that voice / or voices, which most move us / to stay with our work, and life" (*Shen*, 82). The poet gives sound to what he himself has heard rumbling under the "wide floor"; his memory, entrusted to word, is genuinely a "re-calling" (*Shen*, 82).

Although his work begins in that place where the voices sound, he must complete it elsewhere, "in this hollow, manhole-oubliette, / in [his] cup of mountains, with such dregs as these" (*Shen*, 82). The presence of the city yields to his eventual and permanent absence from that place, an exile that jeopardizes his connection to vital supply. Fundamental, his absence unravels threads of continuity that link him to a place and a time. On the one hand, he knows that he

could never return There.
To the town, maybe: to the surface
but not to the place (*Shen*, 85).

On the other hand, he will

never register it, again, so intimately
. . . so as to even try

to live it out
to dream it out,
from [his] own beginning—
since [he has] only one" (*Shen*, 86).

"'Where are we going? Always Home.'" These Odyssean words of Novalis, Martin takes as epigraph.[25] The destination is clear, and there can be no other if one is to avert a final shattering. But the way narrows with each futile attempt to go back and threatens to elude the most valiant of heroes and every nostalgic spirit.

—whatcha do it for then
why throw yr life away

to find a work
that is a way,
an itinerary (*IMR*, 17).

What all must seek, the poet finds in the labor of his work: a way of return, a reconnection that occurs not by moving backward but by the re-calling that bids the past to move forward. In writing the poem, the poet turns toward the past only to find that it has already joined him in the present of his writing:

> It came to me then, as I wrote you,
> that my only way of return
> to the Life, there,
> was through the Work, here,
>
> of speaking out of what I've known,
> of listening to it; and of sounding,
> and resounding, what I cannot know,
> or live, alone, or have forgotten:
>
> of prolonging my attention to the echoes,
> the residual rhythms and tonalities,
> which descend beneath my thresholds
> of hearing, or of speech,
>
> into the basis of speech
> which is the memory of earth,
> damaged, endangered, trembling
> beneath the world we've made.
>
> Attention to the basal echoes
> of the Voice, or voices
> which most moved me: whose vibrations
> reach me here still (*Shen*, 86).

Like the artifact, the poem gives rise to recollection; like the trains' vibrations, it resounds with a history and a prospect. By making present the Voice of *das Fremde*, the poem invites a reconnection to its mystery and demand. The poem is not the Voice, but the medium that enables it again to be heard. "So," the poet notes,

> I must think of our Writing
>
> as a means of conduction: of extending the channels
> we listen through, outside our chambered lives
> into the Life, and the voices
> on that wide floor, under the rooms (*Shen*, 83).

Through the poem the poet returns to a link with his beginning and the vital connections that unify his work and life (*IMR*, 22). From his mountain hollow he returns not to "the town" but to the place of endless supply. There, the re-calling of what has been lost effects a precious and awe-full finding. What history displaces, narrative retrieves.[26]

REDEMPTION

The theme of connections in Michael Martin's poetry illumines this question: Can there be a poetic mending of shattered human experience; can poetry redeem? Although the question invites theological response, any answer must resist religious enthusiasm and romantic theories of poetry. T. S. Eliot's caution yet sobers undue confidence on any front:

> There is only the fight to recover what has been lost
> And found and lost again and again: and now, under conditions
> That seem unpropitious."[27]

Our question, while it does not admit to any final abstraction, does call for a concrete answer in terms of the effect of this one poem, a poem that affirms, even in response to Eliot, that perhaps there is more than "only the trying."

To speak of a poetic mending and of the poem's redemptive character acknowledges that poetry, especially in its narrative capacity, enables connection with realities outside the poem that transform writer and reader. Redemption occurs not within the poem itself, as if it were an intrinsic property of the verse, but rather, it is effected in that space *between* the world that the text makes present and the writer and reader. The poem, as Martin would have it, is the channel or the means of conduction through which the writer and reader are connected to *das Fremde*, the strange Voice that speaks through the poem and addresses the memory and imagination of both the writer and the reader, changing them in the process.

As a channel, a means for connection, the poem mends essential links to that which history has displaced or lost. With Flo, the poem holds up a muddy spoon and bids a reader to envision with Beulah the place where old Meg lived, the place where the narrator now stands with these sisters, and the reader with all three. With the trains on a Birmingham night, the poem emits the vibrations that call readers to hear the resonance of an individual's life history and that of his time. As in an "arthritic" elevator, the poem makes present the stranger who claims the reader with a demand for hospitality and freedom. The poem narrates the making of vital connections in the life of the poet, a making in which the writing of the poem serves as a vital re-calling. The same connections, however, the poem makes available to the reader and to the poet himself who, having lost the lived immediacy of these connections, find them returned to him as a reader of his own writing—or, better, as one who can re-call his own re-calling.[28]

Such mending redeems in two primary respects: it redeems the self from the profanity of disorientation and from the underlying polytheism of fragmentation. First, where neither time nor space has marked contours, a basic profanity occurs, manifest as a chaos pervading human affairs. The absence of boundaries invades the self's own sense of existence, denying any impulse toward accountability and intention and rendering meaning absurd. The resulting disorientation can only threaten a human life with insecurity and deep fear. In the face of such disorientation, however, poetic mending turns to the power of recollection to mark the landscape of a human life. Our geography becomes habitable, proffers a home to which we can belong, only to the extent that we find in it a legacy and a claim: a legacy that connects us to an other who has stood here where we now stand, or stood somewhere else in such a way that echoes in this place of our own struggle; a claim that obliges us to receive and to preserve the contours of a world not simply of our own making. Neither our place nor our time is anonymous. In recollection we hear and pronounce the name they bear; a name that summons other voices to banish fear, to guide, and to identify. As the overgrown potato-patch becomes the place where old Meg once lived, profanity dies to consecration; the spoon that Flo cherishes betokens a reality that redeems from the devouring blur of oblivion, from loss of the recognition that makes us listen at the sound of our own name, our own story.

Second, where life is lived apart from connections, a deep breaking fragments the integrity of any one self and its relations with a community of others and to a common world. As with the profanity of unmarked experience, fragmentation allows no orientation, for it recognizes no constant from which any bearings might be gained. Under its sway, the human story fractures into disjointed episodes, alienating in their tension and dis-tracting, "pulling apart," the lonely self into a myriad of competing allegiances and confusions. Claimed by the very multiplicity of broken experiences, the self lives out an enslaving polytheism, subject to the many forces that converge upon it, yet finally loyal to no one of them.

The poetic mending of Martin's poem acknowledges fragmentation but refuses to surrender to it. The trains are unbroken, not because they are not many, but because underlying their manyness sounds a unified cry that issues a singular demand to follow the tracks to their source and destination, to become oneself as the link that connects their paths. Like the many trains, strangers appear in all their difference yet speak with the univocal Voice of *das Fremde*, clear and steady in its call for freedom, uniting in its bid for common hospitality. Not fragmentation, but unity emerges from the underpinnings of

Martin's connected universe, a unity that depends upon the poet to perceive its signal but that derives from that one Voice that vibrates through the many-ness of human experience.[29] Although no creedal entity, that Voice inflects nothing as much as a deep monotheism, the conviction that reality is ulti-mately one, connected in the knowledge that in all our wanderings we are addressed by our common humanity and the presence whose mysterious freight it bears. Redeemed from endless shatterings, we find in the poem the signs of our vocation, calling and re-calling, the demanding prospect of repair.

NOTES

1. Private communication from Michael Martin to author, summer 1991.

2. A representative portion of the poems that comprise "Mountain-City" was published in a special issue of *The Iron Mountain Review* (4 [Fall 1987]: 3–24) devoted to Martin's drawing and poetry. References here will be made to this version under the designation *IMR*. Further poems from the cycle have been published in *Shenandoah* 43/2 (1993): 76–86 (hereafter referred to as *Shen*). Other references will be to the larger manuscript, designated "Mtn-City" (here cited with permission of the author).

3. On the Lurianic myth of creation see Gershom Scholem, *Kabbalah* (New York: Quadrangle, 1974), 128–44; and Stephen Sharot, *Messianism, Mysticism, and Magic* (Chapel Hill, N.C.: University of North Carolina Press, 1982), 96–97. The Lurianic mythology was creatively appropriated within Hasidism in the tales of Nahman of Bratslav and there gives rise to a theory of imagination and narrative. In that regard, see Arthur Green, *Tormented Master* (New York: Schocken Books, 1981), 337–67; also Arnold J. Band, *Nahman of Bratslav: The Tales* (New York: Paulist Press, 1978), 11 and 285–87. Within modern Jewish thought, see the appropriation of these ideas in Emil Fackenheim, *To Mend the World: Foundations of Future Jewish Thought* (New York: Schocken Books, 1982).

4. See Fred Chappell, "*Approaching History* and the Ambitions of the Modernist Epic," in *IMR*, 29–32.

5. Ibid., 29.

6. This question furnishes the problematic for Hannah Arendt's magisterial work *The Human Condition* (Chicago: University of Chicago Press, 1958), a volume whose influence pervades Martin's verse and whose author is herself a significant figure in "Mountain-City" (see *IMR*, 3–4). My posing of the question recalls as well Richard R. Niebuhr's image of a "radial man," whose predicament was to be accountable to the bombarding force of the world's news that the simplest radio made immediate to any listener. Sitting in one's own living room, the radial person becomes implicated by his or her own knowledge, and suffers under the burden that such knowledge exceeds the scope of any individual's response. See Richard R. Niebuhr, *Experiential Religion* (New York: Harper & Row, 1972), xii–xiv.

7. This surrender approximates the "doom" and "duality" against which Martin Buber contends throughout *I and Thou*, trans. W. Kaufmann (New York: Charles Scribner's Sons, 1970), 100–122. Along with the influence of Hannah Arendt and Paul Celan, Buber furnishes a third stream of perspective that contributes obviously to

Martin's poetry (and may explain the affinity between Martin's work and that of the Lurianic myth that is important to Buber's own Hasidic lean).

8. On the dynamics and effects of such banality, see Hannah Arendt, *Eichmann in Jerusalem: A Report on the Banality of Evil* (New York: Viking, 1964); and Karl A. Plank, "Thomas Merton and Hannah Arendt: Contemplation after Eichmann," in *The Merton Annual* 3 (1990): 121–50.

9. A powerful expression of this sense of connection can be seen in a well-known journal entry of Thomas Merton. He writes, "In Louisville, at the corner of Fourth and Walnut, in the center of the shopping district, I was suddenly over-whelmed with the realization that I loved all those people, that they were mine and I theirs, that we could not be alien to one another even though we were total strangers." Thomas Merton, *Conjectures of a Guilty Bystander* (New York: Doubleday & Co., 1968), 156.

10. For discussion of artifacts in this regard, see Edward Shils, *Tradition* (London: Faber and Faber, 1981), 63–77.

11. On this pattern in treasure stories, see J. Dominic Crossan, *Finding Is the First Act*, Semeia Studies 9 (Missoula, Mont.: Scholars Press, 1979), 22–33.

12. This dynamic is at the heart of Arendt's relating of work (that produces objects) and action (that discloses stories). She writes: "Without being talked about by men and without housing them, the world would not be a human artifice but a heap of unrelated things to which each isolated individual was at liberty to add one more object; without the human artifice to house them, human affairs would be as floating, as futile and vain, as the wanderings of nomad tribes . . . without the enduring per-manence of a human artifact, there cannot 'be any remembrance of things that are to come with those that shall come after'" (*The Human Condition*, 204).

13. As Mircea Eliade has noted, unmarked space is basically uninhabitable. With-out boundary or distinction, space is profane, allowing neither for any sense of orien-tation nor of home. Conversely, when one marks that space, giving it a particular contour, one consecrates its territory and makes it fit for habitation. See Mircea Eliade, *The Sacred and the Profane*, trans. W. Trask (New York: Harvest Books, 1959), 22.

14. Ira Nowinski's photograph of a mound of discarded cutlery at Birkenau's *Canada* shows the powerful resonance that Martin's image has within the landscape of the Holocaust. See Sybil Milton and Ira Nowinski, *In Fitting Memory: The Art and Politics of Holocaust Memorials* (Detroit: Wayne State University Press, 1991), 107. Poignant signs that, even here, someone lived, the abandoned spoons give image to vanished lives no longer present to use these implements in carrying out the meager nourishing of life.

15. Paul Celan, *"Todesfuge,"* in *Poems of Paul Celan*, trans. by Michael Hamburger (New York: Persea Books, 1988), 60.

16. In one sense, this grounds the trains' unity in a common, although partially hidden, symbolic value, or renders it as a metaphorical equivalence. Yet the unity is more than rhetorical. For Martin, the trains are not one because they simply signify in common; rather, they have an unbroken signal because they are one at the underlying level of historical experience, which they symbolize and express.

17. Throughout Lanzmann's nine-hour film, the camera follows the movement of certain trains through the landscape of the Shoah's history. Although the trains are contemporary with Lanzmann's filming, they make present to the viewer intimations of their predecessors, the trains that carried the millions of Jews to their deaths in

Hitler's camps. Lanzmann's use of the trains hauntingly approaches reenactment, as in a powerful ritual.

18. See the cautions of Emil Fackenheim, "Concerning Authentic and Unauthentic Responses to the Holocaust," *Holocaust and Genocide Studies* 1 (1986): 101–120; and Lawrence L. Langer, *Versions of Survival* (Albany, N.Y.: SUNY, 1982).

19. As the Celan inclusio makes clear, the Holocaust provides the fundamental lens through which the other experiences are defined, and not the reverse. Nevertheless, against those whose emphasis of the Holocaust's uniqueness threatens to mystify it or remove it from history altogether, Martin's poem stands as a certain corrective.

20. In literary-critical terms we could speak of the coupling of trains as being metaleptical, that is, bringing into play not only their explicit connection, but the "whispered or unstated correspondences" that belong to their larger fields of reference. On metalepsis, see Richard Hays, *Echoes of Scripture in the Letters of Paul* (New Haven, Conn.: Yale University Press, 1989), 20, following John Hollander *The Figure of Echo* (Berkeley, Calif.: University of California Press, 1981), 133–49. More fundamentally, the point is a semiotic one: signs signify within a system of signs, the whole of which is brought to bear in any given signification. For the semiotic discussion, see Daniel Patte and Aline Patte, *Structural Exegesis: From Theory to Practice* (Philadelphia: Fortress Press, 1978), 7–8.

21. From Paul Celan, *Von Schwelle zu Schwelle* (Stuttgart: Deutsche Verlags-Anstalt, 1961), 38. This quotation returns at a later point within Martin's poem; see *IMR*, 23–24.

22. On this theme see Karl A. Plank, "The Human Face of Otherness," in *Faith and History: Essays in Honor of Paul W. Meyer*, ed. C. Cosgrove, J. Carroll, and E. Johnson (Atlanta: Scholars Press, 1991), 55–60.

23. Arendt's biographer, Elisabeth Young-Bruehl, although not focusing upon Arendt's appearance, confirms Arendt's attraction to "outsiders" and her sense of social difference in herself: "The friends of every sort and also the historical figures with whom Arendt felt special affinities, like Rosa Luxemburg and Rahel Varnhagen, had one characteristic in common: each was, in his or her own way, an outsider. In Hannah Arendt's personal lexicon, *wirkliche Menschen*, real people, were 'pariahs.' Her friends were not outcasts, but outsiders, sometimes by choice and sometimes by destiny. In the broadest sense they were unassimilated. 'Social nonconformism,' she once said bluntly, 'is the *sine qua non* of intellectual achievement.' And she might well have added, also of human dignity . . . Hannah Arendt maintained her independence and she expected her friends to do the same." See Elisabeth Young-Bruehl, *Hannah Arendt: For Love of the World* (New Haven, Conn.: Yale University Press, 1982), xv.

24. Thus Buber describes the inevitable movement from the orientation of "I-Thou" to that of "I-it" (*I and Thou*, 75).

25. As such, Martin's poem creates an interesting intertextual relation with Franz Kafka's parable, translated as "My Destination." For Kafka the journey is always "Away-From-Here," a destination either counter to Martin's movement home, or ironically a reflection of a comparable sense of exile that wants ever to vacate the diasporic "here." See Franz Kafka, *Parables and Paradoxes* (New York: Schocken Books, 1961), 189.

26. A close parallel can be found within the lore of Hasidic narrative. As popularized by Elie Wiesel, the story describes how, in succeeding generations, four *tzaddikim* gradually lost connection to the sources that had sustained them and their communities through past crises. Each rebbe, in turn, loses some portion of the legacy that had

previously sustained, until in the fourth generation no one can find the special place in the forest, or light the fire, or say the prayer. The fourth rebbe, however, Israel of Rizhyn, responds by telling the story that recalls this history, confessing: "'I am unable to light the fire and I do not know the prayer; I cannot even find the place in the forest. All I can do is tell the story, and this must be sufficient.' And it was sufficient." In the eclipse of the way to sacred spaces, rituals, and liturgy, it is the narrative that suffices to reconnect the teller and hearer with that which restores and sustains. See Elie Wiesel, *Souls on Fire* (New York: Summit Books, 1972), 167–68.

27. T. S. Eliot, "East Coker," in *Four Quartets* (New York: Harcourt Brace Jovanovich, 1971), 31.

28. A further implication is that the poet and reader themselves become connected through what they now hold in common, the heard Voice of the poem. As such, the mending combats isolation with the prospect of relation, mediated by the telling of the story, the re-calling of the poem.

29. Note the parallel to H. Richard Niebuhr's distinctive interpretation of redemption in terms of a perception of the "One-in-the-Many." See H. Richard Niebuhr, *The Responsible Self* (New York: Harper & Row, 1963), 108–26. The point is profoundly Buber's as well: an Eternal You speaks through the countless instances of human dialogue, freighting human speaking with a presence of unity and a call for response. See *I and Thou*, 123–68.

5 THE SURVIVOR'S RETURN: REFLECTIONS ON MEMORY AND PLACE

I'm on the track of my rights of domicile
this geography of nocturnal countries
where the arms opened for love
hang crucified on the degrees of latitude
groundless in expectation

Nelly Sachs[1]

If we will have the wisdom to survive,
to stand like slow-growing trees
on a ruined place . . .

Wendell Berry[2]

A place is a form of knowledge.

Herbert Muschamp[3]

MEMORY AND PLACE

A sense of place inhabits us. Like the migration of natural life, our memory knows a homing, an impulse to belong not only to a time but to a place deeply our own. We remember, as pilgrims seeking in regions of lived experience, the site where healing occurs and truth is imparted: the healing of broken continuities whose rupture has made us strangers in familiar lands; the truth about ourselves, our origin and destination. Once we knew that place in the forest and there we were at home amid the sounds of its prayer and the light of its fire.[4] Now we know it no more, except as an absence, a loss that, at odd moments, catches us unaware with sadness or, in sleepless acuity, invades our mind with torment. Yet, loss marks the beginning of memory, and memory, a narrative turn toward that place where we know, if only tacitly, who we are. Memory turns homeward.

In making the past present, recollection runs counter to the unchecked progress of our lives. We live in movement away from home as the passage of time, the growth of experience, and the claim of the contemporary distance our path to places that have vitally identified us in the past. The ties that time obscures, however, memory would recover. No kin to nostalgia, such recollection does not take us back to a lost world, but gives to the past a compelling presence and to the present, a certain depth. Far from home, we remember a somewhere that gives a sense of situation to what we have found, what we have lost, and what we now seek.

If memory recovers a sense of place, place similarly evokes memory. We not only remember places, but remember *in* a place whose terrain may enhance recollection with the resonance of what has occurred there. Places have echoes. We know them as surely as we perceive the land's scars—unspoken witnesses to a legacy that *here* something happened. For the most part, our recollection is shaped by the strange fusion of different settings. We remember an event not only after its time has passed, but often in a setting other than where it occurred. The echoes of one place call out to those of another so that, in remembering, we seem to occupy two worlds. Something *here*, a glance, a fragment of a song, a hint of color, evokes something *there* and, for the moment we stand on the bridge of memory.[5]

A special case, however, occurs when we remember *in situ*, when the setting of our memory and the setting of our remembering are one and the same. The return to a site where something happened in our lives affords a depth and concreteness to memory that would not be quite the same anywhere else. At a distance, memory may become abstract and distorted by romantic ideals of commitments to certain versions of self.[6] In return, however, the true particularity of place counters the impulse to nostalgia or self-interest by keeping before us a reality that is other and more than simply our mental construal of it. The landmarks of place have their own force: They prod us to remember aspects of a situation that we may have forgotten; to retrieve hidden memories that may have eluded us; to see with striking vividness signs that distance or familiarity may have obscured.

Seeking renewal, we would return to those places where something precious was found, where our sense of self was awakened in discovery of a world's welcome. We are also identified, however, and more fundamentally claimed, by our locations of loss. Indeed, human experience tends to fuse these settings, for no place lets us simply hold fast what we have found. Loss is inevitable where life has beckoned at all, and the novelty of today's discovery becomes tomorrow's too familiar source of alienation or anguish. The turn homeward, then, is fraught with ambivalence. There we know the constant sources of our growth, but never apart from the sharpest reminders of our finitude and the terrifying poignancy that issues from it.

No place is immune from the natural dying of all things. We can return to no home without the confrontation of loss and profound ambivalence. But not all of the losses that inhabit a place are natural or simply the function of human finitude. The intrusion of evil in our history has trespassed the private boundaries of land that we have cherished, the intimate places where we came to know our first inklings of hope, where families laughed and cried, where the world hinted at God's mystery. Like unbridled robbers in the night, human agents of destruction have violated the precincts of home, pillaging what was honored within and banishing the rightful residents to a most unnatural exile. Where legions of cruelty have trampled the soil of personal history, we confront not the ambivalence of human finitude, but a more fundamental profanation of space; not the natural loss of particular realities within our domain, but an absolute loss of the ability to be at home at all in that place where once we gathered as a human family. The resulting dilemma is severe: To be at home in the world requires a memory of our origins and, in some sense, a return to the places that have deeply identified us; yet, in the context of evil's radical loss, those very places have become profane and resist any return with the threat of an ominous defilement. How can we return to a ruined place? And how can we not return, if that place has ever been our home?

LANDSCAPE OF THE SHOAH:
RETURN TO A RUINED PLACE

Although we witness daily a sad procession of people banished from the natural claim of home by political, racial, and economic oppression, these displaced persons stand in the shadow of an earlier group of exiles whose plight continues to unsettle our ideas of dislocation and place. No two victims are ever the same, yet neither are they unrelated. The displaced person in our time bears the spectre of those whose exile led to the death camps of Europe, for there in the rubble of human ash we know the radical limit of homelessness. When, in the infamous night of shattered glass, Nazi mobs began their violation of Jewish buildings, they lit the torches whose flames, over the next seven years, would consume much more than place.[7] Where synagogues burn, a people will be robbed of its freedom to reverence life and pursue its meaning; where houses are stormed, a people will lose its right to share life intimately and, as family, to nurture its prospect; where hospitals are invaded and crippled children driven out over shards of glass into the night's cold, a people will be separated from its power to protect life and sustain its humanness;[8] where cemeteries are desecrated, a people will be deprived of its place in history and denied its guardianship of a past and intention of a future. Such violation of place is, always, a sacrilege of person. As in 1938 and its aftermath, to say you have no right to be in this place means finally you have no right to be. The uprooting from home foreshadows an exile from life itself, a captive dwelling in the very domain of death.[9] *Lebensraum* requires *Sterbensraum*.

Survivors of the Holocaust face an unending ordeal in even contemplating return to that ruined place where death made its home. For that place, be it the village from which they were torn or the black landscape of the chimney's shadow, continues to banish them long after treaty and liberation have taken effect. By force of even its single instance, the act of atrocity sets in motion a profanity that lingers in the land, an ever-present reminder that, with the six million had vanished the very sense of home that return would seek. If place and memory could be kept apart, perhaps, then one might return in peace; but, precisely because they cannot, return affects remembrance and remembrance warns that, in this place, one can never be whole again. The memory of an unholy presence exposes the taboo that haunts ruined places: Can one see what happened here and live?

Nevertheless, survivors have returned and testified. In narrative, film, and essay they have made known to us the ordeal of return and something of its significance. Their testimony varies as do their situations: A survivor of Auschwitz returns to the Transylvanian village of his birth where home vanished forever in the dawning of night;[10] a forty-seven-year-old Israeli, one of two survivors of Chelmno, returns to that place along the Narew River where S.S. guards forced him to sing for their entertainment as they were murdering some four hundred thousand Jews;[11] in September 1953 the most prominent of Jewish thinkers, a survivor not of the camps, but of the diaspora, returns to Frankfurt where once he taught at University and *Lehrhaus* and now must speak a word of prophecy;[12] a daughter of the next generation returns to Germany where her father, a "brand plucked from the fire," had written eloquently of the prophets and of the Rambam, and there she risks a holy prayer in that profane place.[13]

The words of those who have returned instruct us in our remembrance and challenge our deeds for tomorrow. With the poet, they remind us that "An awful clarification occurs where a place was."[14] Prophetically, their chronicle warns us that, with the Holocaust, we remember more than an interruption of history, for the shattering of the links that bridge past, present, and future ever involves a deep estrangement from place and a robbery of the very sense of home.[15] The prospect of peace requires a recovery of that sense of home by which we are free to be with others in a particular place. But what extraordinary hospitality can overcome the burden of profanity to host such a return? And, more pointedly, who could welcome its offer?

The testimony of Elie Wiesel, Simon Srebnik, Martin Buber, and Susannah Heschel leads us deeper into the dynamics of return. Although they map no path of safe passage, their reflections illumine the perils of return and, thereby, prepare us for the delicate relation that may yet connect us—victims and those who were not victims—in a pursuit of peace, the sharing of a common world. The survivors' return, so their examples indicate, must confront the discontinuity of ongoing change, the persistence of an unyielding sameness, and a world of concrete others whose existence may either scandalize or assist the survivor in his or her path homeward.

THE OPPRESSION OF CHANGE
AND THE ALIENATION OF THE UNCHANGED

In the narrative account of his return to Sighet, Elie Wiesel recalls wondering, "What would be waiting for me when I arrived? The dead past or the past revived? Total desolation or a city rebuilt again and a life once more become normal? For me, in either case, there would be despair."[16] The prospect that Wiesel describes reflects an inevitable dilemma that the returning survivor confronts. On the one hand, both by intention and simply by the passage of time, the cities and villages of the Holocaust's terrain have changed, often dramatically and always apart from those who, once banished, can return only as strangers. A city rebuilt is not *my* city, and its signs of life may only blur the memory of what occurred in its domain. The markers of normalcy stabilize but, to the survivor, they also indicate that the profound loss no longer has present significance if, in fact, it ever did. On the other hand, the persistence of the unchanging features of that world threatens a similar despair. Can the near-annihilation of a people have made so little difference that, in Wiesel's words, "Nothing had changed. The house was the same, the street was the same, the world was the same, God was the same. Only the Jews had disappeared."[17] The desolated city or the city unchanged is not *my* city either; only the place where exile began.

Time, out of its own momentum, brings change to the landscape of return. Thus, even the most natural of developments frustrates the survivor's return with reminders that the sought-after setting may not exist.[18] However, in the same way that all loss is not natural, so can change result from more than the sequence of todays and tomorrows. Change, in some settings, has its own design. Deliberate intentions to alter and destroy the Holocaust topography fog the path of return with a wicked mist of unreality. Those who facilely beautify, clean, and construct on profane ground risk becoming like those who, in 1943, planted pines at Sobibor: agents of illusion who oppose the truth of remembrance and return.[19]

As Jill Robbins has noted, paraphrasing Maurice Blanchot, "The genocide of the Jews was not just an annihilation, but an annihilation *of* their annihilation." She continues, "The crime includes the attempt to cover up the crime, to . . . 'leave no traces.'"[20] To destroy the trace, however, requires that one silence the surviving witnesses and, with them, the testimony that the land itself might provide. As if to retrieve the testimony or, at least, to deny the authority of the land's enforced silence, Lanzmann's film, *Shoah,* depicts vividly "the pine trees the Germans planted over the mass graves at Sobibor to 'camouflage the traces,' the camp at Chelmno that the Germans levelled, the Narew river in which the ashes of 400,000 Jews burned at Chelmno were dumped."[21] Witness to genocide, the land could not be left alone, for it held the blood that would cry out the tale of atrocity (compare with Gen. 4:10). A place transfigured by horror finds that "the annihilation of annihilation" jeopardizes its final potency, its ability to provoke protest by those who return to view its deep scars. A forest of pines, silent and beautiful in its own right, would deceive when grown over the mass graves: "it wasn't always so silent here."[22]

No portion of Lanzmann's *Shoah* has greater force or poignancy than its presentation of the return of Simon Srebnik to Chelmno. The film opens with Srebnik traveling quietly along the Narew, a route that, in an earlier time, had taken him from the camp to the fields and back again. Chained and under guard, the thirteen-year-old boy with the melodious voice was required by his captors to sing for their pleasure. Now he sings again, gently, and the river listens.

The Narew takes Srebnik to a field, green and peaceful; a field without markers. "It's hard to recognize, but it was here," he says.

> Yes, this is the place. No one ever left here again. The gas vans came in here. . . . There were two huge ovens, and afterward the bodies were thrown into these ovens, and the flames reached to the sky. It was terrible. No one can describe it. No one can recreate what happened here. Impossible? And no one can understand it. Even I, here, now. . . . I can't believe I'm here. No, I just can't believe it.[23]

Chelmno, a maw of death marked by its chimneys; Chelmno, an unbroken, lush field. Such deformation of the land does not take away Srebnik's memory, but gives to it a necessarily paradoxical contour: "this is the place," but it has no markers; "no one ever left here," but no one is there. His return confronts a basic sense of unreality that is derived, in part, from the incomprehensibility of the remembered events themselves. But no less does it derive from the "annihilation of the annihilation." His disbelief signals us in important ways that *this* place is also *not* the place, that this verdant land is not the chamber of flame. What the green field would deny, the land remembers and, with Simon Srebnik, so do we.

Because Simon Srebnik knows both that "this is the place" and "this is *not* the place" he can unmask the lie that would render pastoral the scene of atrocity and domesticate the memory of that place. The presence of the returning survivor uniquely says no to the revisions and reductions that, years later, would continue the "annihilation of the annihilation," that would alter the terrain for self-interested purposes, that would say "this is the place" without a profound awareness that "*this* is *not* the place," that would claim to know what cannot be known.[24] The violation of place, ever a fundamental threat, would finally obscure memory and history's truth. In the changed landscape, the returning survivor finds neither home nor the site that had so profoundly identified him or her. Yet, not without meaning, the return offers a message, a protest for truth: "Here," the survivor says, "I remember."

Not everything, however, has changed. Standing in Chelmno's empty field, Srebnik becomes aware of a striking continuity of silence. He comments;

> It was always this peaceful here. Always. When they burned two thousand people—Jews—every day, it was just as peaceful. No one shouted. Everyone went about his work. It was silent. Peaceful. Just as it is now.[25]

Silence, the ironic marker of this non-place—this place without a trace—furnishes the telling link between Chelmno's past and present. It is a constant voice, audible and unbroken in memory and return. In some instances, silence may deceive, lulling us to forget the screaming agony of a setting's past.[26] It does not do so here. At Chelmno, Srebnik knows the more ominous silence, the lingering backdrop for atrocity.[27] In the undisturbed order of stillness, the survivor finds a haunting reminder that some things do not change at all.

The persistent landscape of the Holocaust's world becomes most prominent in villages such as Grabow, where the permanence of old, carved doors alludes to a time when the unchanged houses on the square belonged to Jewish families;[28] in places such as Wlodawa, where buildings remain the same and the synagogue, already existing before czars ruled in Poland, still assumes its place, although empty—"There's no one to go to it";[29] and in towns such as Sighet where, as Wiesel notes, "buildings, sidewalks, tenements, lampposts—all were just as I had left them."[30] The unchanged town expresses a powerful lure, for it would feign to offer a precious finding of precisely what one had lost. Yet, in its seductive appeal lie the roots of the coldest alienation. The tearing of person and place, like the betrayal of intimates, wounds deeply and leaves unhealing scars. Survivors of catastrophic exile change profoundly in the ordeal, never to be the same again. Returning to the too-familiar setting, they confront the unchanged town's cruelest joke: the survivor's unfathomable loss has left no imprint on the landscape; the suffering, as if it had never occurred, has made no difference.

Where change has not occurred, returning survivors must face the given

tokens of their loss, realizing anew the extent of their deprivation and separation. In a strange land one expects the unfamiliar and, although not at home,
one feels no forfeiture. However, in the land that was once one's own, the very
familiarity of the low, gray houses or the peculiar corner of the market square
exact further sacrifice and surrender of the precious. Different from the sim-
pler loss where something ceases to be, here the survivor knows that something exists, only not for him or her. Estrangement, an acute loss of claim
within loss itself, takes the form of "a house of strangers." Where once the
survivor ate, slept, and loved, another stands instead.

The constancy of setting exposes boldly the singular, telling absence from
this unchanged world. All is in place with only one exception, whose glaring
fact rises in the survivor's consciousness as a screaming indictment of all that
has changed and all that has not. Wiesel describes a moment in his return:

> Scenes and images flitter through my mind's eye. The years roll by,
> disappear into the abyss. Wild thoughts set my brain on fire: speak to
> the living, tear off their masks, reject their obsequious smiles; go from
> house to house, knock on windows, beat down doors and ask the peo-
> ple, "Where are the Jews who lived within these walls?"[31]

Remembrance *in situ* risks confrontation, the meeting of victims and
those who were their torturers, their on-lookers, their usurpers. As memory
gives way to protest, words begin to form that would create a new situation.[32]
Yet precisely here, the force of the old situation expresses its profanity. What
words can be spoken in a ruined place?

THE DIALOGUE OF RETURN

While lecturing in East Germany on the thought of her father, Abraham
Joshua Heschel, Susannah Heschel recalls that there "the Jewish categories of
purity and pollution, holy and profane, suddenly came alive. I started to feel
it was wrong to take the work of my father, who is so precious and holy to
me, and bring it to such a befouled and evil place."[33] The experience of
profanity, a numinous vulnerability to danger, contagion, and deep feeling of
"wrong," assaults the returning Jew from many sources: the lingering nearness
of death and its agents, the obscurity of the markers of good and evil,[34] the
disorientation and experienced sense of unreality.[35] No stronger sense of forbidden line exists, however, than in the victim's meeting of the actual other
who, in this way or that, shared responsibility for the victimization. Return
confronts profanity because it brings into relation the victim and the victim-
izer and, to occupy a common place even for the moment, implies a recognition of the other who dwells there.

Return involves this other. As memory requires a present answering of the past, so does return demand response to the other whose past role forges a present reality in the ruined place. The survivors return to a populated world and cannot finally be alone with their memory.[36] Seeking a glimpse of home, they find the house full of strangers and, with them, the returning Jew can be anything but indifferent. With words or silence the act of return addresses these strangers and situates them in history. Like the survivor, their present has a past; their future, a task.

Lanzmann's *Shoah* gives faces to many of these others. Outside of the church in Chelmno a group of villagers surround Simon Srebnik, eager to welcome his return for "they know all he's lived through."[37] With enthusiasm, they rush to provide their versions of the story as if it were theirs to tell and as if their own zeal did not indict them of the very reality they described. Occasionally they seek Srebnik's nod of approval, yet seemingly without awareness of what they have asked him to confirm. Lost in the midst of their banal cackle, Srebnik is uncomfortably silent. The villagers, caught in the euphoria of their own welcome, do not hear the shattering scream of that silence, and the return goes effectively unmet. No absence of overt hostility can mask this reality: to the villagers, Simon Srebnik has no greater voice in Chelmno's present than he did in Chelmno's past.

The spectrum of others is broader than Chelmno's villagers and includes people of humane openness and courage. Still, their presence is rare and muted under the din of a culture's self-serving noise, a banging accompaniment to the depletion of conscience and criticism. The returning survivor can neither rely on the trustworthiness of the resident others nor take his or her cue from them. Where the other's guilt breeds defensiveness, banality blocks self-cognizance, and even the will to welcome may afflict with self-concern, the survivor returns in jeopardy: The jeopardy that the precious word that he or she has returned to speak will go unheard, or be trivialized, or be caught in a circle of antagonism, the jeopardy that his or her voice will once again have no place.

In Wiesel's *The Town Beyond the Wall*, the character of return, Michael, remembers what another had once told him:

> "Sometimes it happens that we travel for a long time without knowing that we have made the long journey solely to pronounce a certain word, a certain phrase, in a certain place. The meeting of the place and the word is a rare accomplishment, on the scale of humanity."[38]

In a climate of deceptive change, the survivor returns to say, "I remember"; in a milieu of unaffected constancy, he or she voices indictment and protest. Both words express, in the moment of their utterance, a new claim of place, a new sense of situation that allies the survivor with the truth of the land itself. The authority of the survivor's return derives not from the resident others, for it is finally not about them, but from the inalienable right to speak *in* a place the truth about that place, to offer a human word where human beings have lived and died, and to deny the ultimate profanity of anywhere one once was and now is.

The survivor's return does not redeem the land, but seeks to overcome the banishment—the profanity—that would block "the meeting of the place and the word." To a certain extent, a ruined place is ruined forever, for what is lost in a single precious instance cannot there be restored. Yet the profanity that repels, that threatens to make the land uninhabitable, has its roots not in the loss per se, but in the willing failure to allow such an event to address all inhabitants decisively or to fashion a human witness that ever names this place of ruination. Profanity describes the surrender of history to oblivion, to the leveled field in which finally all are lost—except, possibly, the survivor who tacitly knows that "this is the place."

In its moment, the survivor's return, manifesting the living presence of memory, creates new access to the ruined place. Like a rite of purification, the act of return does not do away with danger, but places that which is threatening in an approachable frame.[39] The alien is given human context. Here that human context takes the form of re-marking the land, of exposing within its contours the vital boundaries that separate good from evil, the true from the banal, the kingdom of life from the domain of death. Ruin yet exists, but the survivor has named its locations—Birkenau, Treblinka, Chelmno—and robbed it of its power to obscure the truth or banish the human witness. Although outside all moral categories, the legacy of this landscape creates a claim for human responsibility; no humane tale, the alien chronicle of what there occurred reenters the human story as a warning and call on the lips of the returning Jew.

That certain word that the Jew, after Auschwitz, speaks by his or her very presence articulates an obligation and an overture. Martin Buber's return to Frankfurt in 1953 to accept the Peace Prize of the German Book Trade—a return ripe with the possibility of misunderstanding—occasioned a prophetic pronouncement of that word.[40] Acutely aware of the *churban*, Buber begins his speech with a solemn recognition of what had occurred in this land and intones the stark reminder that here can exist no presumption of forgiveness. Without yielding that deep conviction, he then struggles to discern the face of those resident others gathered in *Paulskirche*, those who people the world to which he has returned.[41] The same memory that drives his indictment requires his discernment as he recalls no simple totality: Where some, by their deeds and intentions, virtually removed themselves from the human sphere, others failed to oppose them, trapped in fears and self-concern; some, at risk of their own death, did fight the incursion of evil and, if to no avail, at least refused to surrender to indifference the plight of another's human life. Only by making such a discernment, only by seeking the face of the resident other, can Buber respond to the voice that cries out from the ruined place. The meeting of word and place coincides with a confrontation of the particular survivor who speaks and the particular other who must, above all, listen and respond as presently addressed. No past pattern of discourse must prohibit the dialogue of return.

The word of return is a present word. It addresses not the burden of the past as a distant item, but as a crisis made present. For Buber, that word heralds a struggle against the *contrahuman* in all its forms, against the demonry that desolated the landscape of Europe and the sacred places of the Jewish heart and that threatens to emerge wherever the human dialogue is broken.[42] It risks profanity for, in Buber's words, "The Jew chosen as symbol must obey this call of duty even there, indeed, precisely there where the never-to-be-effaced memory of what has happened stands in opposition to it."[43] There, in a ruined place, the Jew gives the overture to dialogue and, with the greatest of jeopardy, confirms the human existence of the resident other— not because it is deserved, for it cannot be in this ruined landscape, but because only as such can the survivor vanquish the *contrahuman* in a world where a torturous history has set us to share common places.[44]

Buber seeks a "solidarity that extends across the fronts: the solidarity of all separate groups in the flaming battle for the rise of a true humanity."[45] Whether or not that solidarity is attainable, its goal derives from a keen insight into the spatial dynamics of return: The place that is ours is never ours alone; overcoming the profanity of place requires overcoming the profanity of the resident other. Whether or not the dialogue of return yields "the great peace," its moment of turning "radically changes the situation," the past pattern that has bound victim and oppressor.[46] The dialogue of return, no pacified exchange, exercises the fullest confrontation that remembers, indicts, and seeks to bring back to responsibility the resident other. In dialogue, neither banality nor falsehood can any longer hide this other from the claim of the human voice and the repentance that fights the *contrahuman*. Evil will be denied its mask. As for the survivor, he or she leaves behind vestiges of the victim's role whose words could find no apt expression in either punishment or forgiveness. Turned toward the essential task, the survivor becomes transformed as prophet, proclaiming the challenge of peace in the ruined places of human history.

In his book on the Kotzker Rebbe, Abraham Heschel cites the Midrash that describes the Creator's casting truth into the ground.[47] Entombed in the earth, truth eludes those unwilling to dig into the layered memories of a place. The survivors' return reminds us, nevertheless, that truth *is* in the ground and perhaps only they know where it lies buried. As survivors unearth this truth that is uniquely theirs, they discover neither a restored home nor the recovery of a consumed past. Yet, in the turning over of this very ground, they find the broken signs of a world that identify them decisively and connect us all in the obligation of our time: the larger return to a common humanity.

NOTES

1. Nelly Sachs, untitled, in *The Seeker*, trans. R. Mead, M. Mead, and M. Hamburger (New York: Farrar, Straus & Giroux, 1970), 395.

2. Wendell Berry, "Work Song," in *Collected Poems, 1957–1982* (San Francisco: North Point Press, 1985), 187–88.

3. Herbert Muschamp, in speaking of the U.S. Holocaust Museum, in *New York Times* (April 11, 1993), H32.

4. Note the Hasidic narrative recounted by Elie Wiesel as the prologue to *The Gates of the Forest*, trans. F. Frenaye (New York: Schocken Books, 1982) and in *Souls on Fire*, trans. M. Wiesel (New York: Summit Books, 1972), 167–68.

5. Nelly Sachs, in "Chorus of the Rescued," reflects this potential of the present to evoke memory, even perilously, in the case of the Holocaust survivor. She writes, "Be gentle when you teach us to live again / Lest the song of a bird, / Or a pail being filled at the well, / Let our badly sealed pain burst forth again / and carry us away." Collected in Nelly Sachs, *O the Chimneys*, trans. M. Roloff (New York: Farrar, Straus & Giroux, 1967), 24.

6. On this problem in the context of Holocaust literature, see Lawrence L. Langer, *Versions of Survival: The Holocaust and the Human Spirit* (Albany, N.Y.: SUNY, 1982).

7. *Kristallnacht*, the night of broken glass, occurred throughout Germany during the night of November 9–10, 1938. For discussion of this event see Rita Thalmann and Emmanuel Feinermann, *Crystal Night*, trans. G. Cremonesi (New York: Holocaust Library, 1972).

8. Michael Bruce, a non-Jewish eyewitness of the pogromic events in Berlin, provides the following account: "The object of the mob's hate was a hospital for sick Jewish children, many of them cripples or consumptives. In minutes the windows had been smashed and the doors forced. When we arrived the swine were driving the wee mites out over the broken glass, bare-footed and wearing nothing but their nightshirts." Cited in Leonard Baker, *Days of Sorrow and Pain* (New York: Oxford University Press, 1978), 231–32.

9. As such, the Nazi "Final Solution" preys on the already precarious finitude of human existence in space and time. As the Protestant theologian Paul Tillich noted, "Without space there is neither presence nor a present. And, conversely, the loss of space includes the loss of temporal presence, the loss of the present, the loss of being" (Paul Tillich, *Systematic Theology* [Chicago: University of Chicago Press, 1973], I:195). Tillich's insight aptly reminds that not only is the loss of either time or space thoroughly reflexive, but also tantamount to death. He cites with sober recognition the

author of Job, who employed precisely an image of spatial estrangement to express the reality of death: "he who goes down to Sheol does not come up; he returns no more to his house, nor does his place know him any more" (Job 7:9–10; *Systematic Theology*, I:195). We should be wary of Tillich's perspective, however, in this one sense. For Tillich, the loss of space is simply symptomatic of the conditions of human finitude that imply the self's anxiety, ambiguity, and insecurity. This naturally given threat to human space must be distinguished, though, from the utterly unnatural manipulation of that condition—as in the Holocaust—that not only magnifies the existential crisis beyond all manageable proportion, but fundamentally estranges its victims from the very activity of affirming meaning in the midst of loss. On Tillich and the Holocaust, see Albert H. Friedlander, "A Final Conversation with Paul Tillich," in *Out of the Whirlwind: A Reader of Holocaust Literature*, ed. A. Friedlander (New York: Schocken Books, 1976), 515–21.

10. See the writings of Elie Wiesel that reflect upon his returns to Sighet: "The Last Return," in *Legends of Our Time* (New York: Schocken, 1982), 110–30; and "A House of Strangers," in *A Jew Today* (New York: Vintage Books, 1978), 66–72. See also Elie Wiesel, *The Town Beyond the Wall* (New York: Schocken Books, 1982), a fictional probing of the dynamics of return.

11. See Claude Lanzmann's depiction of the return of Simon Srebnik in the film, *Shoah*. The complete text of Lanzmann's film has been published as *Shoah: An Oral History of the Holocaust* (New York: Pantheon Books, 1985).

12. Note Martin Buber's return to Germany to accept the 1953 Peace Prize of the German Book Trade. Buber's address on that occasion, delivered in Frankfurt at the *Paulskirche*, has been published in several places. See "Genuine Dialogue and the Possibilities of Peace," in Martin Buber, *Pointing the Way: Collected Essays*, trans. and ed. M. Friedman (New York: Harper & Brothers, 1957), 232–39, and in *Men of Dialogue: Martin Buber and Albrecht Goes*, ed. E. W. Rollins and H. Zohn (New York: Funk & Wagnalls, 1969), 20–27.

13. Note the return of Susannah Heschel, the daughter of Abraham Joshua Heschel, whose sensitive essay, "Something Holy in a Profane Place," in *Christianity and Crisis* 46 (October 6, 1986): 338–42, reflects upon her 1986 lecture tour of East Germany on Jewish and Christian dialogue. Abraham Heschel had spoken of himself as a "brand plucked from the fire" in an address at Union Theological Seminary upon assuming the Fosdick Visiting Professorship. See Abraham Heschel, "No Religion Is an Island," in *Union Seminary Quarterly Review* 21 (January 1966): 117.

14. Wendell Berry, "The Slip," in *Collected Poems*, 224.

15. Theological interpretations of the Holocaust have tended to draw heavily on temporal metaphors and perspectives to express the profound crisis of the catastrophe. Note, for example, Emil Fackenheim's important study, *God's Presence in History: Jewish Affirmation and Philosophical Reflections* (New York: Harper Torchbooks, 1972); Arthur A. Cohen, *The Tremendum: A Theological Interpretation of the Holocaust* (New York: Crossroad Publishing Co., 1981); and *The Holocaust as Interruption*, ed. Elisabeth Schüssler Fiorenza and David Tracy (Edinburgh: T & T Clark, 1984). The temporal emphasis is not surprising, given the strong primacy of the category "history" in Jewish tradition and the dramatic sense of temporal discontinuity that the Holocaust introduces. Moreover, the diasporic heritage of Judaism has tended to relativize the importance of place to such an extent that temporal perspectives dominate the theological agenda (note, for example, the implications of Franz Rosenzweig's classic volume, *The*

Star of Redemption, trans. W. Hallo [Boston: Beacon Press, 1972], 298–335). The growing literature of return, however, demands consideration of the fundamentally spatial dimensions of the crisis as well as the temporal.

16. "The Last Return," 111.

17. Ibid., 120. Note also Claude Lanzmann's exchange with a Mr. Filipowicz in present-day Wlodawa: "(Lanzmann): These buildings haven't changed? (Filipowicz): Not at all. There were barrels of herrings here, and the Jews sold fish. There were stalls, small shops, Jewish business, as the gentleman says. That's Barenholz's house. He sold wood. Lipschitz's store was there. He sold cloth. This was Lichtenstein's" (*Shoah*, 18; also see 85).

18. Following again Tillich's insight concerning the interrelatedness of time and space, to return to a given place, but at a different time, is to return, finally, to a different place. In this sense, memory *in situ* may be more of an ordeal than memory at a distance, for the former must contend with the distractions and novelties of what has changed.

19. Even a seemingly innocuous change may be value-laden. Susannah Heschel recalls seeing an empty lot near the Berlin Wall. Walking closer, she noticed a small printed sign that marks the place as the former site of Gestapo torture chambers. An empty lot is a no-place—a place where nothing occurs. Yet, here, the horrible happened and no illusion of non-eventfulness can finally tame the perception aroused by the words on the small sign. As Heschel remembers, "The horror of standing in that space, breathing the air that was suddenly full of screams from those former days was terrifying. Religion gives us psalms and prayers to say when we visit holy places: what do we do when we visit places where terrible evil has been committed?" ("Something Holy in a Profane Place," 339).

20. Jill Robbins, "The Writing of the Holocaust: Claude Lanzmann's *Shoah*," in *Prooftexts* 7 (1987): 252.

21. Ibid.

22. Jan Piwonski, in response to Claude Lanzmann at Sobibor: "That's the charm of our forests: silence and beauty. But it wasn't always so silent here. There was a time when it was full of screams and gunshots, of dogs' barking" (*Shoah*, 10).

23. Ibid., 5–6.

24. Distortion of Holocaust history has taken many forms, both through deliberate strategies of revisionist deceit and sometimes through unwitting reductions. On the revisionist tendencies of Holocaust historiography, see Lucy S. Dawidowicz, *The Holocaust and the Historians* (Cambridge, Mass.: Harvard University Press, 1981); and Norbert Kampe, "Normalizing the Holocaust? The Recent Historians' Debate in the Federal Republic of Germany," in *Holocaust and Genocide Studies* 2 (1987): 61–80. Unwitting reductions pose a unique problem. On this matter see, for example, Lawrence Langer's discussion of Victor Frankl and Bruno Bettelheim in *Versions of Survival*, 1–65.

25. *Shoah*, 6.

26. Note, for example, Jan Piwonski's statement about the silence of Sobibor (*Shoah*, 10; see above, n. 22).

27. Note André Neher's discussion of "scenic silence" in André Neher, *The Exile of the Word* (Philadelphia: Jewish Publication Society, 1981), 212.

28. See *Shoah*, 84–86.

29. Ibid., 18–20.

30. "A House of Strangers," 68.

31. Ibid., 69; note also the version of such an indictment given in Wiesel's novel, *The Town Beyond the Wall*, 133–78.

32. On the antecedence of such protest in Israelite wisdom literature, see Karl A. Plank, "Raging Wisdom: 'A Banner of Defiance Unfurled'" in *Judaism* 36 (1987): 323–330.

33. "Something Holy in a Profane Place," 339.

34. Susannah Heschel refers to an awareness of this sort in a Berlin theater: "One night, in a movie theater, a middle-aged man sitting next to me asked, during the intermission, if I were Jewish. I asked where he was from: Originally Berlin, he said, but, since the war, Argentina. I felt horror; was I sitting next to a Jewish refugee or next to a former Nazi? What kind of place was I in, where good and evil can appear indistinguishable?" (Ibid., 338).

35. Mircea Eliade discusses profane space as a homogeneous expanse, an unmarked place, within which no fixed orientation is possible; see Mircea Eliade, *The Sacred and the Profane*, trans. W. Trask (New York: Harvest Books, 1959), 22. Recall, in this connection, Simon Srebnik's encounter with the absolutely empty field at Chelmno (*Shoah*, 5–6) and its dimensions of paradox and unreality.

36. The possible exception where the Jew is alone with memory may be in the cemeteries, which seem to offer an at-homeness that is absent elsewhere. Note, for example, Wiesel, "The Last Return," 127, and Heschel, "Something Holy in a Profane Place," 340.

37. *Shoah*, 95; for the full account see 95–100.

38. *The Town Beyond the Wall*, 110.

39. See Paul Ricoeur, *The Symbolism of Evil*, trans. E. Buchanan (Boston: Beacon Press, 1969), 29 and 35.

40. On the controversy over Buber and the Peace Prize, see Maurice Friedman, *Martin Buber's Life and Work: The Later Years, 1945–1965* (New York: E. P. Dutton, 1983), 102–30. A distinction might be made between Buber, who immigrated to Palestine in 1938, and the survivors of the camps, whose acts of return must confront a unique memory. Nevertheless, such a distinction should not, in this case, blur the significance of Buber's own return as one who had been persecuted by the Nazis, as one who had prophetically combatted their oppression, and as a survivor of the banishment who retained a deep identification with the Jews of Germany and Europe throughout the war. A telling expression of Buber's perception of the crisis that European Jews were to face can be seen in his post-*Kristallnacht* response to Gandhi; see "A Letter to Gandhi," in *Pointing the Way: Collected Essays*, 139–47.

41. Note that, in the previous year, Buber had declined the invitation to give a public lecture in Hamburg on the occasion of his being awarded the University's Goethe Prize. In a letter to Bruno Snell (January 25, 1952), he gives as his reasons an inability to "overcome the *facelessness* of the German public, which has persisted for me since the events of 1938 and after." He continues to note that the precondition for his speaking publicly remains "being able to regard every *face* that I turn toward as my legitimate partner." (See the excerpt of this letter in *Martin Buber's Life and Work: The Later Years*, 111; emphases mine.) This same dynamic is evident in Susannah Heschel's return to Germany where the concreteness of the resident other raises anew the question of dialogue. She writes, "Perhaps, through an open admission of our own, personal experiences, we can begin to speak with one another. Yet that is both hope and

my fear. Seeing Germans as real human beings, not as mythic figures, entering into relationships with them, is frightening. To stop objectifying and start humanizing Germans threatens the deep commitment I have never to betray my family or my people. My desire is to find a way to break through the Jewish-German barrier without in any way compromising my values, my passions, my commitments" ("Something Holy in a Profane Place," 342).

42. On fighting the *contrahuman*, see "Genuine Dialogue and the Possibilities of Peace," in *Pointing the Way*, esp. 233–34.

43. Ibid., 234.

44. Thus Buber writes, "In a genuine dialogue each of the partners, even when he stands in opposition to the other, heeds, affirms, and confirms his opponent as an existing other. Only so can conflict certainly not be eliminated from the world, but be humanly arbitrated and led towards its overcoming" (Ibid., 238).

45. Ibid., 234.

46. Ibid., 235 and 237.

47. Abraham Heschel, *A Passion for Truth* (New York: Farrar, Straus, & Giroux, 1973), 13.

6 PROCESSION OF THE CRUCIFIED: A LENTEN DEVOTION

You have no God in you! Open the doors, you heavens,
    fling them open wide,
And let the children of my murdered people enter in
    a stream.
Open the doors up for the great procession of the crucified,
The children of my people, all of them, each one a God—
    make room!

                                                Yitzhak Katzenelson[1]

De-Eastered, grave-
tree split into
logs for burning
        Paul Celan[2]

Around 3:00 A.M. on November 10, 1938, gaping darkness
began to spew the flames that were to burn unabated for the next seven years.
On this night, Nazi mobs executed a well-planned "spontaneous outrage"
throughout the precincts of German Jewry. Synagogues were burned, their
sacred objects profaned and destroyed; Jewish dwellings were ransacked,
their contents strewn and pillaged. Shattering the windows of Jewish shops,
the growing swarm left businesses in ruin. Uprooting tombstones and des-
ecrating Jewish graves, the ghoulish throng violated even the sanctuary of the
dead. Humiliation accompanied physical violence: In Leipzig, Jewish residents were hurled into a small stream at the zoological park, where spectators
spit at them, defiled them with mud, and jeered at their plight. A chilling
harbinger of nights yet to come, the events of that November darkness culmi-
nated in widespread arrest of Jewish citizens and led to their transport to
concentration camps. Nazi propagandists, struck by a perverse poetry, gave to
this night the name by which it has endured in memory: *Kristallnacht*, the
night of broken glass. Irony abounds in such a name, for in the litter of
shattered windows lies more than bits of glass. *Kristallnacht* testifies to a
deeper breaking of basic human continuities. Shattered windows leave faith
in fragments and pierce the wholeness of the human spirit.

In that same year of 1938, the Jewish artist Marc Chagall would complete a remarkable painting titled *White Crucifixion*.[3] Here the artist depicts a

crucified Christ, skirted with a tallith and encircled by a kaleidoscopic whirl
of images that narrate the progress of a Jewish pogrom. The skewed, tau-
shaped cross extends toward the arc of destruction and bears particular
meaning in that context. Whatever the cross of Christ may mean, in 1938 it
was circumscribed by the realities of Holocaust: The onrush of a weapons-
bearing mob overruns houses and sets them aflame; a group of villagers
seeks to flee the destruction in a crowded boat, while others crouch on the
outskirts of the village; an old man wipes the tears from his eyes as he
vanishes from the picture, soon to be followed by a bewildered peasant and a

Marc Chagall, French, born in Russia, 1887–1985; *White Crucifixion,* oil on canvas,
1938, 154.3 x 139.7 cm; gift of Alfred S. Alschuler. By permission of The Art Institute
of Chicago.

third man who clutches a Torah to himself as he witnesses over his shoulder a synagogue fully ablaze.[4]

Chagall's juxtaposition of crucifixion and the immediacy of Jewish suffering creates an intense interplay of religious expectation and historical reality that challenges facile assumptions. He does not intend to Christianize the painting, certainly not in the sense of affirming any atoning resolution of the Jewish plight. Rather, in the chaotic world of *White Crucifixion* all are unredeemed, caught in a vortex of destruction binding crucified victim and modern martyr. As the prayer shawl wraps the loins of the crucified figure, Chagall makes clear that the Christ and the Jewish sufferer are one.

Chagall has not been the only twentieth-century Jewish artist to appropriate crucifixion imagery. David Roskies discusses the use of the cross symbol not only in Chagall's painting, but in the literary work of Der Nister, Lamed Shapiro, Sholem Asch, S. Y. Agnon, and the poet Uri Zvi Greenberg.[5] In literature written before World War II (and under the influence of biblical criticism that had emancipated Jesus' image from its doctrinal Christian vesture), these authors used the cross symbol variously; for Asch, the crucified figure in all his Jewishness symbolized universal suffering; for Shapiro and Agnon, on the other hand, the cross remained an emblem of violence and a reminder of Christian enmity against Jews. But to depict the Jew on the cross after the war was to confront a stronger taboo, for to do so required the victim to borrow from the oppressor's cultural tradition. And the potential for being misunderstood would be immense: by fellow victims who would perceive apostasy and betrayal instead of solidarity, by oppressors who would hear forgiving consolation instead of indictment.[6]

We must not misunderstand Jewish appropriation of the cross in the context of Holocaust art and literature. Where used at all, the cross functions not as an answer to atrocity, but as a question, protest, and critique of the assumptions we may have made about profound suffering. Emil Fackenheim puts the matter this way:

> A good Christian suggests that perhaps Auschwitz was a divine reminder of the suffering of Christ. Should he not ask instead whether his Master himself, had He been present at Auschwitz, could have resisted degradation and dehumanization? What are the sufferings of the Cross compared to those of a mother whose child is slaughtered to the sound of laughter or the strains of a Viennese waltz? This question may sound sacrilegious to Christian ears. Yet we dare not shirk it, for we—Christians as well as Jews—must ask: at Auschwitz, did the grave win the victory after all, or, worse than the grave, did the devil himself win?[7]

Questions such as these spring off Chagall's canvas and into our sensibilities. *White Crucifixion* depicts a world of unleashed terror within which no saving voice can be heard or any redeeming signs perceived. Separated from the imperiled villagers by only his apparent passivity, Chagall's Messiah, this Jew of the cross, is no rescuer, but himself hangs powerless before the chaotic fire. The portrayal of Messiah as victim threatens to sever a basic continuity between suffering and redemption (or to use Christian imagery, between cross and resurrection). To have redemptive meaning, the cross must answer the victims who whirl here in torment, for, in the Holocaust, the world becomes Golgotha turned on itself, "one great mount of crucifixion, with thousands of severed Jewish heads strewn below like so many thieves."[8]

However, precisely here the language of redemption seems trivial, if not obscenely blind to the sufferer's predicament. Can one speak of redemption in any way that does not trifle with the victim's cry? Before the mother's despair, words of redemption offer no consolation; instead, like the laughter and music that accompany her child's murder, such words mock her torment and deny the profundity of her suffering. Sign of a Christian gaze, the rhetoric of redemption, no matter how benevolently used, remains the ploy of oppressors even decades later. No one may invoke it for the victim in whose world it may have no place.[9]

That world of the victim has found literary testament in the writings of Elie Wiesel. Although his writings are prolific, few of his works have had the impact of his first narrative, the memoir *Night*. For a decade following the war—years in which he was a stateless refugee in France—Wiesel maintained a personal moratorium on his experience, a pledge of silence that would allow no word to betray the Holocaust memory. On this matter he wrote nothing and spoke nothing, but he listened to the voices within himself. Then in 1956 his memories exploded into an 800-page Yiddish text, *Un di Velt Hot Geshvign* (*And the World Kept Silent*).[10] Over the next two years Wiesel would live with this manuscript, paring away from its pages every letter that was not essential, every mark on the page that might divert from the intense reality of its truth. The result: the stark volume *Night*, some 120 pages that have become a landmark in Holocaust literature. *Night*, too, places the Jew on the cross. It describes the hanging of a young boy who had worked with a well-liked overseer. Both had become suspected of sabotage, and the boy is sentenced to hang, along with two prisoners found with weapons.

> One day when we came back from work, we saw three gallows rearing up in the assembly place, three black crows. Roll call. SS all around us, machine guns trained; the traditional ceremony. Three victims in chains—and one of them, the little servant, the sad-eyed angel. . . .
> The three victims mounted together onto the chairs. . . .
> "Where is God? Where is He?" someone behind me asked.

At a sign from the head of the camp, the three chairs tipped over.

Total silence throughout the camp. On the horizon, the sun was setting. . . .

Then the march past began. The two adults were no longer alive. Their tongues hung swollen, blue-tinged. But the third rope was still moving; being so light, the child was still alive. . . .

For more than half an hour he stayed there, struggling between life and death, dying in slow agony under our eyes. And we had to look him full in the face. He was still alive when I passed in front of him. His tongue was still red, his eyes not yet glazed.

Behind me, I heard the same man asking:

"Where is God now?"

And I heard a voice within me answer him:

"Where is He? Here He is—He is hanging here on this gallows. . . ."[11]

This powerful tableau, haunting in its cruciform reflection, strikes and challenges Christian readers of *Night*. To use the apostle Paul's term, this scene provides the word that *scandalizes*, that makes Christian readers stumble over their expectations and knock down the comfortable prop of resurrection faith. Here, Wiesel's readers confront the new Golgotha. The cross put no final end to the reign of evil, for here crucifixion recurs all over again. Only now the victim is a young boy with the face of a sad-eyed angel; only now the darkness is lit by no Easter dawn, but by the torch of a crematory fire, a fire whose smoke issues an unbroken night; only now God dies, instead of redeeming.

Francois Mauriac, the French Catholic writer and author of the foreword to *Night*, found in this scene not only the center of Wiesel's story but also the essential question for his own appropriation of Christian faith. In 1954 Wiesel, then a young journalist, had occasion to interview Mauriac, who just two years earlier had won the Nobel Prize in literature. The interview proved to be a decisive turning point for both of them: For Wiesel, Mauriac provided the compassionate challenge to tell the story of darkness; for Mauriac, Wiesel made unavoidably personal the plight of the Holocaust child. Upon reading *Night*, Mauriac wrote the following:

And I who believe that God is love, what answer could I give my young questioner, whose dark eyes still held the reflection of that angelic sadness which had appeared one day upon the face of the hanged child? What did I say to him? Did I speak of that other Israeli, his brother, who may have resembled him—the Crucified, whose Cross has conquered the world? Did I affirm that the stumbling block to his faith was the cornerstone of mine, and that conformity between the Cross and the suffering of men was in my eyes the key to that impenetrable mystery whereon the faith of his childhood had perished? . . . But I could only embrace him, weeping.[12]

Mauriac, long a poignant witness to the connection between suffering and love, knew well that the cornerstone of his faith was at stake in Wiesel's narrative. And yet, at the point at which he might have been tempted to proclaim his gospel, he finds that the only fitting response is to embrace the victim, blessing him with tears. The reason is clear: The death of the sad-eyed angel creates a stumbling block not only for Wiesel but for Mauriac; not only for the Jewish victim but for the Christian onlooker who cannot interpret away the scandalous scene without trivializing its grossly unredeemed features.[13] In Mauriac's embrace, human compassion stifles theological conviction, rescuing it from becoming an oppressive utterance. The word of faith gives way to silence, but perhaps therein returns to its authentic ground.

Mauriac's tearful embrace of Wiesel provides us with an emblem that at once interprets the tableau in *Night* and becomes an apt metaphor for Christian devotion to the cross. As an emblem, Mauriac's act keeps before us three fundamental features that should shape Christian response to both the cross of the sad-eyed child and the cross of Jesus: silence, humility, and waiting together for God.

Mauriac's response is, first, essentially silent. The point at which he would announce the victory of the cross gives way to the tacit embrace. In silence his act witnesses to the breaking of an essential continuity in the language of faith, the continuity between words of redemption and the utterly unredeemed circumstances of radical victimization. We lack the words even to describe the plight of the victim, much less the words to make that plight whole. Where all is broken, words of promise turn rotten and oppressive, robbing the afflicted of the integrity of his or her own suffering.

Mauriac's silence is ambivalent; it does not break the word of redemption as much as it hushes its utterance. In light of the Holocaust, the word of the cross can only be a personal and genuine confession. But the onlooker cannot presume to speak for the victims or impose upon their world as reality the expressions of his or her own desire. As the word of the cross shatters any pretentious language of strength, wisdom, and power (1 Cor. 1:18–31), so the word of *Night* stifles any Christian triumphalism. Silence must say no to the human boast.

Second, Mauriac's tearful embrace expresses a profound humility and repentance. We misread the scene if we assume that the writer's tears are tied only to his perception of the victim's tragedy. The conversation between Mauriac and Wiesel begins with Mauriac's recollection of the German occupation of France, admitting his painful knowledge of the trainloads of Jewish children standing at Austerlitz station. As Wiesel responds, "I was one of them," Mauriac sees himself anew as an unwitting onlooker, the bystander, guilty not of acts undertaken, but of acts not taken. The indictment is not Wiesel's but Mauriac's own, born of the self-perception that not to stand with the victim is to act in complicity with the oppressor. Mauriac's tears signify his humble repentance, his turning away from the role of onlooker to align himself with the victim. The observer becomes witness, testifying on behalf of the victim. Crucifixion indicts, for in its shadow one is always the guilty bystander. Humility, such as Mauriac's, puts an end to any assumption of benign righteousness; repentance denies complacency to the viewer of another's passion.

Third, the embrace of Wiesel and Mauriac creates a community of victims and their witnesses who wait together for a Messiah. The powerless, in their very plight, dramatize the need for redemption, enabling others to see themselves more humbly and indicting them when they do not. In the face of the victims, one's own need for God and for human forgiveness becomes blatantly apparent. When one becomes the victims' ally, one receives the reconciling gift that only those victims themselves can offer: the possibility of waiting together for the inbreaking of the Messiah's reign. Waiting together, victim and accompanier effect not redemption, but the community that is its firstfruits.

Crucifixion, be it the cross of Jesus or the nocturnal Golgotha of Auschwitz, breaks the moral continuities by which we have considered ourselves secure and whole. To mend these fragments of human experience lies outside our power. We cannot finally repair the broken world. Yet, as we yield these broken continuities to narrative—to memoir, to literature, to liturgy—we begin to forge a new link that binds storyteller and hearer, victim and witness. But here we who are outsiders must be most careful. We rush to tell the story, confident that it is ours to tell when, in fact, it is ours to hear.

Ours is a season for listening and silence. Not when we speak to victims but when we listen to their testimony do we truly perceive the cross that breaks moral certainties and shatters continuities of power. We who are Christians cannot give our victims the cross, for they are already its true bearers. Rather, it is they who present the cross to us in the form of its awful scandal. White Crucifixion and Night—expressions of Jewish anguish distinctly not our own—return to us the meaning of the cross in its most powerful form. The Jewish testament enables us to see anew what centuries of resurrection enthusiasm have obscured in Christian tradition: the fractured bond between God and the world; the lived moment of forsakenness to which we are vulnerable and for which we are responsible in the lives of one another.

In the world of victims, the language of redemption or victory may alienate, echoing only the speech of oppressors. Although current, this perception is not distinctly modern, but dates at least from the ordeal of an early apostle, himself a Jew. Writing with critical fervor in First Corinthians, the apostle Paul reminds his readers that Christ's resurrection, in its fullest expression, is eschatological, a word spoken in the future; when Christians claim its fullness prematurely, he argues, that word becomes illusory and destructive.[14] To approach the cross with too much faith, to stand in its shadow with certain confidence of Easter light, is finally to confront no cross at all, only the unrepentant echoes of religious noise. Amid the creation that groans for redemption, the church must stand as if *before* Easter: open to its inbreaking, but unassuming of its prerogative. There, in the community of victims and witnesses, the faithful silently wait together for the kingdom of God. There the church must express its humility, for, as the Holocaust chronicles make starkly clear, the Lord whom the church confesses is also its victim.

NOTES

1. Yitzhak Katzenelson, "The Song of the Murdered Jewish People," trans. Noah H. Rosenbloom, in David Roskies, *The Literature of Destruction: Jewish Responses to Catastrophe* (Philadelphia: Jewish Publication Society, 5748/1988), 542 (9.13).

2. Paul Celan, "Solve," in *Poems of Paul Celan*, trans. Michael Hamburger (New York: Persea Books, 1988), 257.

3. Marc Chagall, *White Crucifixion* (1938), oil on canvas, 154.3 x 139.7 cm (Art Institute of Chicago).

4. For further discussion of *White Crucifixion*, see Jane Dillenberger, *Secular Art with Sacred Themes* (Nashville: Abingdon Press, 1969), 34–55; and David Roskies, *Against the Apocalypse* (Cambridge, Mass.: Harvard University Press, 1984), 284–89. *White Crucifixion* is no isolated piece in Chagall's oeuvre. Among the other paintings that use crucifixion imagery, note the following: *Golgotha* (1912), oil on canvas, 174 x 191 cm (Museum of Modern Art, New York); *The Martyr* (1940), oil on canvas, 164.5 x 114 cm (artist's collection); *Obsession* (1943), oil on canvas, 77 x 108 cm (private collection); *The Crucified* (1944), gouache on paper, 62 x 47 cm; *The Soul of the Town* (1945), oil on canvas, 107 x 81.5 cm (Musee national d'Art moderne, Centre Georges Pompidou, Paris); *Resurrection at the River* (1947), oil on canvas, 98 x 74 cm (artist's collection); *The Fall of the Angel* (1923–1933–1947), oil on canvas, 148 x 189 cm (Kunstmuseum, Basel); *The Exodus* (1952–1966), oil on canvas, 130 x 162 cm (artist's collection); *War* (1964–1966), oil on canvas, 163 x 231 cm (Kunsthaus, Zurich); *Jacob's Dream* (1954–1967), oil on canvas, 195 x 278 cm (Musee national Message Biblique Marc Chagall, Nice); *Crucifixion* (1972), black ink, pastel and colored pencils on Japan paper, 76.7 x 5.4 cm (artist's collection). Plates of the majority of these works can be found in the following volumes: *Chagall by Chagall*, ed. Charles Sorlier (New York: Harry Abrams, 1979); and Francois Le Targat, *Chagall* (New York: Rizzoli International Pub., 1985).

5. *Against the Apocalypse*, 258–310.

6. Chaim Potok makes such controversy one of the primary foci for his novel *My Name Is Asher Lev* (Greenwich: Fawcett, 1972).

7. Emil Fackenheim, *God's Presence in History* (New York: New York University Press, 1972), 75.

8. *Against the Apocalypse*, 268.

9. For further discussion of the problem of the Christian gaze and its implications for Christian discourse about the Holocaust and about Judaism generally, see Karl A. Plank, "The Eclipse of Difference: Merton's Encounter with Judaism," in *Cistercian Studies Quarterly* 28/2 (1993): 179–91.

10. Elie Wiesel, *Un di Velt Hot Geshvign* (Buenos Aires: Yel Mundo Callaba, Central Farbond Fun Poylishe Yidn in Argentina, 1956).

11. Elie Wiesel, *Night*, trans. S. Rodway (New York: Avon Books, 1969), 74–76.

12. Francois Mauriac, "Foreword to *Night*," 10–11.

13. On the unredeemed world's challenge to basic convictions of Christian faith, see Karl A. Plank, "Confronting the Unredeemed World: A Paradoxical Paul and His Modern Critics," in *Anglican Theological Review* 67 (1985): 127–36.

14. See Karl A. Plank, *Paul and the Irony of Affliction*, Semeia Studies 17 (Atlanta: Scholars Press, 1987), 11–31.

EPILOGUE

CANTICLES FOR THE AFTERMATH: A RETURN TO THE FOREST

The Hasidic story that Elie Wiesel tells as the prologue to *The Gates of the Forest* has been the unnamed precursor of our volume.[1] The story begins:

> When the great Rabbi Israel Baal Shem-Tov saw misfortune threatening the Jews it was his custom to go into a certain part of the forest to meditate. There he would light a fire, say a special prayer, and the miracle would be accomplished and the misfortune averted.

Whereas the Baal Shem could claim the sacred place, the ritual, and the prayer, his successors experienced a progressive loss of connection to these modes of survival and sustenance. The Magid of Mezritch could not light the fire, although he knew the prayer and the place in the forest; Moshe-Leib of Sasov, after the Magid, knew neither how to light the fire nor how to say the prayer, yet he, too, could find his way in the forest. Such responses sufficed to avert misfortune. Set in the context of pending disaster, each rebbe began by recognizing what had been lost and continued by preserving the fragments whose repair would protect the people once more.

Although they turned away disasters, the threat did not end. Discontinuity, the growing distance from that which had sustained in the past, became near-total. Wiesel continues:

> Then it fell to Rabbi Israel of Rizhyn to overcome misfortune. Sitting in his armchair, his head in his hands, he spoke to God: "I am unable to light the fire and I do not know the prayer; I cannot even find the place in the forest. All I can do is to tell the story, and this must be sufficient." And it was sufficient.

What time and threatening misfortune have torn apart, the story of human struggle would repair. Told to God in the midst of a rending world, the story suffices to connect a teller and a hearer, an absence and a presence, a separation and a return. It starts in each generation with memory's litany of loss and with the recognition of ominous peril; it moves through its own narration to restore and protect. Before its voice, neither jeopardy nor rupture have the final word.

Ours is a time of the aftermath. Although total annihilation was averted by the Jews of our century, the impress of catastrophe yet runs deep and wounds in its very recall. Before its demanding need, we of the aftermath do not know what to say or do; where to go. The knowledge that Jewish lives experienced wire fence, boxcar, and the sight of departing children impedes access to our guiding traditions. These have splintered fine and, with their fragments, no sacred site, prayer, or ritual can be whole as before. Like the *tzaddikim* of the Hasidic tale, we face the situation that demands response hobbled in our ability to navigate a way, to find the necessary language, and to enact the vital deed that guards human life. In this time, any pretense of unshaded confidence means only that we have forsaken the journeys, the words, and the tasks required to be sufficient.

Still, as Wiesel's narrative suggests, the telling of a certain story can protect and transform the human situation. In the aftermath of the Holocaust's disaster, all speech and gesture, as well as every landscape, become potential bearers of this story and are themselves refracted in its light. It is a human duty to testify in behalf of the mother of the wire fence, to become Eve's messenger from the boxcar, to recollect the words that accompanied Blimele to her fate beyond the ghetto—to be the channel through which their voices resound. And what is incumbent upon all must be taken as a religious obligation among the company of the crucified. If the Christian community is to escape its role as marshal of the wire fence, it must bear the story of the Jewish family that suffered in its midst and not apart from its hands. Its act of narrative must give voice to the victim while, at the same time, making confession. With each word, it must listen for the echo of the other side.

Four canticles for the aftermath conclude this writing. Set within the liturgical tradition of a Christian year, each focuses upon some aspect of Wiesel's tale: the ritual of fire, the intercession of prayer, the knowledge of loss, and the marking of place. All strive to charge the images of Christian devotion with a narrative duty and thereby to remember the Jewish mothers who knelt at wire fences and wrote to sons on boxcar walls, the fathers who saw daughters depart forever, and finally, those Jewish children—"each one a God"—whom no parent could protect or save from the darkness.[2]

ASH WEDNESDAY

At Birkenau
the glass-eyed Cyclops
ordered pits to be dug
near Crematorium V.

Then bodies burned
behind a wall of wattle screens.

The Greek Jews could not see
the spring meadow nearby
as they entered the grey mist
with shovels

for the hot ash of kinsmen
rained down on their faces
and into their eyes,
blinding.

O priest!

You smudge my forehead
in Lenten gesture
of mortality,
unknowing.

The ash we bear
is not our own,
but those the flames
made dust.

It is again
the char of kinsmen
that burns and scars
the open face,

that sears now
our darkened cross.

BIRKENAU NATIVITY AND *AVE*

If Bethlehem had been Birkenau
    the Jewish mother would have
    wrapped her package in cheesecloth
    and laid it in the pan of cold water
    Submerged.

Let no one judge her mercy.

If Bethlehem had been Birkenau
    the manger bed would have
    burst into flames
    and blazed in the silent night
    Consuming.

    Hail Mary,
        full of grief.
    May peace be with you.

    Blessed are you and the
        women who knew children.
    And blessed are their lives,
        lost, unrestored.

    Holy Miryam,
        Merciful Mother.
    Pray for us who failed your children
        In the hour of their death.

MICHAELMAS

Michael
the Archangel
wants to prepare
Mercury Pie:

one part the earth in which dead men lay
one part the fire which consumed them
one part the water which bore their ash
one part the air which entombed them
        in clouds of smoke from chimneys.

Michael
the Sign-bearer
wants to bring back
the dead.

I do not
want him
to.

Blessed Michael
Heed not this fear
        to know.

Feed us the food
of our slaughter
lest we starve
in innocence

of who we have been
and may yet be.

Protector of the Dead
Guard those slain in April
and in dark chambers.

Save their words
that we may hear

And turn.

EMPTY TOMB

I. Diptych[3]

According to Luke
   there was a man
   named Joseph
   from the Jewish town of
     Arimathea
a good and righteous man

This man went to Pilate and
   asked for the body
   of Jesus

Then he took it down
   and wrapped it in a
   linen shroud
   and laid it in a rock-hewn tomb

where no one had ever been laid

It was the day of Preparation
The Sabbath was beginning

The women prepared spices
and ointments
On the Sabbath they rested
according to the commandment

When they returned to the tomb

they found no body

Lanzmann records
   testimony of Hanna's father
   Motke Zaidl
   survivor of the Jewish ghetto in
     Vilna
Hanna remembers, he was a silent
man since the time of Sobibor when

Black shirts
   forced him to dig up mass graves
   of *Figuren* and *Schmattes*
   including his mother, three
   sisters, and their children

When the last graves were opened
   he recognized their faces,
   their clothes, too
   he had to open the graves with
   no tools, "Get used to working
   with your hands," they said

In the first grave were twenty-four
thousand bodies, each almost a flat
slab. The deeper he dug, the flatter
the bodies

It was in early January 1944.
The winter preserved the bodies of
those who had been in the earth
the last four months
but others crumbled in his grasp

He worked at a killing pace, beaten
all the time

The Gestapo had ordered: "There are
ninety thousand *Figuren* lying there,
and absolutely no trace must be left
of them

II. Memorial

Here only smoke rises, Joseph,
and gnarled hands paw the winter's earth.
No spikenard scents the stench of pyres,
No sabbath nods to human worth.

Here, your Jew lies here among the
Figuren flattened in trenches.
Here at the Tube's end where mothers
become *Schmattes* and Motke wrenches

the lifeless forms of sisters and
children from the hardened ground
and massive shroud of bone and grit.
Here, Joseph, here is your Jesus to be found.

The women saw no body:
these dead were to leave no trace
as fires burned in the high wind.
Pines were planted in the place

where the camp once stood. They plowed
it under as if to disguise
the ground of Sobibor and
its blackened skies.

Good man, return to the empty chamber
where life became death and words, lies.
Set a marker of stones and remember
that here you once saw the smoke rise.

NOTES

1. See Elie Wiesel, *The Gates of the Forest*, trans. F. Frenaye (New York: Schocken Books, 1982); Wiesel also uses the narrative in Elie Wiesel, *Souls on Fire* (New York: Summit Books, 1972), 167–68.

2. The phrase "each one a God" is from Yitzhak Katzenelson, "Song of the Murdered Jewish People," trans. Noah H. Rosenbloom, in David Roskies, *The Literature of Destruction: Jewish Responses to Catastrophe* (Philadelphia: Jewish Publication Society, 5748/1988), 542 (9.13).

3. The diptych is a rendering of Luke 23:50—24:11 and Claude Lanzmann's filmed interview with Motke Zaiedl and Itzhak Dugin (for the text see: Claude Lanzmann, *Shoah: An Oral History of the Holocaust* [New York: Pantheon Books, 1985], 8–15).

WORKS CITED

Aaron, Frieda W. "A Handful of Memories: Two Levels of Recollection." In *Burning Memory: Times of Testing and Reckoning*, 169–84. Ed. Alice L. Eckardt. New York: Pergamon Press, 1993.

Adelson, Alan and Robert Lapides, eds. *Lodz Ghetto: Inside a Community Under Siege*. New York: Viking, 1989.

Arendt, Hannah. *The Human Condition*. Chicago: University of Chicago Press, 1958.

_____. *Eichmann in Jerusalem: A Report on the Banality of Evil*. New York: Viking, 1963.

Baker, Leonard. *Days of Sorrow and Pain*. New York: Oxford University Press, 1978.

Bal, Mieke. *Death and Dissymmetry*. Chicago: University of Chicago Press, 1988.

Band, Arnold J., ed. *Nahman of Bratslav: The Tales*. New York: Paulist Press, 1978.

Bauer, Yehuda, ed. *Remembering for the Future*. New York: Pergamon Press, 1989.

Ben-Menahem, Arieh. "Mendel Grossman—The Photographer of the Lodz Ghetto." In *With a Camera in the Ghetto*, 97–107. By Mendel Grossman. New York: Schocken Books, 1977.

Ben-Sasson, H.H., ed. *A History of the Jewish People*. Cambridge, Mass.: Harvard University Press, 1976.

Berenbaum, Michael. *After Tragedy and Triumph: Modern Jewish Thought and the American Experience*. New York: Cambridge University Press, 1990.

Berry, Wendell. *Collected Poems, 1957–1982*. San Francisco: North Point Press, 1985.

Bialik, Hayyim Nahman. "In the City of Slaughter." Trans. A.M. Klein. In *The Literature of Destruction*, 160–68. Ed. David Roskies. Philadelphia: Jewish Publication Society, 1989.

Borowski, Tadeusz. *This Way for the Gas, Ladies and Gentlemen*. Trans. B. Vedder. New York: Viking, 1967.

Buber, Martin. *Pointing the Way. Collected Essays*. Trans. and ed. M. Friedman. New York: Harper and Brothers, 1957.

_____. *Israel and the World*. New York: Schocken Books, 1963.

_____. *On the Bible: Eighteen Studies*. Ed. N. Glatzer. New York: Schocken Books, 1968.

_____. *I and Thou*. Trans. W. Kaufmann. New York: Charles Scribners Sons, 1970.

_____. *The Letters of Martin Buber: A Life of Dialogue*. Ed. N. Glatzer and P. Mendes-Flohr. New York: Schocken Books, 1991.

Carmi, T., ed. and trans. *The Penguin Book of Hebrew Verse*. New York: Penguin Books, 1981.

Celan, Paul. *Von Schwelle zu Schwelle.* Stuttgart: Deutsche Verlags-Anstalt, 1961.

―――. *Poems of Paul Celan.* Trans. M. Hamburger. New York: Persea Books, 1988.

Chappell, Fred. "*Approaching History* and the Ambitions of the Modernist Epic." In *Iron Mountain Review* 4 (1987): 29–32.

Cohen, Arthur A. *The Tremendum: A Theological Interpretation of the Holocaust.* New York: Crossroad Publishing Co., 1981.

Crenshaw, James L. *A Whirlpool of Torment: Israelite Traditions of God as an Oppressive Presence.* Philadelphia: Fortress Press, 1984.

Crossan, J. Dominic. *Finding Is the First Act.* Semeia Studies 9. Missoula, Mont.: Scholars Press, 1979.

Daily Prayer Book: Ha-Siddur Ha-Shalem. Trans. Philip Birnbaum. New York: Hebrew Publishing, 1949.

Dawidowicz, Lucy. *The Holocaust and the Historians.* Cambridge, Mass.: Harvard University Press, 1981.

Des Pres, Terrence. *The Survivor: An Anatomy of Life in the Death Camps.* New York: Oxford University Press, 1976.

Dillenberger, Jane. *Secular Art with Sacred Themes.* Nashville: Abingdon Press, 1969.

Dobroszycki, Lucjan, ed. *The Chronicle of the Lodz Ghetto, 1941–44.* New Haven: Yale University Press, 1984.

Douglas, Mary. *Purity and Danger: An Analysis of Concepts of Pollution and Taboo.* London: Routledge & Kegan Paul, 1966.

Dubnov-Erlich, Sophie. *The Life and Work of S.M. Dubnov: Diaspora Nationalism and Jewish History.* Trans. J. Vowles. Bloomington: Indiana University Press, 1991.

Dwork, Deborah. *Children with a Star: Jewish Youth in Nazi Europe.* New Haven, Conn.: Yale University Press, 1991.

Eliade, Mircea. *The Sacred and the Profane.* Trans. W. Trask. New York: Harvest Books, 1959.

Eliot, T.S. *Four Quartets.* New York: Harcourt Brace Jovanovich, 1971.

Ellis, Marc H. *Beyond Innocence and Redemption: Confronting the Holocaust and Israeli Power.* New York: Harper & Row, 1990.

Ezrahi, Sidra. "Dan Pagis and the poetics of incoherence." In *Remembering for the Future*, 2415–24. Ed. Y. Bauer. New York: Pergamon Press, 1989.

―――. "Review of Dan Pagis's *Variable Directions.*" In *The New Republic* 204 (February 25, 1991): 36–39.

Fackenheim, Emil. *Quest for Past and Future.* Boston: Beacon Press, 1968.

―――. *God's Presence in History: Jewish Affirmations and Philosophical Reflections.* New York: New York University Press, 1970.

―――. *Encounters Between Judaism and Modern Philosophy.* New York: Basic Books, 1973.

―――. *To Mend the World: Foundations of Future Jewish Thought.* New York: Schocken Books, 1982.

―――. *The Jewish Thought of Emil Fackenheim: A Reader.* Ed. Michael L. Morgan. Detroit: Wayne State University Press, 1987.

_____. *The Jewish Bible After the Holocaust*. Bloomington: Indiana University Press, 1990.

Feig, Konnilyn G. *Hitler's Death Camps: The Sanity of Madness*. London: Holmes & Meier, 1979.

Felman, Shoshana and Dori Laub. *Testimony: Crises of Witnessing in Literature, Psychoanalysis, and History*. New York: Routledge, 1992.

Ficowski, Jerzy. "I did not manage to save . . ." Trans. K. Bosley and K. Wandycz. In *The Poetry of Survival*, 132–33. Ed. Daniel Weissbort. New York: Penguin Books, 1993.

Fiorenza, Elisabeth Schuessler and David Tracy, eds. *The Holocaust as Interruption*. Edinburgh: T & T Clark, 1984.

Fishbane, Michael. *The Garments of Torah: Essays in Biblical Hermeneutics*. Bloomington: Indiana University Press, 1992.

Fredman, Ruth G. *The Passover Seder: Afikoman in Exile*. Philadelphia: University of Pennsylvania Press, 1981.

Friedlander, Albert, ed. *Out of the Whirlwind: A Reader of Holocaust Literature*. New York: Schocken Books, 1976.

Friedlaender, Saul. *When Memory Comes*. Trans. H. Lane. New York: Noonday Books, 1979.

Friedman, Maurice. *Martin Buber's Life and Work*. 3 vols. New York: E.P. Dutton, 1981–83.

Garber, Zev and Bruce Zuckerman. "Why Do We Call the Holocaust 'the Holocaust'?" In *Modern Judaism* 9 (1989): 197–211.

Gilbert, Martin. *The Holocaust: A History of the Jews of Europe During the Second World War*. New York: Holt, Rinehart & Winston, 1985.

Glatzer, Nahum, ed. *The Passover Haggadah*. New York: Schocken Books, 1953.

Grade, Chaim. *My Mother's Sabbath Days*. Trans. C. Goldstein and I. Grade. New York: Schocken Books, 1987.

Green, Arthur. *Tormented Master*. New York: Schocken Books, 1981.

Grossman, David. *See Under: Love*. Trans. Betsy Rosenberg. New York: Washington Square Press, 1989.

Grossman, Mendel. *With a Camera in the Ghetto*. Eds. Z. Szner and A. Sened. New York: Schocken Books, 1977.

Gutman, Israel, ed. *Encyclopedia of the Holocaust*. 4 vols. New York: Macmillan Publishing Co., 1990.

Halpern, Moyshe-Leyb. "A Night." Trans. Hillel Schwartz and David Roskies. In *Literature of Destruction*, 235–43. Ed. David Roskies. Philadelphia: Jewish Publication Society, 1988.

Hays, Richard. *Echoes of Scripture in the Letters of Paul*. New Haven, Conn.: Yale University Press, 1989.

Heschel, Abraham Joshua. *Quest for God*. New York: Crossroad Publishing Co., 1954.

_____. *Between God and Man*. Ed. Fritz Rothschild. New York: Free Press, 1959.

_____. "No Religion Is an Island." *Union Seminary Quarterly Review* 21 (1966): 117–34.

————. *A Passion for Truth*. New York: Farrar, Straus & Giroux, 1973.

Heschel, Susannah. "Something Holy in a Profane Place." In *Christianity and Crisis* 46 (October 6, 1986): 338–42.

Hoffman, Lawrence A. *Beyond the Text: A Holistic Approach to Liturgy*. Bloomington: Indiana University Press, 1987.

Hollander, John. *The Figure of Echo*. Berkeley, Calif.: University of California Press, 1981.

Jacobson, David. *Modern Midrash*. Albany, N.Y.: SUNY, 1987.

Kafka, Franz. *Parables and Paradoxes*. New York: Schocken Books, 1961.

Kampe, Norbert. "Normalizing the Holocaust? The Recent Historians' Debate in the Federal Republic of Germany." In *Holocaust and Genocide Studies* 2 (1987): 61–80.

Kaplan, Chaim. *The Warsaw Diary of Chaim A. Kaplan*. Trans. and ed. Abraham I. Katsh. New York: Collier Books, 1973.

Katzenelson, Yitzhak. "The Song of the Murdered Jewish People." Trans. Noah H. Rosenbloom. Tel Aviv: Ghetto Fighters' House and Hakibbutz Hameuchad, 1980.

Kepnes, Steven. *The Text as Thou: Martin Buber's Dialogical Hermeneutics and Narrative Theology*. Bloomington: Indiana University Press, 1992.

Kierkegaard, Søren. *Fear and Trembling*. Trans. H. Hong and E. Hong. Princeton: Princeton University Press, 1983.

Klein, Isaac. *A Guide to Jewish Religious Practice*. New York: Jewish Theological Seminary, 1979.

Kraus, Ota and Erich Kulka. *The Death Factory: Document on Auschwitz*. Trans. S. Jolly. New York: Oxford University Press, 1966.

Langer, Lawrence L. *Versions of Survival: The Holocaust & the Human Spirit*. Albany, N.Y.: SUNY, 1982.

————. *Holocaust Testimonies: The Ruins of Memory*. New Haven, Conn.: Yale University Press, 1991.

Lanzmann, Claude. *Shoah: An Oral History of the Holocaust*. New York: Pantheon Books, 1985.

Le Targat, Francois. *Chagall*. New York: Rizzoli, 1985.

Leitch, Vincent B. *Deconstructive Criticism*. New York: Columbia University Press, 1983.

Levi, Primo. *Survival in Auschwitz*. Trans. S. Woolf. New York: Collier Books, 1961.

————. *The Reawakening*. Trans. S. Woolf. New York: Collier Books, 1986.

Levinas, Emmanuel. *Totality and Infinity*. Trans. A. Lingis. Pittsburgh: Duquesne University Press, 1969.

Mais, Yitzchak. *19.9.41, A Day in the Warsaw Ghetto*. Jerusalem: Yad Vashem, 1988.

Martin, Michael. Excerpts from "Mountain-City." *Iron Mountain Review* 4 (Fall 1987): 3–24.

————. "Two Poems: 'On the Sisters' and 'Return Letter.' " *Shenandoah* 43/2 (1993): 76–86.

Mathews, John B. "Hospitality and the New Testament Church: An Historical and Exegetical Study." Th.D. dissertation, Princeton Theological Seminary, 1965.

Mauriac, Francois. "Foreword to *Night*." In *Night*, 7–11. New York: Avon Books, 1969.

Merton, Thomas. *Conjectures of a Guilty Bystander.* New York: Doubleday & Co., 1968.

Midrash Rabbah Lamentations. Trans. A. Cohen. London: Soncino Press, 1939.

Millgram, Abraham E. *Sabbath: The Day of Delight.* Philadelphia: Jewish Publication Society of America, 1965.

Milosz, Czeslaw. "A Poor Christian Looks at the Ghetto." In *The Poetry of Survival*, 52–53. Ed. Daniel Weissbort. New York: Penguin Books, 1993.

Morrison, Toni. *Beloved.* New York: Knopf, 1987.

Mueller, Filip. *Eyewitness Auschwitz: Three Years in the Gas Chambers.* Ed. and trans. S. Flatauer. New York: Stein & Day, 1979.

Neher, Andre. *The Exile of the Word.* Philadelphia: Jewish Publication Society, 1981.

Newman, Judith Sternberg. *In the Hell of Auschwitz.* New York: Exposition Press, 1963.

Niebuhr, H. Richard. *The Responsible Self.* New York: Harper & Row, 1963.

Niebuhr, Richard R. *Experiential Religion.* New York: Harper & Row, 1972.

Pagis, Dan. *Variable Directions.* Trans. S. Mitchell. San Francisco: North Point Press, 1989.

Patte, Daniel. *What Is Structural Exegesis?* Philadelphia: Fortress Press, 1976.

Patte, Daniel and Aline Patte. *Structural Exegesis: From Theory to Practice.* Philadelphia: Fortress Press, 1978.

Penchansky, David. *The Betrayal of God: Ideological Conflict in Job.* Louisville: Westminster/John Knox Press, 1990.

Plank, Karl A. "Confronting the Unredeemed World: A Paradoxical Paul and His Modern Critics." In *Anglican Theological Review* 67 (1985): 127–36.

_____. *Paul and the Irony of Affliction.* Semeia Studies 17. Atlanta: Scholars Press, 1987.

_____. "Raging Wisdom: A Banner of Defiance Unfurled." In *Judaism* 36 (1987): 323–30.

_____. "Thomas Merton and Hannah Arendt: Contemplation after Eichmann." In *The Merton Annual* 3 (1990): 121–50.

_____. "The Human Face of Otherness." In *Faith and History: Essays in Honor of Paul W. Meyer*, 57–73. Ed. J. Carroll, C. Cosgrove, and E. Johnson. Atlanta: Scholars Press, 1990.

_____. "The Eclipse of Difference: Merton's Encounter with Judaism." In *Cistercian Studies Quarterly* 28/2 (1993): 179–91.

Potok, Chaim. *My Name Is Asher Lev.* Greenwich, Conn.: Fawcett Books, 1972.

Quinones, Ricardo J. *The Changes of Cain.* Princeton: Princeton University Press, 1991.

Ricoeur, Paul. *The Symbolism of Evil.* Trans. E. Buchanan. Boston: Beacon Press, 1969.

Ringelheim, Joan. "Women and the Holocaust: A Reconsideration of the Research." In *Signs: Journal of Women in Culture and Society* 10 (1985): 741–61.

Robbins, Jill. "The Writing of the Holocaust: Claude Lanzmann's *Shoah.*" In *Prooftexts* 7 (1987): 249–58.

Rosenzweig, Franz. *The Star of Redemption.* Trans. W. Hallo. Boston: Beacon Press, 1972.

Roskies, David G. *Against the Apocalypse: Responses to Catastrophe in Modern Jewish Culture.* Cambridge, Mass.: Harvard University Press, 1984.

———, ed. *The Literature of Destruction: Jewish Responses to Catastrophe.* Philadelphia: Jewish Publication Society, 1989.

———. "Review of Lawrence Langer's *Holocaust Testimonies.*" In *Commentary* (November 1991): 57–59.

Rubenstein, Richard L. *After Auschwitz.* Indianapolis: Bobbs-Merrill, 1966.

Sachs, Nelly. *O The Chimneys.* New York: Farrar, Straus & Giroux, 1967.

———. *The Seeker.* New York: Farrar, Straus & Giroux, 1970.

Scarry, Elaine. *The Body in Pain: The Making and the Unmaking of the World.* New York: Oxford University Press, 1985.

Scholem, Gershom. *Kabbalah.* New York: Quadrangle, 1974.

Sharot, Stephen. *Messianism, Mysticism, and Magic.* Chapel Hill: University of North Carolina Press, 1982.

Shayevitsh, Simche Bunem. "*Lekh-Lekho.*" Trans. Elinor Robinson. In *The Literature of Destruction,* 520–30. Ed. David Roskies. Philadelphia: Jewish Publication Society, 1989. Also, another translation (unspecified) in *Lodz Ghetto: Inside a Community Under Siege,* 216–30. Ed. Alan Adelson and Robert Lapides. New York: Viking, 1989.

———. "Spring 5702 [1942]." In *Lodz Ghetto: Inside a Community Under Siege,* 250–62. Ed. Alan Adelson and Robert Lapides. New York: Viking, 1989.

Shenker, Israel. "A Life in the Talmud." In *New York Times Magazine* (September 11, 1977), 44ff.

Shils, Edward. *Tradition.* London: Faber & Faber, 1981.

Sokoloff, Naomi. "Transformations: Holocaust Poems in Dan Pagis' *Gilgul.*" In *Hebrew Annual Review* 8 (1984): 215–40.

Sorlier, Charles, ed. *Chagall by Chagall.* New York: Harry Abrams, 1979.

Staff, Leopold. "Foundations." Trans. Adam Czerniawski. In *The Poetry of Survival,* 62. Ed. Daniel Weissbort. New York: Penguin Books, 1993.

Steinmetz, Devorah. *From Father to Son: Kinship, Conflict, and Continuity in Genesis.* Louisville: Westminster/John Knox Press, 1991.

Thalmann, Rita and Emmanuel Feinermann. *Crystal Night.* Trans. G. Cremonesi. New York: Holocaust Library, 1972.

Tillich, Paul. *Systematic Theology.* 3 vols. Chicago: University of Chicago Press, 1951–63.

Trunk, Isaiah. *Judenrat: The Jewish Councils in Eastern Europe Under Nazi Occupation.* New York: Macmillan Publishing Co., 1972.

Weissbort, Daniel, ed. *The Poetry of Survival: Post-War Poets of Central and Eastern Europe.* New York: Penguin Books, 1993.

Wiesel, Elie. *Un di Velt Hot Geshvign.* Buenos Aires: Yel Mundo Callaba, Central Farbond Fun Poylishe Yidn in Argentina, 1956.

———. *Night.* Trans. S. Rodway. New York: Avon Books, 1969.

———. *Souls on Fire.* New York: Summit Books, 1972.

———. "Freedom of Conscience—A Jewish Commentary." In *Journal of Ecumenical Studies* 14 (1977): 638–49.

———. *A Jew Today.* New York: Vintage, 1978.

_____. *The Trial of God*. Trans. M. Wiesel. New York: Random House, 1979.

_____. *The Gates of the Forest*. Trans. F. Frenaye. New York: Schocken Books, 1982.

_____. *Legends of Our Time*. New York: Schocken Books, 1982.

_____. *The Town Beyond the Wall*. Trans. S. Becker. New York: Schocken Books, 1982.

_____. "Foreword to *A Vanished World* by Roman Vishniac." New York: Farrar, Straus & Giroux, 1983.

Young, James E. *Writing and Rewriting the Holocaust: Narrative and the Consequences of Interpretation*. Bloomington: Indiana University Press, 1988.

Young-Bruehl, Elisabeth. *Hannah Arendt: For Love of the World*. New Haven, Conn.: Yale University Press, 1982.

Zelkowicz, Jozef. *In These Nightmarish Days*. Excerpted in *Lodz Ghetto: Inside a Community Under Siege*, 320–49. Ed. Alan Adelson and Robert Lapides. New York: Viking, 1989.

INDEX